# FLORENCE AND JOSEPHINE O'DONOGHUE'S
# WAR OF INDEPENDENCE

BOOKS OF RELATED INTEREST FROM
IRISH ACADEMIC PRESS


The GPO and the Easter Rising
Keith Jeffery

The Northern IRA in the Early Years of Partition 1920–1922
Robert Lynch

Patrick Pearse: The Triumph of Failure
Ruth Dudley Edwards

Myths and Memories of the Easter Rising
Cultural and Political Nationalism in Ireland
Jonathan Githens-Mazer

Republican Internment and the Prison Ship Argenta 1922
Denise Kleinrichert

Our Own Devices
National Symbols and Political Conflict in Twentieth-Century Ireland
Ewan Morris

The Last Days of Dublin Castle
The Diaries of Mark Sturgis
Editor: Michael Hopkinson

# FLORENCE AND JOSEPHINE O'DONOGHUE'S WAR OF INDEPENDENCE

## A Destiny That Shapes Our Ends

Edited by
JOHN BORGONOVO

Foreword by
J. J. Lee

IRISH ACADEMIC PRESS
DUBLIN • PORTLAND, OR

*First published in 2006 by*
IRISH ACADEMIC PRESS
44 Northumberland Road, Dublin 4, Ireland

*and in the United States of America by*
IRISH ACADEMIC PRESS
c/o ISBS, Suite 300, 920 NE 58th Avenue
Portland, Oregon 97213-3644

*Website:* **www.iap.ie**

British Library Cataloguing in Publication Data
An entry can be found on request

ISBN 0-7165-3370-7 (cloth)
ISBN 0-7165-3371-5 (paper)

Library of Congress Cataloging-in-Publication Data
An entry can be found on request

Typeset in 11pt on 13pt Baskerville by
FiSH Books, London WC1
Printed by MPG Books Ltd, Bodmin, Cornwall

# CONTENTS

List of plates and Maps  vi
Maps  vii
Foreword by J. J. Lee  ix
Acknowledgements  xi
Note on the text  xiii
List of abbreviations  xiv
Chronology of events  xv

Introduction  1

PART I THE MEMOIRS OF FLORENCE AND JOSEPHINE
O'DONOGHUE
1  'Loneliness and Homesickness'  9
2  'Illumination'  24
3  'A Job of Work'  46
4  'A Campaign against Public Order'  77
5  'A Hard, Palpable Reality'  90
6  'Mother's Story'  110
7  'To Steal a Child'  125

PART II TAKING TO THE HILLS
8  Love and Terror  141
9  The Letters of Florence O'Donoghue  147

PART III AFTERWARDS
10  Truce and Civil War  193
11  'A Long Life of Devoted Love and Mutual Happiness'  205

Appendix  211
Glossary  215
Biographies  221
Bibliography  238
Index  247

# PLATES

1   Tomás MacCurtain and Terence MacSwiney with Cork No. 1 Brigade officers (Cork Public Museum)
2   Funeral procession of Tomás MacCurtain (British Pathé, ITN Archive)
3   Auxiliary Cadets with armoured car patrol Cork city (British Pathé, ITN Archive)
4   Josephine Brown O'Donoghue and friends enjoy a day of yachting in the early 1920s (Breda O'Donoghue Lucci)
5   Fr Dominic O'Connor (OFM, CAP) (Catholic Diocese of Baker, Oregon)
6   Prominent members of the Cork No. 1 Brigade flying column, 1921 (Fr Patrick Twohig)
7   First Southern Division IRA Convention delegates, Dublin, 26 March 1922 (NLI)
8   The O'Donoghue family in the late 1930s (Breda O'Donoghue Lucci)
9   Florence O'Donoghue speaking at the 1957 Liam Lynch commemoration (Fr Patrick Twohig)
10   O'Donoghue at home with Seán O'Hegarty (Fr Patrick Twohig)
11   Jo and Florrie in their later years (Breda O'Donoghue Lucci)

# MAPS

1   Ireland
2   Munster
3   IRA First Southern Division Brigade Areas

# MAPS

## Map 1: Ireland

## Map 2: Munster

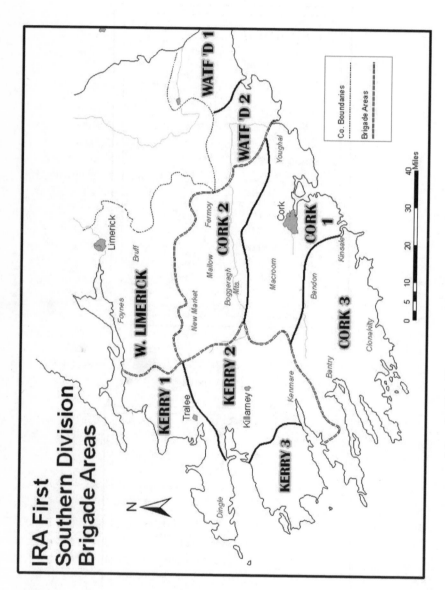

Map 3: IRA First Southern Division Brigade Areas

# FOREWORD

Florence O' Donoghue (1895-1967) and his wife, Josephine (1891-1966), played important roles in the Irish War of Independence. They were pivotal to the struggle in Cork, which in turn was pivotal to the struggle nationally. If Florrie's contribution, as Adjutant and Intelligence Officer, initially for the First Cork Brigade, and subsequently for the First Southern Division, is already broadly familiar, appreciation of his role is deepened by the publication of this Memoir, composed in 1961, but sealed until 2002, and by a number of his letters to Jo, while the incorporation of her own Memoir allows her role to be finally fully appreciated.

The War of Independence was first and foremost an Intelligence war. The poorly equipped IRA had no hope unless they could compensate for their gross inferiority in gun power not only through greater will power, but through superior Intelligence. The role of IRA Intelligence Officers was crucial in levelling up the odds. It is the judgement of John Borgonovo, the editor, that O'Donoghue, a farmer's son from Kerry, was as crucial to the struggle in Cork as Michael Collins, a farmer's son from Cork, was to the struggle in Dublin, different a personality though the quiet O'Donoghue was from the flamboyant Collins.

Nor can this verdict be dismissed as merely a case of excessive editorial pietas. Borgonovo, an American, has already acquired authority on the subject in researching his thesis, *Informers, Intelligence, and the 'Anti-Sinn Féin Society': The Anglo-Irish War in Cork City, 1920-1921*. Besides including a mine of information in his copious notes on the personalities and events mentioned in the Memoir, he also provides illuminating biographical commentary on Florrie and Jo themselves.

Florrie's character, as one of the most thoughtful members of the IRA and IRB, enables the restrained realism of his approach, reflecting rather than declaiming his underlying idealism, ignited by the impact of Easter Week, to carry more conviction than would a more egotistical account.

Of course all autobiographical accounts require probing scrutiny. It seems unlikely, however, that the importance Florrie attaches to Jo's role can ever be disputed. Her contribution may not even have been known to her children until this Memoir was composed, for one of Florrie's declared motives in writing it was to make them aware of their mother's role in the struggle. And what a role it was! Born in Adare, Co. Limerick in 1891, her father an R.I.C. man, for nearly two vital years she supplied O'Donoghue, whom she married secretly in 1921, with the highest quality information on British plans from her inside position as forewoman of clerks and typists in the Headquarters, in Victoria Barracks (now Collins Barracks) in Cork, of General Strickland's 6th Division of the British Army, charged with crushing the IRA in Munster. Her family circumstances take on added piquancy from the fact that Florrie was her second husband, her first, an Englishman, having been killed on the Western Front in 1917. She provides here her own account of the intriguing human interest story of the consequent complicated familial relations.

Although an Intelligence officer was likely to be particularly alert to the importance of 'ordinary' people in a guerrilla war, it may be, at least partly, Florrie's realization of Jo's importance that led him to recognise the significant wider role of women in the conflict. This factor deserves far more attention in evaluations of the extraordinary ability of the IRA to resist vastly superior British power. It might even be argued that the overwhelming British superiority in manpower was partly countered by Irish superiority in womanpower. If few found themselves in a position to play as crucial a part as Jo O' Donoghue, among the many rewards of this engrossing account is the increased understanding it conveys of the importance of the contribution of 'ordinary' women, as well as of 'ordinary' men, to the struggle.

J. J. Lee
New York
January 2006

# ACKNOWLEDGEMENTS

A host of people have made this book possible.

I would be remiss if I did not recognize Florence O'Donoghue for his fine writing, careful research, and the accessible organization of his extensive papers. He made my job very easy indeed.

In the present day, I was very fortunate to find Captain Tom O'Neill (MA, University College, Cork) of Cork, who acted as research assistant and translated the Irish language segments of the O'Donoghue letters. To anyone interested in Cork's role in the War of Independence, I would recommend his work, 'Clonmult, 7 April 1921'. I look forward to his next contribution to the study of this period.

Photographs were made possible through the generous assistance of Breda O'Donoghue Lucci, Sgt Gerry White of Collins Barracks, and Father Patrick Twohig of Mallow. Niall de Barra provided critical help by securing specific photographs in the National Library in Dublin.

In the United States, my lawyer and old friend Laurie Morris Younger generously offered her time and services. Cyndy Comerford spent hours creating maps for me. I also enjoyed access to an excellent Irish library at the United Irish Cultural Center in San Francisco.

My undergraduate history advisor Professor Randall McGowen at the University of Oregon gave me my initial encouragement in this field, which eventually led to this book. While undertaking my Master's work at University College, Cork I was ably assisted by the UCC History Department staff. My thesis advisor Professor Gabriel Doherty offered excellent insight, focus, and encouragement at critical junctures. Thanks also to Ryan Morgan, law lecturer at UCC, for assistance with understanding the Reggie Brown Custody case.

I have visited many libraries during my research, and some deserve special mention. I am grateful to the National Library of Ireland for granting me permission to publish this material. Elizabeth Kirwan and Gerard Lyne of the Manuscripts Department provided much assistance. In Dublin, I was helped by Commandant Victor Byrne (and the late Commandant Peter Young) and the staff at the Military Archives in Dublin, as well as the staff of the University College, Dublin Archives Department. In Cork, I would like to thank the Cork Archives Institute, the Boole Library at University College, Cork, the Cork Public Museum, and the Cork City Library (especially former head librarian Tim Cadogan).

The O'Donoghue children greatly aided my research and publishing efforts. Special thanks should go to Breda O'Donoghue Lucci and her husband Emilio Lucci for their warm hospitality and generous encouragement. This book would have been impossible without their assistance. Thanks also to the late Dr Margaret O'Donoghue who opened her home to me in Lincoln in 1996; and to Dr Patrick O'Donoghue of Brighton for lending his blessing (and fine proofreading skills) to this project.

My research would have been impossible had I not been hosted during my various trips to Ireland and the United Kingdom. Thanks to Niall de Barra, Peter Boyland, and Dr Catherine MacCarthy in Dublin; Chris Murray, Barry Coleman, Kevin Kiely, and Caoimhe Lynch in Cork; James Willcox, Mark Jordan, Kate McKenna, Katie Morris, and Josh Hoffman in London; and the Willcox family in Ampleforth, Yorkshire.

Finally, I'd like to thank my friends and my brother and sisters for their encouragement over the past ten years. This book is dedicated to my parents Roy and Roberta who have always given me their love and support, and remain an inspiration.

# NOTE ON THE TEXT

This book would not have been possible without the permission and support of the surviving O'Donoghue children. Interviews with the late Dr Margaret O'Donoghue, Dr Patrick O'Donoghue, and Breda O'Donoghue Lucci were crucial to my post-war chapter. Breda Lucci also generously provided a number of photographs featured here. Breda and her husband Emilio were most helpful and gracious throughout the publishing process.

The following text appears as Florence O'Donoghue originally wrote it, though in places I have made minor grammatical corrections and punctuation edits for clarity.

This book is intended to offer Florence O'Donoghue's account of his experiences during the Irish War of Independence. It should be noted that at the time O'Donoghue composed his memoir, he was sixty-six years old and was writing primarily for the benefit of his children. While O'Donoghue kept careful record of his activities during the War of Independence period, readers should be aware of the implications of his age and his intended audience.

Historian Gerry White of Collins Barracks, Cork, has undertaken a biography of Florence O'Donoghue. Sgt White's work should provide a more critical examination of O'Donoghue's role during the events of 1916–1923. The editor is eager to see the results of his extensive research.

The Editor's Comments are denoted by a separate font to avoid confusion with the Author's.

John Borgonovo
San Francisco, USA
February 2006

# ABBREVIATIONS

The following abbreviations are used in the notes and references:

BMH    Bureau of Military History (Cathal Brugha Barracks, Dublin)
CAI     Cork Archives Institute
CPM    Cork Public Museum
DDA    Department of Defence Archives (National Library of Ireland)
IWM    Imperial War Museum (London)
MA      Military Archives (Cathal Brugha Barracks)
NLI     National Library of Ireland, Dublin
PRO    Public Records Office (Boole Library, University College, Cork)
UCC    University College, Cork
UCD    University College, Dublin

# CHRONOLOGY OF EVENTS

**1891**  Josephine McCoy born in Adare, County Limerick; her family moves to Cork city eight years later

**1895**  Florence O'Donoghue born in Rathmore, County Kerry

**1910**  Florence O'Donoghue moves from Rathmore to Cork city

**1911**  Josephine McCoy emigrates to Wales

**1913**  Jo marries Coleridge Marchment in Wales
November – Birth of Coleridge Marchment Jr (Reggie Brown)
December – Irish Volunteers founded in Cork

**1914**  Home Rule for Ireland Crisis
August – First World War begins

**1915**  Coleridge Marchment drafted into British Army

**1916**  April – Easter Rising
August – Gerald Marchment born
September – Jo returns to Cork with Gerald, temporarily leaving son Reggie Brown with the Brown family in Wales
December – Florence O'Donoghue joins the Cork Volunteers

**1917**  February – Sinn Féin wins first parliament seat
May – Florrie O'Donoghue sworn into the Irish Republican Brotherhood
June – British officials close Cork's Volunteer Hall
August – British Army begins Passchendaele offensive in the Ypres Salient
October – Coleridge Marchment killed in action
800 Cork Volunteers march to protest a government ban on wearing uniforms
December – Jo takes a position as a clerk with the 6th Division Headquarters at Victoria Barracks, Cork; she is later promoted to head of female clerks and typists

**1918**  February – Florrie succeeds Pat Higgins as Cork Brigade Adjutant
April – Conscription in Ireland bill passed by British parliament; Anti-Conscription pledge signed throughout Ireland
May – Sinn Féin leaders arrested for alleged participation in a 'German plot'
June – Cork city and county declared Special Military Areas; public meetings and gatherings banned

July – Jo loses custody battle with the Brown family; son Reggie remains with the Browns at their home in Cadaxton, Wales

November – Denis MacNeilus shoots Head Constable Clarke; Cork city Volunteers break MacNeilus out of Cork Gaol; First World War ends

December – General Election in Britain and Ireland; Sinn Féin wins 73 of 105 seats; Cork city elects Liam de Róiste and J.J. Walsh of Sinn Féin; Cork Brigade divided into three brigade areas; the Cork No. 1 Brigade territory runs through the middle of county Cork, and includes Cork city

1919    January – Sinn Féin MPs refuse to take their seats in Westminster and form their own Irish parliament called Dáil Éireann; Dáil Éireann declares Ireland's independence from Britain; Tipperary Volunteers kill two policemen at Soloheadbeg

April – Seán O'Hegarty resigns from Cork No. 1 Brigade leadership

June – Josephine Brown first offers her services to the IRA

July – Failed Cork Volunteer attack on British military at Ballyquirk Aerodome

September – Dáil Éireann banned by British Government

December – Florrie offers to use the IRA to retrieve Reggie Brown

1920    January – Cork No. 1 Brigade attacks RIC barracks at Kilmurray and Carrigtwohill; Sinn Féin wins local elections around Ireland. Tomás MacCurtain elected Alderman and eventually Lord Mayor of Cork

February – British spy Timothy Quinlisk killed by IRA in Cork city; O'Donoghue and Matt Ryan attempt to shoot Sgt Ferris, RIC

March – Cork No. 1 Brigade attacks Inchigeela RIC Barracks; 'Black and Tans' first appear on Irish streets; O'Donoghue and Tom Crofts shoot District Inspector MacDonagh; Cork city Volunteers kill Constable Murtagh on Pope's Quay; Cork police assassinate Lord Mayor Tomás MacCurtain; Terence MacSwiney succeeds MacCurtain as Lord Mayor and commander Cork No. 1 Brigade; Seán O'Hegarty resumes Brigade Vice Commander duties; Florrie O'Donoghue goes 'on the run', dedicating himself to full-time IRA duties

April – Cork Coroner's Inquest finds British government officials responsible for Tomás MacCurtain's killing; 300 abandoned police barracks are burned around the country; Volunteers set fire to a number of tax offices and vacated posts around Cork city; GHQ prohibits proposed assault on RIC curfew patrols in Cork city

May – City Volunteers assassinate two policemen suspected of killing Tomás MacCurtain

June – Cork No. 1 Brigade attacks RIC barracks at Blarney and Carrigadrohid; O'Donoghue helps lead both assaults

July – King Street Police Barracks bombed; Anti-British riot in Cork city; Cork city placed under military curfew

August – Cork and Belfast Volunteers assassinate District Inspector Swanzy in Lisburn, Northern Ireland. Anti-Catholic riots follow; IRA prisoners in Cork Gaol begin hunger strike; British Army raids Cork City Hall and arrests Terence MacSwiney; MacSwiney joins the Cork Gaol hunger strike and is deported to Brixton Prison in London

September – Josephine contacts Father Dominic O'Connor and meets Florence O'Donoghue for the first time; Jo begins to spy for the IRA; Volunteers led by Seán O'Hegarty and Florence O'Donoghue attempt to assassinate General Strickland in Cork; Cork No. 1 Brigade assassination squad sent to London for possible reprisals against British Cabinet members if MacSwiney dies

October – Michael Collins provides Florrie with letters of introduction to IRA contacts in England; British Army suffers four casualties in IRA ambush in Barrack Street, Cork; Terence MacSwiney and two other Cork Volunteers die on hunger strike; Unidentified Auxiliary Cadets issue public threats against citizens of Cork city, promising violent reprisals if IRA attacks continue

November – Cork No. 1 Brigade kills six British officers suspected of working for military intelligence; IRA also kidnaps and secretly executes five Cork civilians suspected of informing; unidentified Crown forces set fire to a number of Sinn Féin halls and private homes in an unofficial reprisal campaign; Florrie and Jack Cody travel to Britain to kidnap Reggie Brown

December – Reggie Brown kidnapped from his grandparents' home in Wales; Reggie eventually smuggled back to Ireland and sent into hiding at Alfred and Cissie Hore's home in Youghal; in reprisal for an IRA ambush, Auxiliary Cadets burn much of the Cork city centre; Martial Law declared in Cork city and county; Cork Bishop Cohalon orders the excommunication of any Volunteer taking part in armed conflict in the diocese

**1921** January – City Volunteers ambush an RIC patrol on Parnell Bridge, killing two and wounding five

February – Brigade executes seven suspected civilian informers

and orders others out of the city; Brigade flying column attacks Auxiliary Cadets at Coolavokig, near Macroom; Munster IRA leaders meet to discuss possible cross-brigade cooperation; British Army executes four IRA prisoners at Victoria Barracks
March – In response to the execution of captured Volunteers, IRA units attack unarmed British soldiers around Cork city; six are killed and up to a dozen more wounded
April – Florence O'Donoghue and Josephine McCoy Brown secretly married in Cork city; First Southern Division formed; Florrie promoted to Division Adjutant and Intelligence Officer
May – Florrie leaves Cork city to set up division headquarters near the Cork/Kerry border; Jo remains at Victoria Barracks secretly working for the IRA; Eight police die in an IRA ambush at Rathmore; O'Donoghue family farm destroyed as a reprisal for the Rathmore ambush; Florrie and Liam Lynch inspect IRA units in Kerry, West Limerick, and Cork
June – British Army undertakes 'Great Round-up' encirclement operation around O'Donoghue's headquarters
July – Truce Agreement signed by British and Irish representatives; IRA forces return home without threat of arrest; Jo resigns her position at Victoria Barracks
August – Dáil President Eamonn de Valera and IRA Chief of Staff Richard Mulcahy tour the First Southern Division area
October – Treaty negotiations between Dáil delegation and the British Government begin in London
December – Anglo-Irish Treaty signed; Irish Cabinet splits over Treaty; First Southern Division rejects Treaty; Dáil begins Treaty deliberations

1922    January – Dáil approves Treaty
February – Free State Provisional Government begins to assume governing functions
March – IRA splits into pro- and anti-Treaty factions; IRA Convention meets and declares the organization free of Dáil control. Executive Committee takes charge of the IRA
April – Florrie elected to IRA Executive as Adjutant-General; Anti-Treaty IRA forces occupy Four Courts in Dublin; IRA traitor Patrick 'Croxy' O'Connor shot in New York City
May – Army Unity Letter denounces possibility of civil war
June – O'Donoghue and Seán O'Hegarty resign from IRA Executive over the issue of civil war; Pro-Treaty candidates dominate General Election returns; Anti-Treaty IRA splits outright into moderate and militant factions; Florence O'Donoghue returns to Cork; IRA gunmen assassinate Field

Marshal Henry Wilson in London; Free State Army attacks Four Courts garrison; Moderate and militant factions reunify. Anti-Treaty and Free State forces clash throughout Ireland; Irish Civil War begins

July – Florence O'Donoghue formally resigns from IRA; Cork civic leaders ask O'Donoghue to help with peace negotiations; Anti-Treaty IRA defeated in Dublin

August – Free State Army occupies Cork city; Michael Collins killed by Anti-Treaty forces in Cork

November – Free State Government begins to execute Republican prisoners

December – O'Donoghue and Seán O'Hegarty organize 'Neutral IRA'

1923    January – O'Donoghue acts as peace liaison between Free State and Anti-Treaty forces

February – Neutral IRA peace proposal rejected by IRA Chief of Staff Liam Lynch

April – Liam Lynch killed by Free State troops; IRA declares ceasefire; Irish Civil War ends

# INTRODUCTION

## John Borgonovo

From 1919 until 1921, Cork city was a symbol of violent resistance to British rule in Ireland and the city of 76,000 came to be perceived as the informal capital of the Irish War of Independence. Surrounding areas of County Cork produced the conflict's heaviest and deadliest fighting. The city itself saw some of the most galvanizing episodes of the war, including the assassination of Lord Mayor Tomás MacCurtain, the hunger strike of his successor Terence MacSwiney, and the burning of part of the city centre by Auxiliary Cadet police officers. Less spectacular but equally lethal incidents were common in the city throughout those two years. Citizens grew accustomed to street ambushes, prison escapes, shootings of suspected civilian informers, executions of IRA prisoners, and arson and assassination reprisals carried out by Crown forces. Faced with overwhelming pressure, the majority of Cork's citizens continued to support the rebels, illustrating the British administration's ultimate failure in Ireland.

Florence and Josephine O'Donoghue played leading roles in Cork city's Anglo-Irish drama. Both came from the Catholic middling class of clerks, shop assistants, civil servants, craftsmen, and teachers that dominated the Irish independence movement. Florence (Florrie), a draper's shop assistant, rose quickly through the ranks of the Irish Republican Army (IRA) to become one of the highest-ranking officers in the underground army. Josephine (Jo) was employed as a head clerk in the British Army headquarters and ultimately evolved into one of the most valuable IRA intelligence agents in the conflict. Superficially, each had different personalities. Contemporaries described Florrie as shy, restrained, and pensive, while Jo was considered outgoing, outspoken, and passionate. However, both were highly intelligent, competent in their professions, and dedicated Irish patriots. They were typical of the IRA activists that emerged during the Irish War of Independence.

Modern observers frequently view the IRA guerrillas through two prisms – as bold, brilliant fighters who brought an Empire to a standstill; or as cowardly bullies who terrorized innocents to achieve their goals. While there is some truth in both these characterizations, neither addresses the complexities of the fight in Ireland from 1916 to 1921.

The Irish Volunteers were citizen-soldiers who gradually matured into the formidable guerrilla fighting force known as the Irish Republican Army. Rather than being planned, the evolution to guerrilla war occurred organically, due to a variety of factors. Inspired by the 1916 Rising and devoted to the memories of its martyred leaders, the Irish Volunteers committed themselves fully to the abstract idea of an independent Irish Republic. Their devotion to the Republic intersected with a volatile political situation in the country at the end of 1918. Anger at police repression of nationalist organizations, opposition to conscription into an unpopular war, and frustration at the unwillingness of the British government to meet reasonable Irish self-determination expectations combined to create fertile ground for an insurgency that reached a crescendo two years later.

While academics frequently use 21 January 1919 to mark the beginning of the War of Independence (the date of the Soloheadbeg ambush in Tipperary, which coincided with Dáil Éireann's Declaration of Independence), illegal and underground activities had grown steadily during the previous two years. During this 'phoney war' period (mid-1916 to the end of 1918) the Irish Volunteers learned the lessons of discretion, secrecy, and deception. Chased and harassed by police, the Volunteers began to mask their movements and activities. Drills and meetings previously held in public now took place in secret locations. As the reorganized Irish Volunteers tried to arm themselves, they planned weapons raids, which proved to be excellent rehearsals for future operations against Crown forces. Early leaders wanted by police went 'on the run', creating networks of safe houses and sanctuaries among civilian supporters. Captured Volunteers served their sentences in Republican-run jail wings, which resulted in their indoctrination in Republican philosophy and exposure to military discipline.

During 1917 and 1918 the Volunteer movement built up a body of knowledge that would prove very useful in the coming guerrilla conflict. Problem officers were weeded out, operational procedures developed, and an *esprit de corps* created. When the shooting started in late 1919, the Volunteers hit the ground running.

Florrie O'Donoghue explains the 'phoney war' period as well as any veteran has. Here he traces his personal evolution from apolitical country boy to fugitive guerrilla leader. Surprised by his journey, he suspects fate's intervention along the way. Though he became a top figure in the IRA's Cork No. 1 Brigade, he realistically portrays himself as a novice trying to master a game of life and death. He laughs at his failures, marvels at his victories, and celebrates the naive courage apparent in himself and his colleagues.

In O'Donoghue's letters, we have one of the most significant first-hand accounts to emerge from the War of Independence era. Writing love notes while dodging the British Army, O'Donoghue provides a flavour of life 'on the run' in the Irish countryside during the final ten weeks of the Anglo-Irish War. Late night raids and dramatic dashes for safety contrast with concerns about scabies and the tardiness of return correspondence. His letters illuminate the bravery, bravado, and boredom of daily guerrilla existence. Detailing his thoughts on the military situation, O'Donoghue also offers a snapshot of Republican opinion in the crucial weeks before the Truce of July 1921.

O'Donoghue's self-reflections do not conform with the stereotype of a hardened IRA guerrilla. As someone with an 'innocent and harmless looking appearance' who 'loathes guns', it is difficult to picture O'Donoghue in a trench coat, pistol in hand, staring down a column of Black and Tans. Instead, he consistently reveals more empathy and morality than expected from a 'murder gang' assassin, as was believed by some commentators to represent the sum of the IRA's 1919–1921 campaign.

For O'Donoghue, the IRA Volunteers were self-taught amateurs trying to make do as best they could. Their most effective weapons in the battle against Britain were their personal dedication, ingenuity, and discipline. The rebels lived in poverty, faced imminent death or imprisonment, and retained little confidence in short-term military victory. Mostly they were inspired by the example of the Easter Rebellion martyrs and a semi-religious faith in the cause of Irish freedom. While selfless, O'Donoghue's patriots are not saints. On occasion they steal, kill in cold blood, and allow their vanity to interfere with their duties. They behave as one would expect ordinary people to behave. Sometimes they are brave, sometimes cowardly; sometimes they are generous and sometimes mean. In short, they are ordinary men and women caught up in extraordinary times.

In this tumultuous environment, we meet Josephine O'Donoghue, the remarkable IRA spy in Victoria Barracks. Over the years, various accounts have mentioned Jo's work, but none have provided her full story. In her own words she describes her contributions to the IRA's secret intelligence war, along with the details of her struggle to secure custody of her son Reggie.

As the head of clerks and typists in the British 6th Army Headquarters, Jo enjoyed access to the most sensitive information flowing to and from the British Army in Munster. Her privileged position puts her on par with the most important IRA intelligence sources of the conflict, including David Nelligan and Eamonn Broy.

Facing the possibility of death or long imprisonment, she continued to feed information to the IRA up until the Truce of July 1921.

Josephine O'Donoghue is a powerful reminder of the role played by women during the War of Independence. Women formed a crucial part of the Republican war effort, fearlessly propping up the IRA while acting as intelligence agents, flying column scouts, headquarters clerks, nurses, and safe-house keepers. They also demonstrated against the British administration, wrote and distributed Republican propaganda, and maintained the Dáil's underground government. My abiding image of Republican women comes from a 1921 newspaper description of a British raid on the family farm of fifteen-year-old Mary Bowles, located just outsides Cork city.[1] While British soldiers searched for a hidden IRA arms dump, they stopped Bowles as she casually walked away from the farm. Beneath her bulky dress, the soldiers found two loaded pistols, a bullet-proof vest, and a machine gun. She spent the remainder of the war in a British prison.

The dedication of Republicans like Mary Bowles should not be dismissed nor underestimated. That commitment was the deciding factor of the Anglo-Irish War. As O'Donoghue relates, he and his colleagues willingly faced death expecting no greater reward than a better country for future generations. While both the Crown forces and the Irish Volunteers were prepared to kill for their cause, the Volunteers' readiness to die for their's was the difference between victory and defeat. Britain's loyal subjects in Ireland never matched the rebels' resolve. The Crown forces might have been able to defeat the insurgents had enough Irish Unionists put themselves at risk and provided information about the IRA. Their unwillingness to do so translated into Britain's inability to retain Ireland.

While the Anglo-Irish Treaty of 6 December 1921 did not give Irish Republicans all they demanded, it did result in Britain's departure from twenty-six of Ireland's thirty-two counties. Britain's 55,000 well-supplied and well-funded soldiers and police had proved incapable of defeating an indigenous organization of poorly armed novices.

Ultimately the Irish War of Independence must be viewed as a victory for the IRA. For two years, rebels armed with pistols and a couple of thousand rifles stood toe-to-toe against the most powerful military force on earth. Assisted by large segments of the Irish public, the insurgents controlled vast swathes of the countryside and forced British personnel to retreat into castle-like garrisons. In many areas of Ireland, Crown forces rarely ventured out of their bases, and when they did, it was in clumsy groups that usually failed to locate the rebels. Britain's collective punishment reprisals against the Irish people did not stifle the insurgents, but instead bolstered their support at home and abroad.

In Great Britain, propaganda used to justify so many imperialist adventures failed to maintain public confidence in the Irish campaign. The close proximity of Ireland to Britain allowed intrepid international journalists to investigate the war and eventually refute the British government's claims that it was fighting a small band of terrorists who were holding the Irish people hostage. By the middle of 1921, the British public was demoralized by the Crown forces' inability to destroy the rebels and embarrassed by its government's widely reported outrages against Irish civilians. For Britain's leaders, yielding Dominion Rule to an Irish 'murder gang' became more politically palatable than unleashing a costly full-scale war upon a rebellious people. This decision marked the first in a long series of British defeats at the hands of anti-colonial movements around the world. It can be said that the dismantling of the great British Empire began in Ireland in 1921.

The Irish War of Independence was not the world's first successful guerrilla campaign nor was it the last. The lessons of that conflict, however, are as relevant today as they have ever been. It is remarkable that eighty-six years after Soloheadbeg, intelligent policy makers continue to disregard the power of insurgency. The Irish situation taught us that the military occupation of a foreign country will fail when that presence is opposed by an organized and committed guerrilla force, supported by a significant portion of the civilian population. Britain learned this painful lesson in Ireland in 1919–1921.

To understand the surprising success of the Irish revolutionaries against what was then the world's reigning superpower, one must understand the people who won the war. The accounts of Florence and Josephine O'Donoghue help us to do so.

## NOTES

1    *Cork Constitution*, 14/1/21, 26/1/21; *Cork Examiner*, 14/1/21, 15/1/21; *Cork Weekly News*, 22/1/21; Dan Healy, Bureau of Military History Statement.
2    The memoir can be found in Ms. 31,176, NLI.

# PART I

# THE MEMOIRS OF FLORENCE AND JOSEPHINE O'DONOGHUE

The following narrative can be found in the Florence O'Donoghue Papers held by the National Library of Ireland.[2] The O'Donoghue Papers include letters, documents, photographs, and diaries compiled by Florence (Florrie) O'Donoghue from 1916 until his death in 1967, mostly related to his research into the Irish Revolution (1916–1923). When he arranged the deposit of his papers in the National Library, O'Donoghue requested that all his materials be made public, with the exception of this account written in 1961. It was sealed from the public until 2002.

The narrative was written after the O'Donoghue children were grown, in an effort to record their parents' role in the independence struggle. It appears that O'Donoghue ultimately intended to create a complete account of his role in the 1916–1921 struggle, but did not finish the work.

# 1

## 'LONELINESS AND HOMESICKNESS'

### Florence O'Donoghue

I began to write these personal reminiscences in January 1961, when I was in my sixty-seventh year, and if it be God's will I hope to complete them.

They are not for publication. There are two reasons why it appears to me to be worth while attempting the making of some record, however inadequate, of two lives whose paths have crossed the main stream of our national struggle for independence in their day, lives which have been borne along on that stream in its most turbulent phase, and which in a small way have contributed something to its direction and results.

It is right that all six of you children should have an authentic account of the heroic part, undertaken voluntarily and in disregard of the gravest dangers, which your mother played in the struggle – a story which up to now has not been written. If I take a long time to come to that story it is because I think you will understand better its significance, both for me personally and for the cause we served, if I can enable you to see the background to it through the eyes of one who came to the years of resurgence out of near poverty, without education or training or friends, and who found in the movement worthy ideals and a full life.

The second reason is that I am deeply conscious of the debt of gratitude I owe to your mother for a long life of devoted love and mutual happiness. To her, with homage and tenderness, with love and admiration, I dedicate our story.

\*\*\*

My father said to my mother, 'Don't call him back when we start,' and to me he said, 'Don't look back.' We were standing outside our farmhouse door at Rathmore[1] and I was leaving home for the first time, going to what was for me the strange life of Cork city. The year was 1910 and I was sixteen years old. I had never been further from home than Killarney, where I had gone with my father by road one cold winter's day, and Millstreet where my elder sister Nell had gone as an apprentice to the drapery business the previous year.

Within the narrow boundaries of a child's world in that quiet countryside, one would expect memory to recall as its earliest impression something associated with the family fireside. And yet my earliest clear memory is of the out-of-doors, of snow. My father, knee deep in snow, had taken me on his back into the fields behind our house, and all the world I could see was glistening white and beautiful under the sun.

After that day a number of small events remain as clear pictures but without certainty as to their chronological order; the big collie Dot who gave lifts to us small children on his back, and which I afterwards learned my father had gotten from Lord Kenmare[2]; the black frost in which horses could not travel; the visits of the tailor who made our clothes, sitting cross-legged on the kitchen table, boots off, while he worked; the winter nights when neighbours gathered round the fireside and I went to bed terrified by their stories of ghosts and fairies; the night of the storm in which two rafters cracked under the terrific wind pressure and the thatched roof sagged inwards alarmingly, and the neighbours came with candle lanterns in the darkness to help my father prop it up, their soft black hats tied down with twine under their chins and their strong voices lost in the howling gale.

Associated with these and other early memories, the pale, kind face of my mother is always a part of the mental picture, whether it be of her knitting or mending by lamplight on winter's nights or coming from the milking with the sweet tang of new milk on her hands to see that I was washed and ready for school. My first view of the inside of our two-storied, draughty schoolhouse, with its outside stone staircase and smoking chimneys remains clear because of the impression made on me by the first sight of the head teacher, Master O'Leary as he walked to where I stood timorously at the door. He wore a navy blue serge suit, with a gold watch chain across his waistcoat. He walked slowly on black creaking boots and he carried a whalebone cane in his right hand. I got my share of that cane, or its successors, in due course.

One day at home I remember vividly. Out of the brilliant sunshine my father came into the cool shade of the kitchen from the meadow where he had been mowing. He carried in his hand a brown honeycomb from a moss nest made by wild bees on the ground amid the growing hay. I remember the grateful smile with which my mother took it from his hands, broke off a bit for me and gave the rest to the baby she was just then holding in her lap.

Now I was leaving the familiar shelter of home, too young and immature to know either sharp regret or bright anticipation. As I walked with my father to the railway station I would have liked to look back at the little group of four farm houses of which our house was one, and at the hills on which we turned our backs. The range, extending eastwards from Killarney, which shut in our world to the south was dominated by the twin peaks of the Paps.[3] Since early childhood I had learned to watch for the mountain stream which, after rain, shone like a bright ribbon of silver flowing from the little lake at the base of their rounded breasts. Seen from home, their cairn topped peaks appeared to be clad in flowing robes of misty purple. A closer view which I had one day when I went with my mother to 'the City',[4] where she paid rounds at the holy well on May Sunday, showed me that they were in fact a bleak wilderness of stone and heather. But they never lost their fascination for me.[5]

My father's anxiety was to find someone on the train who would ensure that I reached my destination in Cork safely. To his relief, he found a man whom he introduced as a friend. My father occasionally referred to men, widely scattered in parts of Kerry and Cork, men who I had never seen, as 'friends.' They were not relatives. Thinking about it later I supposed that they were men with whom he had associated in the Land League and Plan of Campaign struggles.[6] He had served a term of imprisonment in Tralee Jail, but when he spoke of it the humorous aspects were the only ones to which he referred, so that I had then no understanding of what the land struggle was about. As the train moved off I looked shyly at my temporary guardian. I never knew his name. I remember him as a solid, silent man with a grey moustache, dressed in a suit of dark tweed. I had never been in a train and the novelty of the changing scene precluded any thoughts of loneliness or homesickness. These were to come later.

In the noise and bustle of Cork station my guardian became vocal long enough to check that my destination was Michael Nolan's shop at 55 North Main Street. He appeared to be in some slight difficulty as to how best to get there, and apparently it was a point of honour with him not to enquire. But he had a solution; we would go to the Butter Market.[7] That was a known base from which he could find any street in the city. He had no thought of getting there any other way other than on foot as he had always done. And so to the Butter Market we walked – then still a place of vast commerce but at the start of its decline – I carrying the light tin box which held my few possessions. From the Butter Market we set off, my guardian with great assurance and I in growing wonder at the sight of all these houses and people, and in due course arrived at No. 55, where the good man refused to part with me until he had been assured that he was handing me over to Michael Nolan in person.

Michael was a cousin on my mother's side. Her family – the Cronins – had many connections in county Cork, while my father's were exclusively in county Kerry, mainly around their ancestral lands at Glenflesk. My cousin had served his apprentice to the drapery trade with his aunt Mrs Collins at Clanbrassil Street, Dublin, and had later worked at Pims in South Great George's Street. When he was about to open his own business in Cork he came to our home on two occasions to ask my parents to allow me to go to Cork as an apprentice. I saw him for the first time on these visits, although his father and brother Con, who farmed at Rathduane, were frequent visitors, and one of my early earliest recollections is of another brother, Tim, who came to our house to make a new cart for the donkey. Michael was the youngest in the family.

At first my parents hesitated. I was the only son in a family of six and normally the eldest son stayed on the farm. In our neighbourhood of small farms emigration was accepted as normal for all except two members of a family, unless the children were brilliant at school and could pass Civil Service examinations, or could find employment in the cities or towns. Even at that time the sons, sometimes the only son, frequently went 'down the country' and were hired as farm labourers for nine or ten months a year. But I was far from being brilliant at school and to my parents this offer of my cousin's seemed a better prospect, an opportunity too valuable to be lightly rejected although it involved a serious sacrifice for them.

And so the decision was made that I should go to Cork. Like many other decisions that has influenced the pattern of my pilgrimage, and enabled me under the Providence of God to come safely through some dangers and difficulties, this first step towards a fuller life than I might have known had my parents been selfish, was one in the making of which I had no part. I have never ceased to be conscious of a deep sense of gratitude to them for their sacrifices on behalf of their family.

The first strong impression made on me by the city was its dry, faintly musty smell, so vividly in contrast with the damp freshness of Kerry mountain air. When I came to 55 [North Main Street] the staff were all girls and some lived in as was the custom in many houses at the time. The house was large, three storied, with bright spacious rooms. The only ill-lighted place was the kitchen, and there the cook-housekeeper Mary Healy ruled with a sharp tongue and iron will.

She was a strange person. In the full blood of womanhood, she had a dark attractive beauty, and a temperament that ranged between boisterous high spirits and fits of the bleakest depression. In a small community where every one's background was common property, she was inordinately secretive and no one ever heard her refer to a relative. She had a good voice and sang through most of her waking hours. The popular ballads of the time were her favourites, those about Cork and its characters particularly; the more rowdy and bawdy they were the greater the gusto in which she sang them. Obviously she had had a fairly good education; ballads were by no means the full extent of her repertory and she was an inveterate reader. She it was who first put Dickens and Canon Sheehan[8] in my hands. She was the first woman I ever saw smoking a cigarette.

Going upstairs for something one mid-morning I found her sitting at the kitchen fire red eyed and weeping bitterly. To my enquiry, she answered, very gently for her, 'You wouldn't understand, child,' and then, fiercely, 'You didn't see me crying. I'm going to sing "If you g'up to the top of the Tower."' (The Tower was an old city landmark.) And sing it she did.

My first year in this strange environment was one of loneliness and homesickness. Occasional walks with Michael Nolan at night and solitary rambles gave me some idea of the geography of the city but no real contacts with its life. In that year Michael's sister Albina came, and a little later his cousin, Gerald Nolan. Gerald had served his apprenticeship in Dublin and had worked later in Glasgow and Edinburgh. He was many years my senior and a bit addicted to drink, so that although we were always good friends no close comradeship developed between us. Later still another cousin, Denis Nolan, came and also a long, gangling lad named MacNamara. The living accommodation was full to the limit and others of the staff lived out.

Books became my solace. My reading was wholly without plan or pattern; anything that came to hand sufficed, from Buffalo Bill and Sexton Blake to Max Pemberton and Jules Verne.[9] There was a recurrent urge to write. I made some secret efforts but had sense enough to realize that the poverty of my equipment made the results worthless. Painting attracted me strongly. At every opportunity I would go and study the prints in the windows of a shop on the Grand Parade, always longing to go inside and explore but never having the courage to do so.[10] I was beginning to feel the attraction of knowledge and to realize sadly how far I was from any hope of grasping these evanescent visions of things beautiful and beyond my ken. Listening to the sermons in the old Broad Lane church of Friars Minor on Sunday nights, I loved the ease of diction and the musical cadences in the oratory even more than the subject matter of the preacher. It was only when I heard a very young priest in SS Peter's and Paul's stumble painfully through a short address that I realized that everybody has to learn.

Distressing though the knowledge of my ignorance was, I lacked the initiative to do anything about it. Unexpectedly Pat Brady provided the initiative. He worked a few doors away and I knew him only casually. One day he told me he was to start on a winter course of night classes at the School of Commerce and asked if I would join also. I did. There that excellent teacher of English, Mr Kennedy, imposed some discipline on my flights of fancy, guiding my reading by lighting for me a path into the vast storehouses of literature. The first prize (which I won at the end of the second session) was an order on a bookseller for (I think) two pounds. I asked Mr Kennedy what I should select. He advised, 'Get a good dictionary and never in your reading pass a strange word without looking up its meaning. Get a copy of Shakespeare and of *The Masters of English Literature,* and if there is anything left a copy of Palgrave's *Golden Treasury.*[11] This was not at all what my untutored inclination would have chosen, but it was priceless advice. I still have those four books. Rathmore National School and the Cork School of Commerce gave me all the education I ever got until I was privileged to join the best university in those days – the national freedom movement.

My first visit home had been at Christmas 1910, and the next in the summer of the following year, on the sad occasion of the death of my sister Molly at the age of ten. Possibly it was in the following year or in 1913 that I was earning enough to purchase a bicycle. I bought it second hand for three pounds from John Murphy, a Castle Street draper and friend of Michael Nolan's, and paid for it in instalments of ten shillings a month. In the next few years I went home frequently on Sundays during the summer months, cycling the ninety miles there and back in a day.

About the same time I joined the Cork Catholic Young Men's Society, where there was a fairly good library, and where I formed the first real friendships with lads of my own age. Those with whom I was most intimate included Keane Harley, Jack Donovan, Fred Eastwood, Tim MacSweeny, and the Stack brothers, Eddie and Jack. We revived a cycling club that had lapsed many years earlier. From it some of us graduated to competing in road and track events. Once again, and not of my own volition, a turn was given to my activities which, looking back, may be regarded as a preparatory phase. I was elected Hon. Secretary of the Club. Later we formed a football club and of that also I became Hon. Secretary. Thus began what has proved to be a lifetime of congenial secretarial work in one form or another down to the present day.[12] 'There is a destiny that shapes our ends...'

There is a medal somewhere which I won in the first fifty-mile road race we held.

[The next-door neighbour's house burns down.]

Michael Nolan took tenancy of the lock-up shop that had been constructed on the corner, and opened it as a men's outfitting store. Gerald and I were installed there, with a young lad, Michael Lehane, who later joined the British Army at the outbreak of the war. In that little shop, which had one exit only and was completely cut off from the upper portion of the building, I continued to work full time until the spring of 1920 when the call came for full-time service in the Volunteers.

[Gerald hypnotizes a prankster and finally emigrates to America.]

Eventually Gerald's restless feet were on the road once more – to America this time. He died there at an early age. I was then given charge of the shop, with Denis and Michael Lehane as assistants. Denis did not stay very long. One Sunday night he left a note for Michael and, without a word to anybody, walked out. It was years later that we heard he had arrived in the United States. MacNamara had left before this time and my sisters Nell and Albina had come to Cork. When Michael moved to Blackrock we took over a tenancy from him of the upper part of No. 55. When Lehane left to join the British Army, Walter Leo Murphy of Ballincollig came as an apprentice and worked with me. We became very good friends.

In the early years of the twentieth century, Ireland struggled to secure a measure of autonomy from Britain in the form of Home Rule. Championed by Charles Stewart Parnell and his Irish Parliamentary Party during the 1880s, Home Rule for Ireland was debated in the British House of Commons for over a generation. By 1913, the ruling Liberal Government of Henry Asquith moved to pass a watered-down Home Rule Bill, largely to maintain its governing majority through the support of Irish nationalists.

The passage of the Home Rule Bill sparked Britain's worst constitutional crisis since the reign of King Charles. Fierce resistance came from Ireland's Ulster Unionists, led by Edward Carson, who feared Catholic hegemony in the new arrangement. Britain's Conservative Party strongly supported Ulster's intransigence, motivated by both ideology and politics, as it recklessly used the issue as a wedge to try to drive the ruling Liberal Government from office.

The Ulster Unionists threatened civil war if Home Rule was implemented. They formed their own militia, the Ulster Volunteer Force (UVF), and organized tens of thousands of volunteers who took a pledge to defend Ireland's Union with Great Britain by arms if necessary. When the British Government ordered some army units into strategic locations in Ulster, British Army officers at the Curragh Camp expressed reluctance to operate against the Unionists, and were supported by some of the Army's most senior staff (especially the

Ulster-born General Sir Henry Wilson). Ultimately the Liberal Government backed down from their challenge and refused to censure the 'Curragh Mutiny' leaders.

Meanwhile, Irish supporters of Home Rule, inspired by the example of the UVF, organized their own paramilitary body called the Irish Volunteers. The quasi-militia commanded by the Gaelic scholar Eoin MacNeill, was led by militant nationalists, including members of the secret Irish Republican Brotherhood (also known as the IRB). Seeing the Irish Volunteers' growing popularity, the constitutional Irish Parliamentary Party (led by John Redmond) assumed control of the body, but IRB militants remained its driving force. Tens of thousands of Volunteers marched and drilled openly across Ireland, though they remained practically unarmed. While most contemporary observers considered the Irish Volunteers play-actors rather than soldiers, their appearance accelerated the country's drift towards open conflict.

In August 1914, at the height of the Home Rule crisis, the First World War erupted in Europe. A patriotic fervour broke out in Great Britain and Ireland. Mass army recruitment meetings were held across the country, and thousands of Corkmen were among those who answered the call for military service. The British Government postponed implementation of the Home Rule Bill until after the war's conclusion.[13]

After the outbreak of the war in 1914 a wave of propaganda swept the country, directed at getting the maximum number of recruits for the British forces. Sustained and intense, with the glamour and the glory emphasized in a thousand ways, it took many a young lad with no better appreciation of issues than I had, so completely off his feet that the appeal was irresistible. A few with whom I was fairly intimate, Michael Lehane, Jack Stack, and Tommy O'Meara, joined up. We talked about it, but to the suggestions that I should go with them I did not respond. My refusal had nothing whatever to do with the national question or the issues involved, because my ignorance on both heads was profound. My decision was, I think, dictated by about equal parts of an instinctive dislike of what I had seen of British soldiers with their swaggering ways and flashy uniforms in the streets of Cork, lack of initiative, and a sense of responsibility to my parents and sisters. The whole weight of such opinion as I had any contact with, newspapers, periodicals, public speeches, and private discussions, was unquestionably pro-British. I never at the time heard a note of doubt or protest, or anything but admiration for England and a hatred for Germany.

War was then a novelty. It made me recall one of my earliest memories, that of Mickey Walsh, an intelligent but illiterate neighbour, coming with the latest newspaper on Sundays so that my father could read for him the latest news of the Boer War. Mickey called it 'the wor.' He was enthusiastically pro-Kruger[14] and with his excellent memory, would, before the reading session began, lay down a mental situation map of the position as given in the previous Sunday's news.

Mickey made a living cutting bogdeal, disinterring the stumps and roots of primeval forest long buried in bogland, hacking them into small pieces with his axe, and sending wagon loads of them by rail to Cork. He once went to hospital in Killarney – a rare occurrence at that time in our locality, but a wonderful event for him that provided material for long disquisitions on the wonders of the world. When leaving the hospital, so he used to relate, the doctor advised him that for some days he should steep bread in tea and eat it with a tea spoon. Mickey's comment was, 'A Mhuire then, yes, for fear I'd ate too much of it with a big spoon.' He or his brother Seamus would take care of us children in the rare occasions when both father and mother were away from home together at a fair, a funeral, or a wedding.

To return to 1914–15. I was still attending night classes at the School of Commerce. Cycling trips and visits to sports meetings had given me a fair knowledge of the immediate countryside, and I read much by candlelight. Most of what I read was fiction, but occasionally it bore in on me, in passages describing a country or giving glimpses of its history, a sense of how very little I knew of my own country or of its history. But the kind of interest or curiosity that would have made me seek information was lacking. Ignorance was not sufficiently depressing to act as a spur, although I was beginning to be aware of the vast undiscovered fields of colour and beauty and variety in life. For a time poetry wove its spell, but it was English poetry – or at least anything that was Irish made no illuminating connection with the life around me.

The so-called National school education of those days was certainly misnamed. It nourished no natural feelings of love of country; it told children nothing of the story of their own land, except that which was so remote that the link between it and the living present was lost; nothing that would cause pride in their own localities was ever mentioned. That, I am sure, was not the fault of the teachers but of the system they were obliged to operate. One of my teachers whom I always remember with gratitude did something to defeat the system, by utilizing the play hour (on wet days when we could not go outside the school) to read us Scottish patriotic songs. Denis Breen would have given us some spark of nationality had the system permitted him to do so.

I had no smallest inkling that the large ring-fort from which my home parish got its name was a survival from an ancient past, that ordinary people lived out their lives there in another age, built their stone-roofed underground passages and raised the immense earth banks against the wild beasts of the surrounding forests.[15] To us children it was merely a haunted place, sacred to the fairies, which no one would plough or meddle with on pain of dire misfortune. I did not know that the 'City' was the scene of one of the surviving folks tales of ancient days, nor that all this land had in later times been swept with fire and sword by foreign invaders, till not a human voice nor the lowing of a cow could be heard between the Rock of Cashel and the far sea at Dingle. I did not know that I had been born and reared on the edge of Sliabh Luachra, a nursery of poets which had produced Aodhgán O'Rahilly, greatest of the Gaelic singers and ranked by scholars as one of the great poets of the world; and that after him from the same nursery came Eoghan Roe O'Sullivan, living and wandering in near poverty and making almost the last songs of a broken Gaelic civilization. Neither did I know that a man of my own name, Geoffrey O'Donoghue, had attained the poetic stature of being ranked with O'Rahilly, O'Sullivan, and Pierce Ferriter.[16]

Although the Volunteer organization had been started in Cork in December 1913, I have no recollection of having seen or heard anything of it until after the outbreak of the war. Even then, amid the band playing and flag waving of the recruiting campaign, it made no permanent impression. None of the lads I knew were Volunteers or had any information about the movement. We went on with our cycling, a bit of boxing and gymnastics, and games of Gaelic football. And so it was that when the Rising came in 1916, it came out of a world and out of causes of which I knew nothing. But I had an indirect connection with it that I was not aware of until nearly a year later.

At the outbreak of the Great War, Irish Parliamentary Party leader John Redmond committed the Irish Volunteers in support of Britain's war effort. Redmond hosted mass recruiting meetings and encouraged his Home Rule followers to join the British Army. Thousands of Volunteers answered his call, believing their loyalty to Britain would be repaid with the passage of Irish Home Rule. However, the militant IRB-controlled wing of the Volunteers violently opposed recruitment for the European War. The issue split the Volunteer movement into two separate organizations, the Irish Volunteers (now militant Irish Republican) and the National Volunteers (moderate Home Rulers also called Redmond Volunteers). The vast majority of Volunteers joined the Redmondite organization, though it never gelled as a body and disappeared within four years.

The Irish Volunteers retained a small but strong core of militants around the country, and probably numbered around 10,000 members by early 1916. The body did not have an explicit independence programme, but its rhetoric and public drilling pushed a separatist agenda.

During the first year of the war, leaders of the Irish Republican Brotherhood decided to stage a rebellion using the Irish Volunteer organization.[17] They requested assistance from Germany, which agreed to land 20,000 rifles on the Kerry coast to arm the insurgents. The uprising planning took place in utmost secrecy, excluding even the Volunteers' moderate Chief of Staff Eoin MacNeill. Many of the Volunteers probably supported a rebellion in principle, though more than a few thought such an action tantamount to suicide.

A week before the Rising, Volunteer headquarters ordered all units to conduct countrywide manoeuvres on Easter Sunday. Some Volunteers correctly guessed that these manoeuvres were in fact a cover for an insurrection. By this time, Volunteer Chief of Staff, Eoin MacNeill, had finally learned of the Rising plans, and reluctantly agreed to support the venture. The rebels planned to land the German arms over the weekend, and distribute them to the Munster Volunteers on Easter Sunday. The latter would then march on the capital in support of the Dublin Volunteers, who intended to occupy the city centre. On Good Friday, however, the German arms ship *Aud* was intercepted off the Kerry Coast by the Royal Navy and scuttled by its crew in Cork harbour. When Eoin MacNeill learned of the loss of the *Aud* and its 20,000 rifles, he moved to stop the insurrection. On Saturday, the day before the national Volunteer mobilization, MacNeill issued a public counter-order cancelling the Sunday manoeuvres. He sent couriers to key Volunteer commanders around Ireland (including Cork's Tomás MacCurtain) to notify them that the uprising was off. MacNeill's countermand resulted in much subsequent confusion throughout the country. With the Volunteers' arms now resting at the bottom of Cork harbour and their units ordered to stand down, the Rising seemed to collapse before it had begun.

Facing imminent defeat, IRB leaders instructed Dublin Volunteer units to assemble on Easter Monday. This smaller body (numbering about 1,000 men and women), bolstered by James Connolly's Irish Citizen Army, seized control of the city centre and issued a proclamation declaring an Irish Republic. The Rising leaders now recognized their rebellion had no hope of military success, but considered the action a protest in arms.

Since Volunteer units around the country had been specifically ordered by Eoin MacNeill to take no action, the Dublin insurgents largely fought alone. The battle in Dublin raged for five days, until superior British firepower overcame the rebels. Hundreds of combatants and civilians had been killed and Dublin city centre lay in ruins. The British Army executed thirteen of the Rising leaders in the days following the Rising.

Initially the Irish public overwhelmingly rejected the Rising, but that opposition disappeared within a few weeks. The insurgents' spirited defence stirred national pride in some. Others objected to the British Army's drawn-out execution of the Rising's leaders. The rebels' willingness to die for the cause of Irish independence also seemed to strike a chord around the country. Within months, public opinion swung firmly in favour of the insurgents.

In Cork, the Rising had been a debacle. On Easter Sunday, about a thousand Volunteers assembled around County Cork to receive the *Aud* arms, but because of MacNeill's cancellation order they were dismissed that evening. Rumours of fighting in Dublin reached Cork the next day, but proved impossible to verify due to a news blackout and a British cordon around Dublin. Cork commanders Tomás MacCurtain and Terence MacSwiney felt they could not act without clear and definite orders from Volunteer Headquarters in Dublin, and those instructions never arrived. Armed men guarded Volunteer Hall in Cork city, and a tense stand-off existed between them and the British forces. By the end of the week, a clergy-brokered agreement saw the Volunteers deposit their arms in City Hall under the care of neutral parties, while the British agreed to take no offensive action against the Volunteers or their weapons. Two days later, after the Dublin insurgents surrendered, the British Army seized the Cork Volunteer arms and arrested MacCurtain, MacSwiney, and other Cork Brigade leaders.[18]

The entire episode galled Cork Republicans. They felt as if they had let down their counterparts in Dublin and were ashamed that their inaction could be interpreted as cowardice. A year later, MacCurtain and MacSwiney were court-martialled for their conduct during the Rising by both the Volunteer Executive and the IRB. Both bodies eventually cleared the two leaders of wrongdoing, since they had indeed followed orders issued by the Volunteer chain of command. However, Cork's failure during the Rising had a profound impact on Cork's Volunteer movement.

First, the Corkmen were motivated to clear the cloud hanging over their organization. This created an aggressive spirit and desire to start fighting as soon as possible. During the next four years of conflict, Cork Volunteers moved to the forefront of the movement, and Cork city became an unofficial capital of the Irish rebellion. Second, a schism grew between Tomás MacCurtain (along with other moderate Volunteer leaders in the city) and a more militant wing composed primarily of IRB men led by Seán O'Hegarty. MacCurtain believed the confusion of the Rising could have been avoided had the IRB not undermined the Volunteer chain of command. He resigned from the IRB and tried to instil greater discipline in the Cork Brigade. The IRB militants, however, intended to fight at the next opportunity, with or without the blessing of their moderate Volunteer leaders. Seán O'Hegarty, the head of the Cork IRB and the Vice-Commander of the Cork Volunteers, instructed IRB members to defend their arms at all times. This order would figure prominently in two significant episodes in the city in 1918 and 1919. Finally, the Rising amplified tensions between Volunteer leaders in Dublin and Cork. In time, Cork would act largely on its own against the British, with little deference to Volunteer General Headquarters in Dublin. This would become a major factor in the run-up to the Irish Civil War.

Tomás MacCurtain worked hard to reorganize the Volunteers in 1917 and 1918. Some militants still suspected his commitment to physical force, but MacCurtain's aggressiveness in the ensuing months helped rehabilitate his image. He brought the Cork Brigade up to fighting strength, and like much of his rank-and-file, he became impatient to restart the war begun in Dublin on Easter Monday, 1916.

## NOTES AND REFERENCES

1    Rathmore is a village in County Kerry, located between Killarney and Millstreet, on the Cork/Kerry border.
2    Valentine Augustus Browne, Fourth Earl of Kenmare, was the prominent landlord of the Killarney Lakes region. He left Ireland in the 1880s, during the Land War.
3    The twin peaks are a Kerry landmark known in Irish as An Dá Chích Dannan, or the Breasts of the Goddess Dana, who was the mother of the mythical Tuatha De Dannan ('the race of Gods who are called her people'). See T.J. Barrington's *Discovering Kerry, Its History, Heritage and Topography* (Dublin: Blackwater, 1980).
4    Known in Irish as Cathair Chrobhdearg and located at the base of the Paps, 'the City' had been a place of worship since the pre-Christian period.
5    For details about this area, see T.J. Barrington's *Discovering Kerry*, p. 167.
6    During the Irish Land League's 'Plan of Campaign' in the 1880s, County Kerry saw frequent non-violent and occasionally violent land agitation. Disorder occurred in O'Donoghue's native Rathmore, where there were occasional outbursts of 'chaos'. See L. Curtis 'Landlord Responses to the Irish Land War, 1879–87,' *Éire-Ireland Journal of Irish Studies*, Fall/Winter 2003; and Margaret O'Callaghan, *British High Politics and a Nationalist Ireland* (Cork: Cork University Press, 1994), pp. 122–40.
7    The Shandon Butter Exchange was located in the city's Northside. In the

nineteenth century it was the centre of Cork's thriving butter industry.

8    Canon Patrick Sheehan of Doneraile, Co. Cork was a popular novelist who celebrated rural Ireland.

9    These were adventure stories and thrillers for young adults. Buffalo Bill and Sexton Blake were pulp fiction characters, the former an Indian-fighting buffalo hunter from the American West, while the latter was a more physical, less intellectual version of Sherlock Holmes. Max Pemberton wrote crime short stories of the 'rogue school', and Jules Verne penned juvenile classics such as *20,00 Leagues Under the Sea* and *Journey to the Centre of the Earth.*

10    O'Donoghue's youngest daughter Breda later became a successful painter and sculptor. Her painting of Seán O'Hegarty hangs in the Crawford Municipal Art Gallery in Cork.

11    *Palgrave's Golden Treasury of the Best Songs and Lyrical Poems in the English Language,* edited by Francis Turner Palgrave (London: MacMillan, 1875). See Florrie's letter to Jo dated 27 June 1921 for his continued appreciation of a good dictionary.

12    Over the years, O'Donoghue served as secretary to the Bureau of Military History, the Cork Congo Comforts Committee, the Cork County Gaol Memorial Committee, the Cork Tóstal Council, the Diarmund Lynch Memorial Committee, the Neutral IRA, the Old IRA Men's Association, the Memorial Committee of the IRA Cork No. 1 Brigade, and the Terence MacSwiney Memorial Committee.

13    For a general background of the Irish Home Rule Crisis, and the state of Ireland at the outbreak of the First World War, see D.G. Boyce, *The Irish Question and British Politics, 1868–1996* (London: Macmillan, 1996), pp. 47–58, and *Nationalism in Ireland* (London: Routledge, 1995), pp. 259–90; George Dangerfield, *The Damnable Question, A Study in Anglo-Irish Relations* (Boston: Little, Brown and Company, 1976), pp. 28–123; R.F. Foster, *Modern Ireland 1600–1972* (London: Allen Lane, 1988); Joe Lee, *Ireland, 1912–1985* (Cambridge: Cambridge University Press, 1989), pp. 7–23; F.S.L. Lyons, *Ireland Since the Famine* (New York: Scribner, 1971); and Nicholas Mansergh, *The Irish Question 1840–1921* (Toronto: University of Toronto Press, 1975), pp. 192–239, and *Unresolved Question, The Anglo-Irish Settlement and Its Undoing, 1912–1972* (New Haven: Yale University Press, 1991), pp. 27–78.

14    Paul Kruger, President of the South African Republic during the Anglo–Boer War (1899–1902). This conflict was closely followed in Ireland, and many Irish separatists cheered the Boers' fierce resistance to the British Army. Irish Republicans later studied the lessons of this war, especially the skilful use of guerrilla tactics by the Boers, and Britain's brutal response (resulting in the deaths of 28,000 Boer civilians interned in British concentration camps). See Florrie's letter of 5 May 1921.

15    In Irish 'Rathmore' means 'big ring fort'.

16    Sliabh Luachra is an area in the mountainous bogland beyond Rathmore where a series of ancient Irish settlements was located. In the seventeenth century it was one of the last strongholds of Gaelic Ireland, and O'Donoghue here lists a number of its famed Irish-language poets.

17    For general information about the Easter Rising, see Max Caulfield, *The Easter Rebellion* (Dublin: Gill and Macmillan, 1995); Michael Foy and Brian Barton, *The Easter Rising* (Gloucestershire: Sutton Publishing, 1993); and Robert McHugh (ed.) *Dublin 1916* (London: Arlington Books, 1966).

18    O'Donoghue's biography, *Tomás MacCurtain, Soldier and Patriot* (Tralee: Anvil

Books, 1955), offers a comprehensive examination of Cork city during the Rising. His assorted research on the subject can be found in his papers in the NLI. The collection includes excellent primary accounts and correspondence from participants. Two Volunteer veterans also discuss the Cork situation during the Rising in the *Capuchin Annual*: see Liam Russell, 'The Position in Cork', *Capuchin Annual*, 1966, pp. 371–80; and Senator James Ryan 'General Post Office Area', *Capuchin Annual*, 1966, pp. 379–80. Ryan hand-delivered MacEoin's cancellation order to MacCurtain on Easter Sunday.

# 2

# 'ILLUMINATION'

## Florence O'Donoghue

On Easter Sunday 1916, when I was very busy in the shop, a first cousin of mine, Pat O'Connor, called. He was a Post Office clerk in Dublin, having taken first place in Ireland in a Civil Service examination. He lived next door to me at home but was a little older and had left home some years before I did. He appeared to be distraught. He was on his way back to Dublin from the funeral of another brother, Denis, who had also been in the Civil Service but who died at home. He began to talk in a rambling way, to the general effect that he had to come to see me before he went back to Dublin, that he knew I had not been able to get home for the funeral, that he had to say goodbye to me, and that I would never see him again. I foolishly put all this down to the effects of his brother's death, of whom I knew he had been very fond, and to the drinking inseparable from a funeral in the country. I was very busy and could not go out with him then, did not particularly want to, and got rid of him as soon as I could. The last thing he said was that I would never see him again. That was the simple truth. He was killed somewhere around Earl Street or Thomas Lane off O'Connell Street in Dublin on the Friday of Easter Week. His body was not found, or (if it was) was one of those buried without being identified, and it was some time before his death was established.[1]

I did not know he was a Volunteer. In fact he was also a member of the IRB, which probably accounts for the fact that he knew the Rising was timed for Easter Sunday. Efforts had been made to persuade him to remain at home over the weekend after the funeral, but he had insisted, without giving any reason, that he had to be back in Dublin on Sunday. We had not met for about two years before that. On that occasion we were home on holidays at the same time. We had made a round of visits to relatives and had climbed Caherbarnagh one day, got caught in a sudden fog on the top, and had to slither our way blindly downhill until we came on a little lake which gave us an idea of our location. He had not then or on any other occasion said a word to me on any matter of national concern. He must have thought I was a bad prospect or too immature. Intellectually he was brilliant, but my memory of him remains that of a gay and charming companion who talked exceedingly well. A monument to his memory now stands in the village of Rathmore.

For me, as for thousands of others, the Rising was an illumination, a lifting of the mental horizon giving glimpses of an undiscovered country. It created an interest more intense and absorbing than anything in my previous experience. It raised questions so vital and immediately personal that study of them became an imperative necessity. Out of what kind of Ireland, unknown to me, had it come? What manner of men were these who had put their names to the brave, inspiring words of the Proclamation? What was this idea of national freedom for which they had fought and sacrificed themselves?

The two who first emerged for me as personalities whose minds I could contact were Pearse and MacDonagh[2] – mainly perhaps because some of their writings became available soon after the Rising. For a time the others remained merely names – names I had never heard. But Pearse alone would have been enough. I began to read under a new light, to study, to think. And gradually as I began to understand something of the truth in the connection between Ireland and England, conviction grew until it was a passionate belief that these men who had fought in Dublin were right, that they represented the real Ireland submerged under the one I knew.

'In the name of God and of the dead generations from which she receives her old tradition of nationhood, Ireland through us summons her children to her flag and strikes for her freedom.'[3] There it was, simple, inescapable – something that called insistently to an instinct latent or smothered in all of us. During that summer after the Rising there was a wave of what I can describe only as national pride. A fresh, exhilarating wind was blowing in Ireland. Of the lads with whom I discussed it, none withheld admiration for the brave men who had challenged fortune. But in Leo Murphy alone I sensed a reflection of my own feeling that acceptance was not enough, that there was also a call to serve.

Neither of us knew anybody who was a Volunteer, nor did we know if we would be accepted as recruits. But sometime in the winter of 1916–17 we decided to go to the Volunteer Hall and offer our services. Here again the initiative lay more in Leo's character than in mine, though I feel sure that in one way or another, once I had reached conviction in my own mind, I would have been driven into service in some form. We were accepted without question or formality.

At first I was not impressed by what I saw – rather the reverse. My recent reading had included much that idealized and gave a romantic glamour to the national struggle for freedom. I found it hard – impossible in fact – to relate these poetic conceptions to the stark reality represented by groups of shabby youngsters gossiping in the Volunteer Hall or muddling through some clumsy drill. It amazed me that I knew nobody. These lads were different to any I had made contact with through the Catholic Young Men's Society, the School of Commerce, the Gaelic football or cycling clubs, and at first I felt that I did not quite understand them. Of my earlier companions, Keane Harley was one of the very few who later joined the Volunteers, and he had then left Cork to take up a post in the Munster & Leinster Bank, first at Bruff [Co. Limerick] and later at Dame Street, Dublin, of which Branch he ultimately became manager. I remember how I used to scan the faces for someone I knew, and with what joy I saw at last one business friend – Seán O'Donoghue of Mitchelstown, who was employed in Dwyers. During the Civil War Seán was shot dead by Free State soldiers while a prisoner.[4]

> The Irish Volunteer organization was structured along British Army lines, in companies, battalions, and brigades divided geographically. For example, a company area encompassed a village, or a parish, or a city neighbourhood. A number of companies formed a battalion (typically a district or large town), and a number of battalions a brigade (usually a county, or a part of a county). Unit strengths varied, as a company roll could range anywhere from twenty to 150 Volunteers. The Cork No. 1 Brigade was the strongest in Ireland (7,800 Volunteers), and by the truce of 1921 the Brigade's two city battalions together numbered about 2,000 men. (However, the Volunteers never had remotely enough weapons to arm more than a fraction of these men.)

Even in the city the Volunteer organization was on a territorial basis. Company areas were clearly defined, and one had no choice except to join the Company in whose area one lived. I had the good fortune to be in the area of one of the best Companies in the city. If a few of its officers and some of its members had scant respect for any laws, foreign or native, if occasionally they were not above preying on the wealthy commercial life around them, nevertheless they were wholly reliable, intrepid men whose loyalty to the organization was absolute. They circulated in certain friendly pubs; they drank but were not drunkards. Some were skilled tradesmen, following their crafts wherever the job took them, independent, at times truculent, sturdy characters without a trace of subservience. They could plan a job as well as any staff I ever knew. For a time I could find no logical basis for their patriotism. They knew little of history ancient or modern, and cared less. It was a puzzle to me why they were Volunteers at all. And yet, when it came to the test, they proved their courage, their loyalty, and their readiness always to take the post of greatest danger.

These men did not of course comprise the whole Company. One of a very different stamp with whom I became friendly was Matt Ryan, a fine type of Tipperary man, whose fate it was to be killed in the Glen of Aherlow in the Civil War. For some unaccountable reason, he and I were picked by the tough men as two of a party of about twelve for a raid for arms in the house of a Captain Clarke at Farran, about twelve miles from the city. The raid was unauthorized and wrong for two reasons – there was a general order against raids on private houses, and it was outside the Company area. Neither impediment troubled these pirates, and as I was unaware of the order, that aspect did not worry me either. There was a prospect of getting a gun – my immediate ambition just then. The information we had was that there were some rifles, revolvers, and swords in the house. Some resistance was possible and the best time to raid was when the family assembled for dinner in the evening.

It was my first experience of a Volunteer operation – if it can be called that. I did not feel too happy about it. The contrast between it and 'Our camp fires now are burning low; out yonder waits the Saxon foe,' seemed fantastic and absurd. The foe in this case probably wasn't a Saxon anyway, I thought, and I felt an uneasy guilt at the idea of invading with arms the privacy of a man's home, whether he was a foe or not.

We went out in two cars and, as usual with the men in charge, the staff work was good. We arrived when dinner was on. Possibly there were guests, for there were about fourteen or fifteen men and women in evening dress in the dining room. The plan was simple like all good plans, and everyone knew his part clearly. One harmless looking lad to ring the front door bell, the others out of sight until it was opened, then all in very quietly; one to the phone, one to control the back exit, two to the kitchen and servant quarters, two to search for arms, one on the front door, and the remainder to the dining room. Our appearance in the dining room unannounced caused some alarm, but nothing more at first. It was explained that this was a raid for arms, we did not wish to cause any disturbance; if the arms were handed over we would depart quietly, and if they were not we would have to search. Guns had been kept out of sight up to this. The move towards resistance which came suddenly from the men was checked by the firing of one shot, which fortunately did no harm. The arms were found, and we left as quickly as possible. Although the result added a few good weapons to the Company's small stock, I still felt unhappy about the raid. Coming back to the city I was told that if there should be any enquiries by the Brigade, of course I knew nothing whatever about it. But, whatever the poets said, this was reality.[5]

No outdoor parades or training took place, or could take place at this time. The drill indoors was monotonous and I thought of little value. I was getting bored. Leo Murphy, also bored but with more initiative, began to spend his nights and Sundays trying to organize a Volunteer company in his native Ballincollig. It was a bad area, dominated by a large military barracks, and Leo was having a difficult time. But he persisted, and eventually succeeded in building up a Company and later a Battalion of four companies of which he became Commandant, in what had been a virgin area for the organization.[6]

Quite clearly I had reached the point where a decision had to be made. Involuntarily my thoughts went back to something said to me by the fat, matronly cook-housekeeper who had replaced Mary Healy at No. 55. She had glittering green eyes, and the girls found that she could be persuaded to tell fortunes. At one session they had insisted that I let her read my hand. Two things only she said – 'You are not half as determined as you pretend to be,' which struck me as true enough; and, 'You are coming to the time when you will have to choose one of two roads in life. One is going to bring you a lot of crosses and trouble. I don't know which you are going to take.' Now, nearly half a century later, I have no regrets for the choice I made, whatever the other road may have led to.

Up to the end of 1916 I had not got to know any Volunteers other than those in my own Company, and of these I knew only a few really well. I had not found in talks with them any reasoned or logical programme of action by which we could hope to achieve national freedom in arms. I was looking for too much of course, but it seemed to be necessary. There was light and airy talk of fighting that I wholly distrusted. I could not see any weapon with which to fight, I could not see anybody being trained seriously to fight, and I could not see or think of any plan that gave us the remotest chance of success in a fight.

I began to assess myself what we had on our side – a handful of the population mostly poor, untrained, almost unarmed; a lot of frothy patriotic sentiment; and an organization, the small bit of which I could see, was apparently futile and without a policy. There was something more of course, but I did not realize it then. I tried to reckon what was against us – a regular army and police force, well entrenched in solid barracks, trained, well fed, and supplied with all the materials of war; the power and influence of all that was solid and wealthy in the community; and the long established machinery of Government. It looked hopeless.

Two voices called then, one the cautious, practical voice of the work-a-day world, that regarded this playacting as soldiers as not quite respectable and suited only to the lower orders. I got much good and well-meant advice to the general effect that I would ruin my business prospects if I continued to associate with the rabble. The other voice came out of something deeper. It was quiet, assured, spoke only to the heart, and knew no doubts. There is an obligation to do what you believe to be right; be not afraid, go forward, this is your destiny. And so a decision was made. But I did not and could not afford to neglect my ordinary employment. I had always kept close touch with home, frequently cycling the ninety miles there and back on Sundays. When I told them I was going on with my Volunteer work, my mother thought I was doing a foolish thing, and I can well understand how it must have appeared so to her. I think my father understood, but even his approval only came later.

Three strong figures led the Volunteer movement in Cork. Tomás MacCurtain, Terence MacSwiney, and Seán O'Hegarty had been active in the city's Gaelic cultural revival. A clerk, traditional musician, and Irish-language teacher, MacCurtain proved a personable leader and capable administrator as he headed the Cork Brigade following the Redmond split of 1914. He was ably assisted by Terence MacSwiney, a charismatic teacher, playwright, and member of a formidable Republican family (his sister Mary was a national leader of Cumann na mBan, and younger brother Seán became a prominent Cork city Volunteer officer). MacSwiney's skills as an orator and writer helped him grow into one of the most celebrated figures of the Irish War of Independence period.

Seán O'Hegarty also acted as a key organizer during these early days. As the centre of the Irish Republican Brotherhood in Cork, O'Hegarty breathed new life into the secret society. A postal clerk, he had even recruited an IRB circle in the Cork Post Office. O'Hegarty knew MacCurtain and MacSwiney from Irish language and cultural activities in the city, and with them co-founded the Irish Volunteers in Cork. In 1914, British authorities had him dismissed from the post office and ordered out of Cork city, though he was never charged with a crime. Decisive, quick-witted, and sharp-tongued, O'Hegarty proved an excellent military leader.

Early in 1917 the effect of the release of the interned Brigade officers was soon apparent.[7] There was a more purposeful activity; one sensed the presence of a steadier hand on the helm. I saw Tomás MacCurtain and Terence MacSwiney for the first time, but their minds were completely out of my reach.[8] Although it was less than two months before they were re-arrested, much had been done by that time to give a new impetus to a now rapidly expanding organization. Up to the Rising there had been one Battalion of four companies in the city, of which Seán O'Sullivan was Commandant. In the rapid expansion of 1917 two Battalions were formed in the city, with Terry MacSwiney as Commandant of the First and Seán O'Sullivan of the Second.

In the first months of 1917 a notice appeared in the [Volunteer] Hall to the effect that a Cyclist Company was being formed. It directed that those interested should hand in their names. Here was something I could do which promised to be more interesting than the routine drill parades. I put in my name. Twenty-five or so Volunteers were got together one night and told to elect officers.[9] This was the usual procedure at the time. I knew perhaps half of those present; many like myself were country lads. A man I had never seen before, who was a little older than the rest of us and appeared to be well known to most, was unanimously elected Captain. He was Denis MacNeilus, a Donegal man who had been in the Volunteers in Cork from their formation. The reason why I had never seen him was that he had been on night work where he was employed at the Shell factory in North Main Street. He was an engineer and a very highly skilled craftsman. To my astonishment he proposed me for the position of 1st Lieutenant and to my greater astonishment I was elected unanimously. I do not know whether there was any pre-arrangement, I never enquired, but this was a complete surprise for me.[10] There it was again, the unforeseen turn of events creating a decision in which I had no part. Very soon I discovered that I had come into touch with a kindred spirit. In his thinking on the national question MacNeilus had arrived at the same state of mind as myself, and by the same road, but much earlier. We spent many a happy night in argument, plans, and dreams. He had an alert, active mind, a very practical intelligence, and a cold Northern manner. He was an Irish speaker, having learned the language, as he told me, from a Scotchman in Manchester.

We discovered that we had quite good material in the Cyclist Company. Neither we nor anybody else knew anything about cyclist training. We bought any British [Army] manuals we could lay our hands on (the only ones available to us), and applied our common sense to the principles laid down. We were practical to the extent that we never allowed ourselves to lose sight of our own circumstances. MacNeilus went on night work again soon after we started, so that, except on Sundays, command and training of the Company fell to me. I discontinued attendance at the School of Commerce, gave little attention to the Cycle or Football clubs, and began to devote all my spare time to Volunteer work.

A period of happy activity commenced. An officers class, held in the fields on the outskirts of the city early on Sunday mornings, gave us a gruelling as severe as a modern commando course. A series of indoor lectures covered the usual elementary military subjects. Terry MacSwiney gave a couple of lectures on the writing of orders, but I made no intimate contact with him then. In none of the lectures can I recall any faintest hint of a plan of action or any suggestion of the kind of struggle that developed three years later. The training was orthodox and based on British [Army] manuals.

The urge to write, never wholly suppressed, reasserted itself. Amongst other publications I had been reading was the *Irish World*, a weekly published by P.S. O'Hegarty. I did not know P.S. then or anything about him.[11] With a good deal of diffidence and misgiving I sent him my first efforts. He published them and asked for more. Thereafter I wrote an article weekly for him for about two years until the paper was suppressed. I think not more than half of them got past the censor and almost all were mutilated – a not unusual experience at the time. I looked over some of them recently. There is nothing in them worth preserving, nothing that had not been better said before. I was merely churning out ideas I had absorbed in study, but I suppose they were good propaganda at the time.[12] I even wrote some bad verse, all of which has fortunately perished, except one small bit which I see in the *Irish World*.

In April or May 1917 I was sworn into the Irish Republican Brotherhood. This was a secret, oath-bound society, small in numbers but comprising only carefully selected personnel. Its previous existence was known since the Rising, but this was the first indication I had that it was being reorganized. The pre-Rising strength in Cork did not exceed twenty, and at the time of my initiation it was still under fifty, although there were then over one thousand Volunteers in the city.

It was organized in Circles of ten or twelve under a leader called the Centre; Circles were grouped to form Districts under a District Centre; these in turn formed a County Organization under a County Centre. At the top was a Supreme Council, the majority elected, a few co-opted. It was a close-knit, practical, hard-headed body, and it evoked an extraordinary spirit of loyalty and brotherhood amongst its members. It was not propagandist; it sought rather to find and bind together men of good character who had themselves reached the conviction that there was no solution to the problem of achieving national freedom except through the use of physical force.[13]

It was good to find such men. They knew their own minds; they had a clear and definite objective; and they had an intelligent and practical approach to the realities of our situation. After the Rising no one was admitted who was not a Volunteer. Despite the obvious dangers of a secret body inside the Volunteer organization, I think what the IRB contributed as a hard core of opinion outweighed the disadvantages. At the date of the Truce I was County Centre for Cork city and county. The number of members in Cork city and county was then 580.

I do not think that in 1917, or indeed during the following years of struggle, any of us thought very much about forms of government. I had no clearer definition of national freedom than that envisaged by the ejection of British troops and British machinery of government out of the country. Republicanism was no more than a convenient expression, not a faith or a belief in a particular form of government. There was a clear and desirable objective (as we thought), and all our energies were devoted to studying how best to use such means as we had or could acquire, to attain it.

Contemplating what we had in men and arms, in spiritual and material resources, I was then unable to see any immediate or even remote prospects of success in the kind of insurrection that had become traditional. At the same time, I was not insensitive to the resurgent spirit of the time, our expanding organization, and the vast change in the climate of public opinion. If the people remained steadfast in their new-found faith, if there was good leadership, something might be achieved. If we were to fight sometime, somehow, certain things would be needed which we could begin to acquire now – organization, discipline, training, arms. In that light I set to work with my small Company. Responsibility for training forced me to study hard myself. The available manuals could not be allowed to obscure the fact that we would never have most of the facilities they accepted as normal in an army. We had to seek the underlying principles, and adapt, improvise and relate them to our very different circumstances.

Parades were held on two nights each week and almost every Sunday. The ability and endurance of the men were tested in long Sunday rides into the country and in some night exercises. MacNeilus and I made the training progressively difficult, and soon we had a good idea of the individual capacity of each man. Allowance had to be made for poor or unsuitable bicycles. The machines were of course the property of the men themselves; each man had to meet the cost of upkeep and wear and tear himself. All were trained to do normal running repairs. As MacNeilus was on continuous night work, we had a 2nd Lieutenant elected. He was Denis Kennedy, the genial son of a Dungarvan doctor, and he was then an Engineering student at University College.

In the early months of 1917 I made my first official contact with one of the Brigade officers. I had to see Brigade Adjutant Pat Higgins about some matter connected with the Cyclist Company. He was tall and thin, hook nosed and sallow featured, with shoulders slightly hunched and an ungainly habit of tucking his hands backwards into the sleeves of his raincoat. His hair and moustache were wiry and coal black, he drooped a little and sounded weary. To me he seemed aged, though he was not in fact more than ten years older than I was. I was disappointed. Anything that looked less like a soldier and an officer I could not well imagine. Later, when I got to know Pat well, I came to appreciate the lively intelligence of this whimsical and charming man. He had a fund of stories and one may be worth recalling.

He was born at the Powder Mills, Ballincollig, and the house in which he lived was one of a number on the land attached to Ballincollig military barracks. In his young days there were soldiers in the British Army in this post who were not alone Irish speakers, but who knew practically no English and used Irish habitually as their normal language. (What tragedy there is in that.) Some of them lived in married quarters in houses which had a common entrance gate with that of the residents in the Powder Mills, and on which a sentry was always on duty. The gate was closed at night and a small wicket used. One night late one of the Irish speakers and his wife arrived at the closed wicket for admission. The Cockney sentry on duty challenged, 'Who goes there?' The Irishman replied, 'Seán O'Domnal agus a Bhean.' The sentry grumbled, 'I can't open the big gate. Come in Seán O'Domnal but you'll have to leave the bloody van outside until the morning.'

At the beginning of June 1917, the Volunteer Hall was closed against us by an order of the military authorities, after a demand that we should evacuate it had been refused. Thereafter each Company had to find alternative accommodation for indoor training wherever it could. My company was allowed the use of the Blackpool Sinn Féin Club rooms at Watercourse Road.

Tomás and Terry had been arrested with some other officers in February and deported to England. They were released in the middle of June at the same time as the prisoners who had been sentenced to terms of penal servitude after the Rising.[14] They resumed their posts at once but it was not until October that I had any close contact with them.

In that month a general order was issued for public parades in uniform on Sunday the 21st [of October]. These parades were primarily a gesture of defiance of a British prohibition on parades or the wearing of a uniform. Secondarily, they were a recruiting and propagandist effort. The city's eight or nine hundred men paraded outside their closed Hall in Shears Street. Only a minority had full uniform, but all made the best show possible, with Volunteer caps, bandoliers, belts and puttees. No arms were carried. Police and detectives were very busy as we assembled.[15]

I remember that Sunday particularly well for two reasons. It was the first time I wore a uniform and the first time I spoke to Tomás MacCurtain. That first tunic of mine – I remember we later put it on the light shell that was the body of Michael Fitzgerald, after he had died on hunger strike in Cork Jail in October 1920. Terry was dying in Britxton – died a week later in fact.[16] Tomás was dead and the whole world was black about us. One of the many things that remain vivid in my mind out of that grim month, was the shock of amazement I got in the cold, candlelit mortuary in SS Peter's and Paul's on that raw October night when we took Fitzgerald's body out of the coffin in which it had been brought from the Jail, to fulfil his last wish that he should be buried in uniform. He had been a burly lad; now I could lift his poor body as if it was that of a little child. His face too was childlike and peaceful. My first tunic was buried with him in Kilcrumper.[17]

Preparing to move off from Shears Street in the parade, Tomás came to where I was in charge of the Cyclist Company. He said, 'Can you meet me tomorrow night at eight?' I said of course I could, unless we were all in jail tomorrow night. He smiled and said, 'Well maybe. I'll tell you now what I want you to do.' Rapidly and concisely he explained that it was necessary to organize lines of communication by means of cyclist dispatch riders, from Brigade Headquarters in the city to every Battalion headquarters in the country. I was to take charge of this work and use the Cyclist Company for the first stages of these lines of communication. I would be appointed Brigade OC Communications and would attend Brigade Council meetings in future.[18] I was to submit a plan to him as soon as possible.

My first reaction was, by God, here at last is a man, maybe a great man. In his early thirties, medium sized, stocky, alert, soldierly, clear, concise, calm, with a gift of precise expression and wrinkles of humour round his blue eyes – so much I gathered while he spoke. He had a personality that was very attractive, but I sensed something else which I got to know well later, hard to define but seeming to me compounded of a complete absence of vanity, entire unselfishness, a dedicated integrity, and sincerity.

My second reaction was, 'Me? Why? I don't know how many Battalions there are; I don't know an officer in charge of one of them outside the city; I don't know the first thing about this job; I'll make a mess of it.' Thinking about it during the day, I grew more intimidated by the prospect and thought of asking to be excused undertaking the job. That passed however. I sought out Pat Higgins during a break when we were in a field near Blarney. Pat tucked his arms further up his sleeves, hunched his shoulders, looked at me quizzically and said, 'Young fellow, you're going to be busy.' However, he gave 'out of his head' a list of the twenty Battalions with their HQ locations and the names of the officers in charge as far as he could remember them. He made the sensible suggestion that I should put them down on a map of the county and see how the best routes to them could be worked out.

Tomás, Terry, and some others who wore uniforms were arrested the next day.[19] I must have been unrecognised or regarded as of no consequence because no attempt was made to arrest me. The prisoners went on hunger strike and were released in a few days under the Cat and Mouse Act.[20] I chewed on the job I had been given with all the keen earnestness of youth and inexperience. When I saw Tomás towards the end of the week he gave my proposals immediate approval, told me to go ahead as fast as possible, and to report to him when the system was ready to operate.

Once I had accepted the responsibility I put every bit of care and thought and ingenuity into making the scheme sound and workable. I remember the principles I worked out for myself to guide me. First: safety and secrecy, to be attained by picking reliable men, using numbers instead of names of men or units, keeping the routes as far as possible off the main roads and by-passing police and military posts. Next: speed and reliability, to be attained by not making the stages longer than the average man could do at a speed or at night or in bad weather – ten to twelve miles, maximum fifteen. And finally economy of man power; to be attained by making the main routes serve the largest possible number of Battalions, with short branch routes stemming from them where necessary.

With so large an area to be covered, I had pointed out that the work would take time to complete in the most distant stages, as I wished to cover every route myself and see and instruct the men appointed. I hardly realized what I was taking on because almost all the work had to be done on my only free day – Sundays. With the authority and support of the Brigade Commandant I made it a rigid rule that no names would be used in dispatches, and no locality mentioned in connection with any unit. Thus if the police did intercept a DR [Dispatch Rider] and find his dispatches (and we worked out some good methods of concealing them) they would gain no information as to who the OC was or where a particular Battalion was located. A very detailed British Intelligence report captured in May 1921 showed that even then the British did not know where our Battalions were.

MacNeilus was on continuous night work but was sometimes free on Sundays. I left the Cyclist training to him and to Denis Kennedy, and began to acquire for myself an intimate knowledge of the county Cork bye-roads on my Sunday organizing journeys. All through the winter I kept at it, and by March 1918 I had covered every point on the seven routes radiating from the city that could by any stretch of effort be reached in a day and a night on bicycle. Being wet was not unusual, I did not mind it very much. What I hated was the cold. I could be happy in a warmer climate than ours. But I was never once ill.

There remained the distant ends of the routes that could not be reached in a day's cycling from Cork. Roads were of course very different then to what they are nowadays. Tarred stretches were few on main roads, entirely absent on bye-roads; loose stones, mud, and potholes were the normal winter fare. The distant points were covered by leaving the city after work on Saturday nights (usually about midnight as we worked up to 11 p.m. on Saturdays), cycling to near the required point, and then if there was an hour or two before first Mass, crawling into a hay barn somewhere and getting a little sleep. On some of these trips MacNeilus came with me, on some Denis Kennedy, but most of them I did alone.

I can fix the date of one of these journeys accurately because it was the Sunday on which the Anti-Conscription pledge was being signed at the Church gates throughout the country – 21 April 1918.[21] Denis Kennedy and Denis McCarthy (another member of the Cyclist Company), came with me. We left the city about midnight on Saturday, taking the Inchigeela/Ballingeary Road for Bantry. It was intensely cold when we reached the Pass of Keimenigh in the small hours of Sunday morning. After trying to eat some sandwiches we had brought with us, McCarthy got ill and we had to walk slowly to the top of the Pass. After an early breakfast in Bantry, we attended Mass and later had a meeting of the local Battalion Council.

At Caheragh on the way to Skibbereen, McCarthy had to drop out. A strong head wind had made the going very tough. We were an hour behind schedule at Skibbereen, and after a long meeting with the Battalion Council, efforts were made to get us to stay overnight. It was fifty-five miles back to Cork. Denis Kennedy decided to stay, but as I had to be at work at nine the next morning, I set out alone at about 7 p.m., reaching Cork very tired just on midnight – a round trip of about 140 miles in twenty-four hours.

Two others of these journeys I remember well. One on a day of endless rain and mud when Justin McCarthy and I organized the Dunmanway route, and the other a Saturday night trip with MacNeilus over Nadd to Kanturk and Newmarket. We got a couple hours sleep in a hay barn without disturbing the farmer's dog. The man of the house did not quite know what to make of us at first, but insisted that we have a cup of tea anyway. At Newmarket that day I met Seán Moylan for the first time.[22]

Out of all this I got something priceless, something which I value as one of the precious privileges of my fortunate generation of Irishmen. I got the beginnings of an intimate knowledge of that splendid body of men who were the backbone of the Volunteer organization in this county. Ireland never had more faithful or unselfish sons, never had more earnest or willing workers, never had braver or better soldiers. I got sincere comradeship and friendships that have deepened with the years, surviving even the clash and bitterness of Civil War. I got to know that generous and courteous hospitality which still lived on unspoilt in the countryside. And I began to appreciate that quiet courage with which the older people were ever ready to wish God's blessing on the dreams and schemes of turbulent youngsters.

The Brigade Council meetings gave me contact with the men who controlled the Brigade, and an insight into their policy and problems. No one sitting at these weekly meetings could doubt for a moment Tomás MacCurtain's ability to control and if necessary dominate the Council. But he exercised his authority with a gentle if firm hand, seeming to gather it always from the corporate opinion of the meeting, but invariably making the final decision himself. He could be persuasive, patient, and humorous. Here I met the Vice Commandant Seán O'Hegarty for the first time. In some ways a more forceful character than Tomás, he had a fine intelligence and a faith and determination that literally blazed in his eyes when he was moved. He was then slight, sallow, with a heavy black moustache, magnificent eyes, and an intellectual forehead. He had not MacCurtain's genial imperturbility, nor half his humorous tolerance and understanding of human frailty. It was rarely that their views clashed on any serious matter; in fact the only such clash which I can remember before the one which caused Seán's resignation (and which I will come to later), was a stupid row precipitated in Cumann na mBan by two groups of jealous women, relatives of almost everyone on the Council except myself. I do not remember the details of that row now, nor had I much interest in it at the time, but it was unpleasant and it took several months to patch up.[23]

Here too I came into intimate contact with Terence MacSwiney, then OC First Battalion. A little above medium height, dark hair always worn long with a lock falling over his forehead, [he had] a sallow, rather attractive face with a sensitive mouth and blue eyes. Serious, fluent in Irish or English, [he was] always eager to accept any duty. At that time he impressed me as a dedicated, cultured man, gentle and thoughtful. Without being able to define the difference satisfactorily then or now, I felt that his mind was not the mind of the average Volunteer; in him all their finer qualities predominated; it seemed that the fire and passion in him had been schooled into calm restraint. The OC Second Battalion was Seán O'Sullivan, a man of fine commanding presence and good looks, and the most impressive figure amongst the officers. He spoke well, with easy confidence, out of a shallow mind. He personified all the fine airy hillside talk I had come to distrust. He faded out when the fight began. The Brigade Adjutant was Pat Higgins whom I already mentioned. Seán Murphy, the Brigade Quartermaster, was a cautious, hard-working officer and a friend of Tomás'. He had limitations and did not retain his post after 1918. He was replaced by Joe O'Connor, a brother of Father Dominic's.[24]

That was the normal group who comprised the Council, although all Battalion Commandants were members and some attended occasionally. Michael Leahy of Cobh, T.J. Golden from Donoughmore, and Tom Hales from Ballinadee were the most frequent visitors. All these men had given years of service to the national cause, some of them for many years before the foundation of the Irish Volunteers, and all had served in the Volunteers since their inception. I was therefore, both in years and in service, very junior. I had nothing to contribute to the Council except what concerned my own responsibility for Communications. I was still so shy and diffident that although I had begun to be able to express myself mostly on paper I still found it an ordeal to speak at a meeting.[25] Mostly I was silent.[26]

By 1918, the Irish Volunteers was a semi-legal organization. It was not banned, though its members were prohibited from owning arms, drilling, marching, or wearing uniforms. The RIC kept the Volunteers under close observation, monitoring public meetings for possible sedition and frequently arresting Brigade leaders. This harassment forced the Volunteers to get into the habit of disguising their movements and avoiding loose talk. Their improved security discipline proved invaluable in the coming years.

Meanwhile, the separatist political party, Sinn Féin, exploded throughout Ireland. Under the leadership of Arthur Griffith and Eamon de Valera (the most senior surviving commandant of the Easter Rising, who proved much more adept at politics than war), the party mobilized popular sympathy for the Easter Rising and attracted vibrant new blood into Irish politics. Sinn Féin vigorously contested three by-elections, handing the Irish Parliamentary Party a series of defeats. The Republicans built an effective national grassroots organization and aggressively

challenged both the British government and Ireland's fading constitutional political parties.

Sinn Féin and the Irish Volunteers remained different organizations,
providing two separate wings of a national independence front
(Cumann na mBan formed a third). While the Volunteer organization
had at this time no stated policy of armed insurrection, it was clearly
moving in that direction. The Volunteers themselves were largely young
men who frequently saw physical force as the answer to every independence question. Sinn Féin members, however, tended to be more
moderate, older, and less confrontational. In the early days of the War
of Independence, Sinn Féin's leaders frequently opposed armed
resistance against the British. While the Volunteers usually assisted Sinn
Féin election campaigns, many Volunteers remained suspicious of all
parliamentary politics.

Ignorant of these Republican complexities, British authorities saw
membership of the two bodies as interchangeable and frequently
harassed and arrested the better-known Sinn Féin activists. These arrests
proved counter-productive. The jailing of elected officials, frequently on
dubious and trumped-up charges, aroused public resentment of the
British Administration; physical-force militants often replaced many of
the imprisoned moderates; and the police activity warned the Volunteers
of a pending crackdown, giving them time to move their organization
underground.[27]

The whole movement was still largely in the open. Companies were
holding regular training parades, but the mass public parades in
uniform had been discontinued, it being considered that they had
served their purpose and that there was nothing to be gained by
inviting further arrests. Gradually we began to adopt a policy of
evading and not provoking arrests. Terry had been arrested in Dublin
in March. Many of the most important officers, including Tomás and
Pat Higgins, went on the run to the extent that they did not sleep at
home nor go about openly, although they carried on their normal
Volunteer duties. The rest of us stopped wearing uniforms and
covered our activities in such a way as to give the police the impression
that we were only nominally active. Substitutes were named and
notified for each officer of any importance – the substitute to take up
duty immediately on the arrest of the officer whose 'shadow' he was. I
became the shadow for Pat Higgins, Denis Kennedy for me and so on.
Police activity was confined mainly to observation; arrests were usually
for public speeches or for arms found in raids.

My journeys to the country Battalions gave me contacts and
opportunities that Tomás was quickly to avail of. More and more he

gave me all sorts of missions that were outside the scope of my own work; more and more he relied on my reports, and when he went on the run would sometimes arrange to come with me on journeys. I remember those Sunday trips with delight. He was a good cyclist and a charming companion. He was interested in everything. Somehow he preserved his tolerant good humour in the face of such incidental troubles as bad weather, punctures, people late for appointments, things not done that should have been done, disappointments about meals – all these things, small in themselves, that would irritate another never unduly bothered him. And yet he was not lax or easy-going with anyone. He was ahead of us all in his practical thinking, but he had the patience and vision to nurse rather than drive the solid building up of organization, discipline, and steadiness.

In February 1918 he asked me if I would take the post of Brigade Adjutant. On my enquiring about Pat Higgins he said that Pat himself was anxious to be relieved, that with what was before us a younger and more active man was necessary, and that I had all the contacts. I said there were several suitable officers with longer service and more experience, some of them better equipped educationally and as Irish speakers than I was. I thought they would resent being passed over. He then did something I have many times recalled with astonishment. He gave me the character estimations of the officers I had mentioned, some of which surprised me and some that I disagreed with strongly. The subsequent years of trial proved that in no single case was his estimation in error.

He demolished my arguments and I agreed to take the post. It was an honour I was proud of, although I had no illusions either about my own limitations or about the heavy work involved. At the next meeting of the Council, Pat resigned and proposed me to replace him, speaking highly of the work I had done. Tomás must have prepared the ground because the appointment was unanimous.[28]

The Adjutant is the maid-of-all-work in every army and at every level. I did not know that then, but made ample discovery of it for myself in the following years.[29] Armies, even an amateur one like ours, tend to follow a pattern. I was in that post until I went on promotion to the Division in April 1921, and it was a liberal education. Everything administrative and much besides came into my hands. Soon there was no smallest aspect of Brigade activity into which I had not poked an inquisitive nose. There was something exhilarating in that sense of creative activity, in building up, binding together, cementing, in the spiritual as well as on the physical plane, the malleable, fiery material at our disposal.

It was fiery material and there were frequent fireworks. The organization was still growing, expanding, and finding its feet. New companies were being formed in places where none had existed, old companies were being divided as they grew unwieldy, and Battalions were being recast to conform with terrain and with an eye to the future. The Parnell split was still a live issue in many parts of the country.[30] Families that had been on opposite sides would not work together in the Volunteers. If a man from one side or the other became company Captain, those on the other side would sulk, start sniping operations, or resign. The system of election of officers obtained right through the organization, and while it was on the whole satisfactory, occasionally it put into office the plausible talker rather than the capable worker. But the countrymen made few mistakes of this kind.

The whole situation became complicated by the wildfire spread of the political organization – Sinn Féin. National opinion was rapidly swinging over to us, bringing with it, along with many earnest and excellent people, elements we regarded, rightly or wrongly, as not wholly disinterested. There appeared to be a real danger that the national character of the movement and its national objective would be watered down or weakened by this influx.[31] Party politics had dominated public opinion for so long that it was difficult for those who had been immersed in its conflicts to accept the new conception of national service; and more difficult still to accept it from a younger generation. We were in the dilemma of either keeping Volunteers out of the political organization and thereby taking the risk that it would become a menace to our aspirations, or allowing them to go in and thereby distracting them from their primary duties and responsibilities. The compromise solution was that a limited number of officers and men went into the Sinn Féin organization, sufficient to exercise a reasonable degree of control and to ensure that the national claim was not endangered.

No Volunteer was forbidden to join the political organization. Many of our best officers went into it, some from political ambition, some because there was no other way to control it locally, and some on instructions. Political activity did not appeal to me. I had no aptitude for it, and I thought it better to try to do one thing well than two indifferently. Seán O'Hegarty and Joe O'Connor were the only other Brigade officers who did not participate.

I have no recollection of being very conscious of it at the time, but in fact what was happening was that the whole of nationalist Ireland was organizing itself voluntarily in a loose but effective way. There was a spirit of unity of purpose, although no clear policy as to method existed, even for the Volunteers. This unity of purpose and the fact that there were organizations suitable for everyone, all having a common objective, were factors of tremendous significance in mobilizing national strength. Apart from the IRB, the Volunteers, Cumann na mBan, and Sinn Féin, there were organizations for boys and girls, and welfare bodies in which the older people could participate. Above all, many fresh minds were thinking seriously on the old problems presented by alien domination. The contacts with that thought (which my organizing gave me), inspired unbounded faith in the shrewd, reflective countrymen I had met. There was nothing flashy about them. They were practical, intelligent, and sincere; they knew what they were doing and what they wanted to do; and they were learning how to combine to do it.

I remember a particularly happy summer, although I cannot now be certain whether it was that of 1917 or 1918. It was usually possible for us to have one free evening each week. We were all learning Irish. Joe O'Connor, Matt Ryan, and I would cycle to Inniscarra (a lovely spot on the Lee six miles west of the city,) and there after a swim, read *Séadna*,[32] try out our limping Irish on each other, or talk in the long summer twilight. Occasionally there were others in that group – Jerry Murphy, a brother of Leo's, now Professor of English at University College Galway; Tadg Barry, a journalist, later shot by a sentry while a prisoner at Ballykinlar Camp;[33] Seán Scanlan, one of the city Company Captains, who died some years ago; and Jim Doherty, a friend of Matt Ryan's.

I think that summer must have been 1917 because Matt Ryan and I decided to go to Banna Strand on Easter Sunday for the anniversary of Casement's landing.[34] We left Cork about midnight on Easter Saturday, reached Killarney just after sunrise, and cooked our breakfast beside the little stream crossing the main road on the Tralee side of town. We cycled on to Tralee, heard mass, and joined the Tralee Volunteers in their march to Banna Strand. In the evening we pushed on to Tarbert, stayed the night there, and on Monday cycled into Limerick and back to Cork. What did we do that 200 mile trip for? I suppose, in part anyhow, the desire to see Banna; the desire to see the Kerry lads and compare them with our own; and youth, good health, and high spirits.

## NOTES AND REFERENCES

1    Patrick O'Connor was probably killed during The O'Rahilly's charge up Moore Street. See Dan Cronin 'The Life of the Late Jim Dempsey', *Sliabh Luachra*, Vol. I, No. 4, June 1987, p. 18; and T. Ryle Dwyer, *Tans, Terror, and Troubles, Kerry's Real Fighting Story 1913–1923* (Cork: Mercier Press, 2001), p. 311. British forces burned both the O'Connor and the O'Donoghue farms as a reprisal for the Rathmore Ambush in May 1921.

2     Patrick Pearse, educator and writer, acted as president of the newly proclaimed Irish Republic. Thomas MacDonagh, poet, author, and literature professor at UCD was (along with Pearse) one of seven signatories of the 1916 Proclamation. Both were executed days after the Rising.

3     From Pearse's Rising Proclamation (read on the steps of the Dublin General Post Office on the first day of the rebellion), declaring Ireland's independence.

4     The militant Republican periodical *Wolfe Tone Annual* included Seán O'Donoghue in its Civil War list of 'unauthorized murders'. His entry reads simply: 'Commdt. Seán O'Donoghue – Murdered in Cork on September 28, 1922.' *Wolfe Tone Annual,* 1962, p. 25.

5     O'Donoghue enrolled in 'G' Company of the Brigade's First Battalion. Freelance actions such as the unauthorized arms raid Florrie describes, were symptomatic of a discipline problem with aggressive IRA units in the city. On 17 November 1920, members of 'G' Company shot the popular RIC Sergeant O'Donoghue without Brigade sanction, apparently because he was an easy target. See Peter Hart, *The IRA and Its Enemies,* (Oxford: Oxford University Press, 1998), p. 13.

6     On 26 June 1921, Commandant Leo Murphy was killed by a British raiding party that surrounded his Third Battalion Council meeting in Waterfall. O'Donoghue later organized a memorial to mark the spot where he fell.

7     There were two classes of Irish prisoners from the Easter Rising. A number of Volunteers were charged with specific crimes, tried by British military court-martial, and when found guilty, sentenced to a prison term. An even larger group of Volunteers were detained without trial and deported to prison in Britain. The Cork Brigade officers were among this latter group. The British Government released the detainees first. Some months later, those convicted of crimes were pardoned and released.

8     After the Easter Rising, the British deported 141 Cork Volunteer leaders to internment camps in Britain. Tomás MacCurtain and Terence MacSwiney were among those imprisoned at Frongoch Camp in Wales.

9     IRA units usually elected their own officers.

10    As MacNeilus was an active IRB member, his election may have been pre-arranged by the IRB.

11    Patrick Sarsfield O'Hegarty was a founder of the Sinn Féin Party and a prominent Republican propagandist and intellectual. He was a Corkman and the brother of Brigade leader Seán O'Hegarty.

12    The IRB financed the *Irish World.* Years later, O'Donoghue's friend Diarmund Lynch inquired about a piece in the *Irish World* that sounded familiar. O'Donoghue replied, 'You are right in thinking the article was mine. In fact, all my very immature efforts at political propaganda are in this publication. Their only interest now is as a reflex of youthful enthusiasm.' O'Donoghue to Lynch, 2 July 1949, Ms. 31,283, NLI.

13    Following the Easter Rising, Michael Collins reorganized the IRB and became its new head. Most prominent IRA leaders during the 1919–1921 conflict were also members of the IRB.

14    Both were deported to a village in England and detained without charges or a trial. The British authorities paid for their upkeep, but the detainees were confined to a small area. See O'Donoghue, *Tomás MacCurtain,* p. 126. In 1917, Kerry Volunteer leader Billy Mullins was deported to Yorkshire in similar circumstances and wrote a fine account of his experience. See Mullins, *Memoirs of Billy Mullins* (Tralee: Kenno Ltd, 1983), pp. 76–98.

15   The *Cork Examiner* wrote of hundreds of 'orderly' Volunteers marching from the city 'in an approved military formation'. *Cork Examiner*, 22 October 1917.

16   In October 1920, Terence MacSwiney died on hunger strike in London's Brixton Prison. IRA prisoners in Cork Gaol were also striking at the same time, and two of them, Michael Fitzgerald and Joseph Murphy, died.

17   Kilcrumper Cemetery in Fitzgerald's hometown of Fermoy, Co. Cork.

18   A Brigade Council was a meeting of the Brigade Staff, often joined by commanders of individual Battalions. These conferences were somewhat democratic and the Brigade Commander acted as a kind of meeting chair.

19   Most of the prominent Volunteer leaders in Cork city were arrested, including Seán O'Sullivan, Fred Murray, Pat Higgins, and Roibeárd Langford. In a showing of their increased popularity, the prisoners were cheered by bystanders while being marched to court (*Cork Examiner*, 1 November 1917 and 8 November 1917).

20   The 'Cat and Mouse Act' enabled British officials to release a prisoner before their sentence had been completed, but re-arrest them any time thereafter, to complete their term. This allowed authorities to discharge Republican hunger strikers, but then return them to prison once they had regained their health.

21   The Anti-Conscription pledge was part of Ireland's concerted national movement against mandatory service in the British military. The pledge was supported by Sinn Féin, the Irish Parliamentary Party, the All-for-Ireland League, the Irish Labour Party, and the Catholic hierarchy. In 1918 hundreds of thousands across Ireland signed it. The pledge read: 'Denying the right of the British Government to enforce compulsory service in the country, we pledge ourselves solemnly to one another to resist conscription by the most effective means at our disposal.'

22   Seán Moylan successfully commanded the Cork No. 2 Brigade flying column and later the brigade.

23   Cumann na mBan was the Republican women's organization that closely coordinated with the Volunteers. Two factions of the Cork Cumann na mBan refused to recognize each other's authority in the city. The dispute was finally settled with the 'extinction' of the faction led by Mary MacSwiney and the wife of Seán O'Hegarty. See Ms. 31,282 (2), NLI.

24   Father Dominic O'Connor served as Brigade Chaplain. Joe O'Connor was one of Florrie's closest associates to survive the conflict.

25   Cork veterans used that term when describing O'Donoghue to author Seán O'Callaghan. See his book *Execution* (London: Muller, 1974), pp. 57, 58, 186. See also Tom Barry, *Guerilla Days in Ireland* (Boulder, CO: Roberts Rinehart Publishers, 1995), p. 158; and Seán Moylan, *Seán Moylan, In His Own Words* (Millstreet: Aubane Historical Society, 2004), p. 119. Professor John A. Murphy of UCC described O'Donoghue during an interview with me on 17 September 1996. He had considered buying the O'Donoghue home in Cork city during the early 1960s.

26   Observers typically described O'Donoghue as shy. The *Cork Examiner* wrote that O'Donoghue was a 'man of few words'. Professor John A. Murphy of UCC told me that O'Donoghue was quiet and shrewd. Seán Moylan used the latter term, depicting O'Donoghue as 'shrewd, brainy'. Tom Barry wrote, 'Shrewd, calm, and capable, I rated him as one of the ten best officers I met during my membership of the IRA.'

27   Joost Augusteijn's, *From Public Defiance to Guerrilla Warfare* (Dublin: Irish Academic Press, 1996) provides an excellent summary of the Volunteers' evolution during the 1916–1919 period.

28    After resigning his Brigade post, Pat Higgins moved into the political side of the struggle and served with the Dáil's Department of Local Government in Cork city. He became a vice-guardian of the Cork Workhouse, which was frequently used for covert Volunteer activity. Along with fellow vice-guardian Seamus Lankford (the future husband of the Cork No. 2 intelligence officer Siobhán Creedon Lankford), Higgins was targeted for assassination by British forces but escaped. See Siobhán Lankford, *The Hope and the Sadness* (Cork: Tower Books, 1980), pp. 256–62.

29    In a military organization, the adjutant acts as a kind of secretary. An adjutant typically writes orders, manages personnel matters, and organizes inter-unit communication.

30    Charles Stewart Parnell led the Irish Home Rule and Land League 'Plan of Campaign' movements during the 1880s. At the height of its success, his Irish Pariamentary Party was shattered when Parnell married a divorcee named Katherine O'Shea, with whom he had carried on a long affair. The Catholic Church denounced Parnell, and his party split amid great recriminations. In Cork city, supporters of the Irish Parliamentary Party (pro-Parnell) and the All-for-Ireland League (led by Cork's anti-Parnellite, William O'Brien) frequently brawled with each other during election campaigns.

31    The Republicans distrusted former adherents of the Irish Parliamentary Party (IPP). The Redmond/Parnell party had dominated the country for almost forty years and its Westminster manoeuvres had still failed to achieve Home Rule. Many Volunteers believed the only way to obtain independence was through physical resistance to British rule, and that continued dependence on constitutional politics would result in defeat.

32    *Séadna* is an Irish-language folk tale written by Peadar Ua Laoghaire (Peter O'Leary), a Catholic priest from County Cork. The novel became a popular teaching text for Irish students in the early twentieth century.

33    Ballykinlar Camp was a British prison for Republican detainees located in County Down.

34    In 1915 and early 1916, Sir Roger Casement headed the IRB's pre-Rising negotiations with Germany and helped organize the *Aud* arms shipment. On the eve of the Easter Rising, a German submarine landed Casement on Banna Strand, a beach in County Kerry. Casement was promptly captured by local police and hanged for treason a few months later.

# 3

# 'A JOB OF WORK'

## Florence O'Donoghue

By the beginning of 1918, the First World War was three-and-a-half-years-old. Bloody combat on the Western Front had used up armies at staggering rates and began to exhaust the combatants' manpower. In Ireland, the war had already lost much of its glamour and recruiting for the British Army dried up to a trickle. In late March 1918, the German Spring Offensive broke through the Allies' frontline in France, causing Britain's top generals to appeal for immediate reinforcements. On 18 April 1918, the British Parliament passed the Military Service Bill, which introduced conscription in Ireland to help alleviate the Army manpower shortage (conscription was already employed everywhere else in Britain). But the Irish public rallied against conscription, supported by Catholic Bishops who encouraged defiance. Irish members of parliament withdrew from Westminster in protest, and the Irish Volunteers threatened armed resistance, resulting in a large influx of new recruits into the organization.

During the spring and summer, the British Government tried to suppress opposition to conscription. Parts of Ireland, including Cork city and county, were proclaimed Special Military Areas, resulting in the banning of meetings and public gatherings, including GAA matches. Sinn Féin leaders were arrested and deported under dubious charges of participating in a 'German Plot' to undermine the British war effort. However, this repression only stiffened Irish resolve. In the end, national unity and the threat of physical resistance (rather than constitutional politics), defeated conscription. The British government recognized that enforcing conscription in Ireland would require more soldiers than it could yield. The Military Service Act was repealed, handing physical-force adherents a significant victory.[1]

The threat of conscription in April 1918 brought a large number of new men into the Volunteer organization. Some remained, but the majority dropped out again when the danger passed. For some months it appeared to us that the British were determined to attempt to put the Act into force. A plan of resistance for the Brigade was worked out, the main feature of which was (in the best tradition) that we should take to the hills. It is certain that resistance would have been determined and sustained; whether it would have been successful is another question.

No matter how poor our efforts at soldiering may have been, and no matter how reluctant the average countryman was to put pen to paper, it was inevitable that when organization had been put on a sound basis (as it was in 1918) and regular reports insisted upon, a substantial volume of correspondence would develop. Besides correspondence with Tomás (who was on a tour of the Battalions, and from whom a stream of notes and memoranda flowed back to Brigade HQ), contacts had to maintained with GHQ and the neighbouring Brigades. (We had one Battalion Adjutant who always spelt bayonet 'banit'; I thought he was one up on the Yanks. His name was McNamara and for some unfathomable reason he always wrote it 'McManara').

Much of the correspondence was in my department. I had a rule against it coming to the shop where I worked, and also against persons calling there indiscriminately. There were two reasons – first because I was beginning to realize the need for covering my activities from the eyes of the police; and second because I knew Michael Nolan would disapprove. I was determined to give him no cause of grievance, either by any neglect of my work for him, or by what he would regard as undesirable callers. He had ceased to talk about it, but I felt his silent hostility. He had the honest if foolish conviction that my association with the Volunteers would injure his business. I honestly believe that it brought him more business than it ever lost him, and (God be good to him, he died in near poverty) I think he realized this himself later, because he said to me some years before his death that he never had a day's luck since I left him. Of course, it was not altogether a question of luck.

In connection with the first reason there is a curious thing. The shop was on the corner of North Main Street and Castle Street. Police were still doing ordinary patrol duty. One policeman on this beat, McCoy, was a customer of mine, and occasionally he would come in for a smoke and a chat, or on a wet day stand in out of the rain. Leo Murphy and I never quite knew whether he was friendly or otherwise. He knew we were Volunteers, was frank about the fact that he knew, but never made the slightest effort to get information. Later in 1920 and 1921 he had a bad name. It was well known to them then [the RIC] that I had gone on the run, but I was still around town and saw him several times in circumstances he could hardly have failed to see me. He was the one policeman who would unquestionably have been able to identify me, and I always believed that if he had set out to get me he would have been successful. I gave him credit for having a good streak in him.

A last point about the shop, though this is anticipating a little. Seán O'Hegarty became very concerned later that I would be caught in what he called 'that bloody rat trap' – it had only one door on to the street and no exit at the back or upstairs – and he did everything possible to induce me to leave it long before I did. He could never be reconciled to the reasonable argument that I could not afford to leave my job. Leo and I were well aware of the hopelessness of escape out of it in the event of a raid. We could not very well keep arms there but did the next best thing we could think of, kept two four-pound hammers handy under the counter.

In view of this position about the shop, a depot for dispatches was essential. We found it in the newsagent's shop of the sisters Sheila and Nora Wallace in Augustine Street. I had been getting my papers there and had known them for some time. They lived over the shop, they worked from eight in the morning until midnight, and neither of them was very robust. But if any two women deserved immortality for their work in the following three or four years, they did. After the Volunteer Hall was closed against us, Wallace's became to all intents and purposes Brigade Headquarters. It became the normal meeting place for Brigade officers for everything except formal meetings; it became the point of contact for the countrymen, and the depot for dispatches and messages of all kinds. It became an indispensable part of the organization, and the more we went underground (as we did from then onwards) the more indispensable it became. Sheila and Nora came to know everybody and everybody's status; they became experts at side-tracking persons with no serious business, and at making appointments for us at times at which we could keep them. Nothing that I could say about their tact and discretion would express adequately my appreciation of the manner in which they did a most difficult and valuable job.[2]

In the little kitchen behind the shop some of us were sure to assemble every night that we were free. Often there was work to be done; sometimes it was for no more than the exchange of gossip and the latest news. The regulars were Seán O'Hegarty, Joe O'Connor, Matt Ryan, Dom Sullivan,[3] and myself. Occasionally we had also Tomás MacCurtain, Fred Murray, and Ned Lynch. There began that close friendship between Seán O'Hegarty and myself in which there has never been a break, down the years. I think at first it was a sort of father and son relationship; he kept a protective eye on me all through the struggle; I saw it in a thousand little ways and in many a gruff kindly word when things were bad. He was married and had no children of his own.

The year 1918 marked the development into a deep and untroubled conviction of my faith in the justice and logic of our claim to national freedom. Without fundamental change, it has governed and guided all my subsequent actions and decisions in matters of national concern down to the present day. But there were two other questions with which I had to wrestle before I felt free to give unquestioning allegiance to the cause – first, the moral responsibility undertaken in killing our enemies; and second, my personal reaction to death.

For the first I could not accept any plausible or pseudopatriotic sentiment as sufficient, nor could I dismiss it on the ground that one would be merely obeying orders. I felt it as a personal responsibility; I wanted some rock-solid ground for the moral authority of those who issued the orders. I had to find a justification that was logical and complete, and which did not outrage reason or conscience. Without that, the taking of human life was to me unjustified and a crime.

With Father Dominic's wise guidance I found the principles in Catholic teaching which satisfied me completely.[4] Put in the briefest and simplest form, they are that a nation which is unjustly invaded has the right to resist the invader and the right to use every lawful means to try and eject him. That right is not extinguished by reason of the fact that the invader, by superior force, has annihilated the lawful government of the invaded country and established himself as the supreme and unquestioned master. It still lives on in the people. Nor is it extinguished by reason of the length of time the invader maintains his conquest, nor by the fact that his government of the invaded country is temperately administered. It still lives on in the people. Not merely have the people the right to combine for the purpose of trying to eject the unlawful invader, but when his superior force makes combination impossible, they still have the right in small groups or even as individuals to resist injustice, to resist unlawful occupation, and if need be to kill the invader. There is even more than a right to resist. There is a duty. It is the moral duty of the people of the nation to resist and endeavour to eject the invader; and that duty again extended down to even one lone man who stood for the right against injustice on behalf of his people.

Contemplation of possible death evoked at first emotions of sadness but not of terror. To be killed, in youth, so much undone, unknown, not experienced; so little achieved, so many ambitions unfulfilled; an end of me, an end of my family in the male line;[5] the grief of those who loved me and would sorrow thereafter; the plight of those dependent on me. Would my father and mother understand? Would I be a coward when the moment came? I knew nothing of real pain; I had never been seriously ill or severely hurt. I was terrified of torture. What of the 'undiscovered country' after death?

Gradually I came to see that life was God's gift, to take from me when He would; that I should go forward with confidence, unafraid, doing what I so sincerely believed to be right. Thus I came to the peace of complete acceptance of death if it was the will of God. It imposed only the obligation of trying to live so as to be always prepared for the call. The possibility of death never troubled me afterwards, even at moments when it seemed imminent; but for some curious reason that I do not understand, I had occasional fleeting presentiments of being shot treacherously in the back in some dark place. There was one short street that for preference I would avoid at night. Cowardice? I just don't know.

In October 1918, while Tomás was attending a Volunteer Executive meeting in Dublin he was stricken down by a severe illness and did not return to Cork until December.[6] Seán O'Hegarty was acting Brigade OC in his absence, and it was under his direction that the rescue of Denis MacNeilus from Cork Jail was carried out. I will include nothing about that matter here which has already appeared in my published account,[7] but there are some things I did not mention for publication. The whole question of the defence and security of such arms as we had was a difficult one. Most men owned their own weapons and kept them at home. There was an order that they should resist being disarmed. Raids were taking place, and arms were being lost with a detrimental effect on morale. We recognized it, but we recognized also that to expect a lone man to confront a dozen armed raiders with a revolver in circumstances where he had little or no hope of survival was asking for rare heroism. The mental climate for that kind of resistance was not very general, nor could one reasonably expect it to be at that early stage.

MacNeilus was one of the officers who had always declared his own intention of defending any arms in his custody if he was raided. His position was even more difficult than that of the average man because he acted as armourer for the city companies and always had a number of arms on hand for repair. In fact he spent most of his spare time on this job.

On 4 November 1918, a party of police raided Denis MacNeilus' lodging house to search for illegal arms. MacNeilus grabbed a pistol, and in the ensuing struggle shot and seriously wounded Head Constable Clarke. After a long brawl, police reinforcements led by District Inspector Swanzy subdued MacNeilus and a second Volunteer who had come to his assistance. During the days following MacNeilus' arrest, it appeared that the wounded policeman might die. If he did, MacNeilus faced a murder charge and possible death sentence. Inspired by their colleague's spirited resistance, Seán O'Hegarty and Florrie O'Donoghue resolved to save him.

When Seán and I decided to rescue him out of jail, and we had decided it the morning he was taken without consulting anybody, I called a formal meeting of the Brigade Council for Seán's house that night, telling them what it was for. Seán O'Sullivan, OC Second Battalion was 'sick' and could not attend. Terry [MacSwiney] was a prisoner at the time and Fred Murray was acting for him as OC First Battalion. He attended but obviously disliked the project. At the second meeting on the following night, after I had been in to the jail and had come back with a plan of rescue in my head, Murray objected to the use of arms in the attempt at rescue and to risking the lives of six men to save one from the gallows. He walked out on us. Truth compels me to record these things although I do so with regret. That of course was the end of O'Sullivan and Murray; they were allowed to fade out later without comment.[8]

Florrie visited MacNeilus twice inside the Cork Gaol, to study the prison routine in order to devise a break-out. He also told his friend to be prepared for a rescue attempt. Florrie developed a simple but effective escape plan. Every weekday, visitors could appear at the gaol front gate and request to see a prisoner for a one-hour period. A guard admitted the visitors through the front gate and walked them a few steps to a small waiting room structure, located in between the front gate and a second interior gate. Meanwhile, the prisoner would be collected in the cell house (located inside the interior gate), and taken downstairs to the building's visiting room. Once the prisoner arrived, a guard would unlock the interior gate, usher the visitors through it (locking the gate behind), and walk them across a small yard to the visiting room, located inside the cell house.

O'Donoghue decided to send three pairs of Volunteers to the prison on visiting day. In order to avoid suspicion, each pair would request to see a different prisoner. The rescuers' entrance was staggered and timed so that the first pair of Volunteers would be with MacNeilus inside the visiting room while the other two pairs were ready in the waiting room. At a pre-arranged time, the pair in the visiting room with MacNeilus would subdue the visiting-room guard, leave the cell house, and then move towards the locked interior gate. The second and third pairs would disable the warder in the waiting room, and use his keys to unlock the interior gate, opening it for the MacNeilus party now waiting on the other side. The reunited group would use the same keys to open the front gate and lock the door behind them, sealing any pursuing staff inside the gaol. Outside, a Volunteer covering party holding extra bicycles would detain pedestrians, cut the prison phone lines, and then conduct MacNeilus to a prearranged safe house.

We had no difficulty whatever in getting all the men we needed for the job; we could have got ten times as many. My plan was so delicately balanced on a time schedule that any slightest departure from it or any absence of complete understanding and co-operation between the six men going into the jail, would inevitably have ruined it. I wanted to be one of them but Seán would not hear of it. He made it an order that I was not to take part, and we had our first and almost our only disagreement. We had the happy thought of picking one man of each of the three pairs and letting him pick the man he wanted to go with him. The first man selected was the tough Captain of my old 'G' Company, Joe Murphy. Joe had worked in England and had carried a gun for years. He asked for Martin Donovan and he could not have asked for a better man. Martin was as cool and as poker-faced as himself. In addition, although not a big man, he was a physically powerful one. The other two pairs, Christy MacSweeney and Paddy Healy, and Frank McCarthy and Jerome Donovan were equally reliable. All did their parts excellently. There was, amid the tension and postponement, one amusing incident. Frank McCarthy went in dressed as a Christian Brother – a ruse to allay possible suspicion on the part of the warders. On the night before the rescue we got him to try on the suit and clerical collar we had provided at 56 Grand Parade.[9] When he had self-consciously got himself into the outfit one of the others made some facetious remark. Frank, in a sudden fit of temper, tore off the collar and hat, dashed them on the floor, and declared that he would not wear them or be made a laughing stock of for any bloody rescue operation. He was persuaded to relent.

The MacNeilus escape proceeded almost perfectly. There was one moment of fear for the covering party when a detail of British soldiers approached the prison while the raiders were inside. Without detecting anything amiss, the soldiers marched past the covering party and through the gaol front gate, passing unknowingly beneath a Volunteer who was then atop a pole cutting the prison phone line. Inside the gaol, the plan worked like clockwork. The first party in the visiting room with MacNeilus knocked their warder unconscious, and handed a gun to the prisoner. The three then dodged sentries in the prison yard and arrived at the locked interior gate. The second group in the waiting room jumped their single warder, tied him up, and then unlocked the interior gate for the MacNeilus party. The seven men then dashed through the front gate to freedom.

The only miscue occurred when MacNeilus emerged from the prison. As his rescuers celebrated and congratulated each other, MacNeilus grabbed the first available bicycle and rode off in the wrong direction, not realizing he was alone. In the confusion, his rescuers did not see him leave. By the time MacNeilus turned around, the rescue party had already dispersed and he was left on his own. The fugitive rode to a friendly residence outside the city and sent word of his presence to Florrie, who had been scouring the city for him. Eventually they were reunited and Florrie passed MacNeilus to a pre-arranged hiding place in the countryside near Macroom. MacNeilus remained on the run for the next two-and-a-half years.

The MacNeilus jailbreak gained much publicity and raised the morale of Republicans around the country. The *Cork Examiner* called it, 'One of the most extraordinary and carefully planned coups of its kind ever brought off in the history of Irish, or, indeed, any other prison.'[10] The rescuers' use of pistols was not lost on physical-force proponents. Today, the prison escape remains largely overshadowed by events in Cork over the next two-and-a-half years. However, at the time it was a bold strike along the lines of the Fenians' celebrated attack on the Manchester Prison Van in 1868.

The reactions of Murray and O'Sullivan came as a shock to me. Here for the first time was the first real test and we would be fools not to face up to its implications. I wondered at the mental unpreparedness of these senior officers, older and more experienced than I was. I wondered if they had thought over the logic of their positions; if they had ever thought that the first and primary duty of a solider is to be prepared to give his life for the cause he serves. It was not for me to judge them, but one had to realize that here was a new problem. Later a few other city officers faded out, presumably for the same reasons.

The war in Europe ended on the day of the MacNeilus rescue. The British Government immediately decided on a general election, which of course included Ireland, and it was held in December. The Irish Parliamentary Party, hitherto dominant, was reduced to a few seats; Sinn Féin got an overwhelming majority and in January established Dáil Éireann as the national parliament. A native Government was set up in defiance of British rule for the first time in one hundred and twenty years. The nation was thenceforward committed to the Republic by popular vote. The Volunteers gained a constitutional status as the Army of the Republic. The expression of the will of the majority of the people, and the consequent acquisition by the Volunteers of the status of an Army of the people and of their lawfully elected Government, which made such a tremendous difference in the mental outlook of many men, was not for me personally a fundamental matter. I regarded it merely as the better and more explicit expression of a latent but valid right. Similarly, the contrary effect produced later on by the Bishop's purported Decree of Excommunication left me completely unmoved and undisturbed.[11]

In the 1918 General Election, Sinn Féin won seventy-three of the 105 seats, while the Irish Parliamentary Party was reduced from eighty to six seats.[12] The Republicans swept almost every district outside of Ulster. The victory was not an outright mandate for revolution. Much of the electorate wanted to support Sinn Féin's independence petition submitted to the Versailles Peace Conference (which was supposed to secure the rights of small nations, the purported war aim of the Allies). In addition, many Sinn Féin candidates downplayed their party's independence programme, the Irish Labour Party abstained from the election, and the demoralized Irish Parliamentary Party failed to contest a number of seats. Nevertheless, Sinn Féin's election victory signified clear and unified public support for Irish self-determination, and a dramatic increase in the party's popularity.

In Cork city, there could be no doubt of Sinn Féin's new power. The General Election results were: Walsh (Sinn Féin) 20,801; de Róiste (Sinn Féin) 20,506; Talbot-Crosbie (Nationalist) 7,480; Sullivan (Nationalist) 7,162; Williams (Unionist) 2,519; Farrington (Unionist) 2,254.[13]

The Sinn Féin MPs refused to take their seats in Westminster and formed a separate assembly called Dáil Éireann, electing Eamon de Valera its president. Dáil Éireann proclaimed itself the elected body of the Irish Republic declared in the 1916 Easter Rising. The new national parliament created a shadow government, complete with underground ministries to undermine the British Administration in Ireland. President de Valera called for a boycott of British government functionaries, including the country's police force, the Royal Irish Constabulary. Financed by a national Dáil Bond, the underground government proved particularly successful with arbitration courts that largely supplanted the British legal system.[14]

At this stage, the Irish Volunteers was an independent organization led by its own elected Army Council. The Army Council was located in Dublin and known as General Headquarters (or GHQ). Army Council members headed their own departments (for example, Michael Collins served as Director of Intelligence) under the command of Chief of Staff Richard Mulchay, and their positions were ratified by an annual

Volunteer convention (though no convention could meet for the next three years). In 1919, GHQ announced that the Irish Volunteers would swear allegiance to Dáil Éireann as the parliament of the Irish Republic. The Volunteers then placed themselves under the command of Dáil Minister of Defence, Cathal Brugha, and eventually became known as the Irish Republican Army.

The IRA frequently enabled Dáil ministries to function, by providing manpower and occasional intimidation in support of Dáil authority. Most important, the Volunteers enforced the Dáil's police boycott, which slowly destroyed the RIC – the most effective counterinsurgency body in Ireland.

There emerged in the election another aspect of the dilemma that had arisen with the rise and expansion of Sinn Féin. A number of our best officers became TDs and were never afterwards able to give their undivided attention to Volunteer duties. It was a whittling of our strength that had to be accepted in the interests of overall unity of purpose.

Tomás [MacCurtain] declined nomination for Parliamentary honours. Terry [MacSwiney] stood for mid-Cork and was elected unopposed. In fact there was no contest in Cork outside the city. For polling day, a number of Volunteers were drafted in to protect voters at the booths and maintain order. They marched in from neighbouring districts on the previous night and were billeted on straw in a large two-storied building in Drinan Street. Cumann na mBan cooked for them and Tomás put me in charge for the period of occupation.

In preparing for the election, a Committee was set up on which the Brigade had two representatives – Seán O'Hegarty and myself. We found an early tendency to play down any too positive references to the Republic, and we had to contest the argument that the primary purpose was to win the two city seats. The candidates, J.J. Walsh and Liam de Róiste, appeared to endorse the view that voters would shy away from too blunt a definition of the objective. Possibly we were over sensitive on the point, but we insisted successfully on having the undiluted programme put fairly to the people. These two seats were won easily.[15]

Looking back now, it is not difficult to see that so far as the struggle for freedom was successful, its achievements must in part at least be attributed to the combination of parallel efforts in the military and political spheres. Nor is it to be doubted that such military success as we had was influenced by the impact of events, such as those connected with the MacNeilus rescue. No normal army can have such opportunities of testing its personnel before battle. Ordinary training does not bring a man face to face with the grim realities of war in the same way that the circumstances of our position did. We had relatively large numbers; we could never arm more than a fraction of them; only a comparative few would ever do any actual killing. Yet nearly all were tested in the routine of movement, and care and custody of arms in such circumstances that actual risks had to be taken, and their reactions were a standard by which to judge them. We were not thrown headlong into a fight. The struggle developed slowly out of minor clashes, thus giving the Volunteers and the people generally a gradual acclimatization to the atmosphere of war.

We got two other useful ideas out of the MacNeilus rescue. One was that the enemy organization opposed to us was slow and ponderous, and most certainly had blind spots. We were of course immeasurably weaker in arms and in all the sinews of war, but could we not use our widespread organization, and our flexibility and simplicity of control to good purpose against the blind spots? The second idea was that we were completely ignorant of the enemy except in the most general and fragmentary way. We never made any attempt to study closely his organization, routine, morale, equipment, and personnel. Was there any reason why we should continue to remain in so dense a state of ignorance? We thought not. Out of these ideas our intelligence service was born; or rather I should say was born locally, because [Michael] Collins was developing similar ideas in Dublin, though we did not know it then. Later, when an all over effort was made to develop an Intelligence service, we found that we were a bit ahead of the country generally.

In fact our contacts with Dublin were slight enough at this time. My recollection is that I had been to GHQ twice before the end of 1918. I had met [Richard] Mulcahy and Collins, Gearóid O'Sullivan, Dick McKee, and Peadar Clancy.[16] None of them had made any greater impression on me than the average good officer of our own Brigade. What remains clearest in my mind is that I was shocked by Mulcahy's deliberate, cold-blooded blasphemy. I attributed it to a weakness of character, a desire to appear tough and ruthless. Maybe it was a pose adopted to impress the country boys. I found Dublin rather addicted to that sort of thing. Not that I was squeamish, even then. I had had the benefit of hearing Seán O'Hegarty's vigorous and comprehensive command of bad language, and I had yet to meet anyone who could excel him when he was thoroughly roused; Collins could curse explosively and violently with the best; and Jim Grey, our Brigade OC Transport, had a brand of scurrility all his own of which he was a most efficient exponent. But I had never heard anything that revolted me in the same way as Mulcahy's impassive, unemotional blasphemy.[17]

During the intensive development in 1918, the whole county had been organized parish by parish, and the whole network gathered into a tight integrated body. It was obvious to us then that a Brigade of this size and territorial extent was unwieldy and incapable of efficient control with the means and personnel at our disposal. GHQ decided to divide the county into three Brigade areas; we in Cork No. 1 retaining the middle strip running form Youghal to the county boundary west of Ballyvourney, and including the city; Cork No. 2 in the north and north-east; and Cork No. 3 in the west. We were satisfied that the necessary calibre of officer material existed in each area, that the best man would probably be elected, and that they would be suitably replaced in their own commands.

Just after Christmas 1918, Michael Collins came down to attend the meeting of the Battalion officers convened for the formation of Cork No. 3 Brigade and the election of its officers. This was the last visit by any GHQ officer to the South. It was the last occasion on which we saw any of them except when one or other of us visited Dublin.[18]

Collins, MacCurtain, and I attended the meeting in Dishure, Terelton. We went out the previous night in a car (what luxury!), slept three of us in a double bed, and talked into the small hours. I liked Collins. He had a mobile, expressive face, quick wit and a quick temper. He was gay, boisterous, optimistic, bubbling with dynamic energy. That would not have made a man of him of course, but behind the dashing exterior there was a keen intelligence, great strength of character, steadiness, determination, and vision. He had the qualities I thought we needed most in our leaders.

The meeting was entirely practical. There were no speeches. It was realized that men were being voted into posts of responsibility that could be passports to early graves. For some elected it meant just that. As I had to be at work, I was unable to attend the meeting for the formation of Cork No. 2 Brigade held a few days later. Tomás presided at that meeting; Collins had returned to Dublin. Heavy snow fell the night we were at Dishure. It had frozen over the next day as we skidded and slithered our way back to Cork. All the same, I thought this a much superior mode of transport to the bicycles on which we had been tearing all over the county, and I began to discuss with Tomás the question of whether the Brigade could not in some way or other acquire a car. The one we used that day was either hired or loaned, and the driver was not one of us.

Tomás had a genius for making friendly contact with persons who may be useful to the organization. He must have given thought and consideration to this matter in advance (and often far in advance of actual developments), because whenever a question arose of getting someone outside the organization to do some particular work, Tomás could always put his hand unerringly on the right man. The fact that he was never wrong in these selections was one of the constituents in his high status as a leader. Now he told me there was a lad named Jim Grey working in a garage in Beasley Street; there were two of them, father and son, but it was young Jim I should see. He was not a Volunteer and the elder Jim had been in the British Army. Unpromising as it seemed to me, I went and talked to the son. The eventual result was that he became the Brigade Transport officer, and there never was a better; but the story of how he got us his first Brigade car comes a little later.

The potential crisis created by the existence of the secret IRB organization inside the Volunteer movement came to a head for us in the summer of 1919. Many of the more responsible leaders had come out of jails and internment camps in 1917 with the firm conviction that there was no further need for a secret movement, that the IRB should be allowed to lapse, and the whole future struggle be based on the open political and military organizations. They included de Valera, Cathal Brugha, Austin Stack, MacCurtain, and MacSwiney. But they had reckoned without the astuteness, tenacity, and organizing ability of Collins, who had virtually taken control of the IRB after the Rising, re-organized, expanded, and infused new life into it, and who now refused very determinedly to wind it up or even curtail its activities. I will refer to this only so far as it affected me personally. In pursuance of the policy agreed upon, neither Tomás nor Terry had taken any active part in the IRB since their release from internment. On the other hand, Tomás had taken no steps to suppress or discourage it in his area. Seán O'Hegarty was County Centre and Brigade Vice Commandant. The relations between Tomás and himself continued to be personally friendly and co-operative, but this thing had been in the background for a year or more without ever becoming an acute issue.

Relations of genuine personal friendship had developed between Tomás and myself, and between Seán and myself. I had the confidence of both of them, I knew both sides of the case, and I was in a position of some difficulty. I had to make my own decision as to whether I would remain in the IRB or not. Neither of them would advise or influence me either way. After mature consideration I decided to continue as a member, believing that such an organization was still necessary in the circumstances of the time. I told them both of that decision as soon as I made it. It never made the slightest difference in the generosity of Tomás' friendship nor in the extent to which he gave me his entire confidence.

The local crisis developed out of the action of one of the tough men in my old 'G' Company, Harry Varien. He was an IRB man and almost always carried arms, partly I suspect with a view to 'pickings' as much as to any necessity imposed by his Volunteer duties.[19] He could always plead Volunteer duty and this was so elastic a thing in our circumstances that no one could contradict him. One night around the end of April 1919, he was going home very late when a policeman attempted to stop and question him. Harry was in what was for him a normal condition at that hour of night, but by no means drunk. In fact I have some doubts whether anything procurable in this island would have made him drunk. He was abrupt and uncomplimentary to the policeman and that poor fellow foolishly attempted to arrest him. Harry promptly pulled the gun and fired – with no intention of killing him, or so he said afterwards. The policeman was wounded seriously but did not die. Harry went home to bed in no ways perturbed. He did not know what he was stirring up.

The shooting caused an outburst of intense police activity, in the course of which the houses of many Volunteers were raided and a few of them arrested. The Volunteer organization as such had little or no hope of discovering who did the shooting, but Seán knew the next day and told me. I was in a spot. For a moment I salved my conscience by reflecting that if anyone was to tell Tomás, Seán himself should do so.

I was very unhappy about it. The occurrence created a surge of feeling out of all proportions to its importance. Some Volunteer officers denounced it; everyone wondered who had done it and why. The policeman concerned was a harmless person. The issue was forced by the arrest of Fred Murray and his positive identification by the wounded policeman (wrongly of course) as the man who shot him. I then told Tomás who had done the shooting and the lid blew off everything. When Varien was questioned, he declared truculently that he had Seán O'Hegarty's authority to carry a gun and use it if need be. That was good enough for him and he was making no apologies to anybody. In effect we could all go to hell.

His interpretation of Seán's instructions was not entirely accurate of course. The instruction was that men should defend their arms, but this was of small consequence. What was vital was that the event raised for Tomás in the most positive way the question of his authority as officer commanding the Brigade. He could not ignore it, no matter how reluctant he was to do anything that would cause a break in organization that had been built up with so much labour. Seán would not and could not be expected to abate anything of his IRB authority, but was quite willing to work in co-operation with the Volunteers provided they were on his road. And this was the heart of the trouble. There was then no definite Volunteer policy, and there was a fairly strong section who thought of the Volunteer organization in terms of a potential threat to the British, as something with which to back up our political demands. Another section quite sincerely thought any attempt to do anything by force of arms was utterly mad and would destroy the country. Many had eyes on the [Versailles] Peace Conference and some faith in the fine principles concerning the rights of small nations that had been so cynically preached by [US President Woodrow] Wilson and [British Prime Minister David] Lloyd George.

Knowing that compositions of the Volunteer mentality at the time, knowing the absence of official policy, and believing that whatever was attempted would emanate from the driving force of the hard core of the IRB men within its ranks, I had become convinced of the necessity for maintaining the organization [the IRB], not withstanding all the difficulties and dangers of dual control. Now the difficulty came home to me very forcibly. Fortunately in Cork it was not complicated by any bitterness or personal ambition. Both Tomás and Seán were acting out of a strong sense of duty. Seán resigned his position as Vice Commandant of the Brigade and returned to the ranks as an ordinary Volunteer. It was not a complete solution, but it was a gesture to the authority of Tomás, and it left Seán's IRB position intact. Terry replaced him as Vice Commandant of the Brigade.[20]

I was considerably agitated over my own position, now more complicated by reason of the fact that Seán held no rank. I knew that any day something could arise which would confront me with the dilemma of dual allegiance. I had so much of Seán's confidence in the IRB matters, that I feared a situation in which it would conflict with the loyalty I owed to Tomás and to the Brigade. Without consulting anybody, not even Joe O'Connor who was in a similar position but without the added complication of close association with Seán, I decided to offer my resignation from the position of Brigade Adjutant to Tomás. When I did so, he asked me if there was any reason other than the IRB one. I said there was absolutely none, but that I felt the difficulties of the IRB position to be so serious in my case that it was better to resign now than to embarrass him in a crisis. He said in that case he would not allow me to resign nor mention the fact that I had offered my resignation. He assured me again that the IRB position would not make the smallest difference as far as he was concerned to our mutual trust and co-operation. It never did down to the day of his death.

Meanwhile something had to be done to save Murray (an innocent, however weak he proved to be in the MacNeilus case), from at least a long term of imprisonment. An alibi was the obvious defence, but when the lawyers examined the available evidence they found it weak and we had to search for a Capuchin priest who had been with Murray late on the night of the shooting. He was Father Gabriel Harrington. I do not now remember how the matter became so urgent, but I remember clearly that on the night we discovered he was on holidays at Courtmacsherry, Tomás decided that I should go down at once and persuade him to give evidence. Christy Canny drove the car. It had an old-fashioned acetylene lightning, with rubber tubes and the carbine containers on the running boards with the lamps. It was late and the roads were deserted. It was my first night journey in a car. The patterns made by the headlights on bush and stone, the rolling white ribbon of road, the sense of speed through the cool night air – these in some way gave me a feeling of fascination and wonder which made me begin to take a poor view of the bicycle.

I got Father Gabriel out of bed and he readily agreed to give evidence at the trial. He had been with Murray that night and knew that Fred had a knee injury at the time that made it impossible for him to be at the place where the shooting occurred. At the trial in Cork, the Special Jury agreed, but the Crown had the case transferred to Dublin, where, despite Father Gabriel's honest and truthful evidence, Murray was convicted and sentenced to twelve months' imprisonment. The view taken by Father Gabriel's religious superiors is indicated by the fact that within a week of the trial he was transferred to the United States.[21]

Although the other Brigade officers were 'on the run', Joe O'Connor and I continued in our normal employments. In both our cases the police appeared to have written us off as of no consequence. We began to take very deliberate and continuous steps to maintain that valuable position, mainly by avoiding any open association with prominent persons or activities. My dinner hour was reduced to fifteen minutes; for the remainder of the hour I was at the Wallace's attending to dispatches and routine matters. From the moment the shop was shut, every night was devoted to Volunteer work and every Sunday to some trip to the country. The reduced size of the Brigade area made it possible to reach any Battalion on bicycle in a day; organization had vastly improved; one could be sure that when a man was ordered to be at a particular place at a particular time he would be there, and when something was ordered to be done it was done.

From the date of the MacNeilus rescue, his safety became my willingly undertaken responsibility. He was a man who could not bear inactivity. We planted him out in the country Battalions and moved him round as he got restless. While he could occupy himself at night with Volunteer duties, there was little he could do in the daytime since it would be too dangerous for him to be abroad openly. He was not a country man and did not take easily to life on the land. The result was that he worked out his spare time prodigally in writing abstruse letters to me on subjects ranging from interpretations of old Omar to the Malthusian theory of population. What was worse, he expected me to answer them.

Usually when he wished to move to a new location and I had found a suitable place for him, I went out to accompany him on the journey. As he never went unarmed after the rescue, these were always armed expeditions. We were both a bit vain about our proficiency in map reading. On one of these moves that vanity was well and truly knocked out of us. He was in Reinaree, south of Ballyvourney, and I was moving him to a place near Upton. I left Cork on the bike on a Sunday, timing myself to arrive at the place where he was (thirty-five miles from the city), at dusk so that we could leave on the second leg of the journey (about twenty-two miles), immediately after dark. I would still have fifteen miles to do to get home, and I wanted to get in before daylight. As soon as I had had something to eat we set out in the sleety March night.

The roads were vile. The procedure was to memorise from the map two or three cross-roads or road junctions ahead with approximate distances, go on to that point, check, and memorize another bit off a wet map in the light of a bicycle lamp and continue. We got across the [River] Lee alright and into the tangle of bye-roads south of it. Soon afterwards (one gets a kind of instinct about roads) it occurred to both of us about the same time that the one we were on was not the one we had visualized from the map. The next cross-roads proved conclusively we were wrong. We tried to see how we could have made a mistake but failed; the road we had taken should be the right one according to the map. It was not. That took the starch out of us.

We ploughed back through the mud and loose stones to the last point we had definitely identified. Yes, the road we had taken was the one we wanted according to the map, yet we knew it was wrong. Hell and damnation! Here were a pair of us who had been teaching map reading for almost two years and this spider's web of bohereens had beaten us. To this day I do not know the explanation. As the map was of no further use to us, we decided to head straight south by the aid of an occasional view of the stars – or rather as straight south as the twisting roads would allow us. To make an enquiry, apart from its undesirability from a security point of view, would have been the final blow to our pride, and anyway it was one o'clock in the morning.

I knew there was an east–west road from Crossbarry to Bandon that I would recognize when I saw it, and if we kept going south we were certain to strike it somewhere. MacNeilus had an odd sense of humour that made it incumbent on him to manufacture a joke with much industry and produce it solemnly at moments like this. We had been silent for quite a while, concentrating on dodging loose stones and pools of rainwater, when suddenly he said, 'I know what's wrong with this road.' I knew about five things wrong with it myself at that moment, but I also knew him so well that I sensed a joke and said, 'I'll buy it,' or whatever was the current slang. He said, 'They found it was too long and they had to put bends in it to make it fit.'

Reckoning on a time basis, I thought we should have reached the east–west road. It had not appeared and I was beginning to be a little uneasy. A light appeared ahead. We approached cautiously and saw that it was in the window of a house a little way off the road. The last shred of our pride was jettisoned; we decided to enquire. I threw the bike against the wall, opened the iron gate, and walked up the short gravel path. Almost at the door I looked up and saw the RIC sign over it. Crosspound police barracks! I knew where we were then but did not stop to make an enquiry. The road I was looking for was only a few hundred yards away.

That was the only occasion on which we had this kind of trouble. Before and after it we did many similar journeys relying on the map; and sometimes we met at night at a previously agreed point selected from the map and communicated to each other in code. In fact all communication between us in regard to these moves was invariably in code.

I believe that the hand of Providence saved me, for the first of many times, from death or arrest that night. When we came to the house where I was leaving MacNeilus, the owner was waiting up for us and had the kettle boiling. I took a cup of tea and started for Cork at once. I was wet, I feared the rain had got into the mechanism of my automatic pistol, and I wanted to get in before daylight. I was tempted to take the main road home. Although there was little difference in miles, it was far less hilly and had a better surface than the bye-road I usually used on this route. Providence, training, caution – something positive anyhow – urged me to take the harder way. I discovered the next day that two lorries with military and police, going on a raiding mission to the very area I had left MacNeilus, had gone out the main road at the time I came in the bye-road. Had I come back by the main road I would have run into them. The Crosspound police had been waiting up for them when I almost knocked on the barrack door. Tommy Kelleher, to whom I would have called if there had been time, was arrested that morning. He was the local Company Captain.

During 1919 I kept contact with the officers of the other two Brigades in the County, particularly with Liam Lynch and George Power, OC and Adjutant Cork No. 2 [Brigade], and with Tom Hales and Liam Deasy, OC and Adjutant Cork No. 3 [Brigade].[22] In fact these contacts were well maintained up to the formation of the First Southern Division in April 1921. In visits within our own Brigade, Terry [MacSwiney] was with me on a few occasions, and in that year I got to know him well. He had read widely, he was particularly conversant with the issues in the American Civil War, and he could always be interesting on a variety of subjects. Where he differed from Tomás mainly was that he did not have MacCurtain's shrewdness or intuitive knowledge of countrymen. Neither had he O'Hegarty's lashing tongue or rapier-like intelligence. He was a gentle soul and it was part of our tragedy that he had to be a soldier. He never looked well in uniform.

In July he took charge of what was to have been our first action for the capture of arms from the British military. It was a miserable failure. The American [Army] forces had partly completed the construction of an aerodome at Ballyquirk near Killeagh.[23] Work had been suspended when the war ended, and a party of British troops were billeted in the buildings and maintained a guard. The Fourth Battalion, in whose area the post was, suggested that it would be possible to attack it successfully at night and capture the arms. They did not have in the Battalion sufficient arms to give the raid a chance of success. I am not quite certain whether the attempt became a Brigade effort, or whether it was a combination of the First and Fourth Battalions. Anyhow it was men from these two Battalions under Terry's command who participated.

Paddy Healy and I cycled to Ballyquirk on a Sunday and made as close an inspection as we could of the dispositions of sentries, guard room, billets, and so on. On the information we brought back Terry made a plan, sound enough I think, though possibly assuming a degree of control that he would have been unable to exercise in a fight in the dark. Nobody had any better one to suggest and he went ahead with preparations very confidently. The plan was never put to the test.

The attack was timed for midnight. In the evening, the First Battalion men were sent off from the city on bicycles in two and threes, with instructions to assemble at a point near the aerodome under cover at 11.30 p.m. They were armed with revolvers only. The Fourth Battalion men were to assemble at another point close by at the same time. Terry, Joe O'Connor, Dan Donovan,[24] and I left the city in a car carrying all the First Battalion rifles (twelve, I think), at a time when Jim Grey (who was driving) reckoned would get us to the assembly area by 11.30. Jim had planned a route on the bye-roads and we had left that entirely to him. He had 'borrowed' the car, and we were not long on the road when I felt that he was not happy about it. Soon it began to give him trouble and there were frequent stops. Finally there was a complete breakdown that Jim told us would take him some time to put right. He began to work on the car in the dark (we had been driving without lights) making heroic efforts to control his tongue. Once when Terry moved away out of earshot he exploded into a growling, blistering profanity, pronouncing a solemn curse upon the car, its several parts, its antecedents, its manufacturer, and its owner with a fine impartiality, confiding to us that we would be here until morning with our load of rifles, but for so and so's sake not to tell him – meaning Terry.

Perhaps two hours later he got the car going again and soon afterwards we went astray. Jim was so flustered by this time that it was hard to blame him. I blamed myself for not having taken precautions against the possibility. Eventually we got to the point of assembly about 2 a.m. to find that everyone had left except a local lad. They had assumed when we did not arrive by midnight that we had run into trouble, and as there was no question of attempting the attack without the rifles we were carrying, they had decided to call it off for that night. Terry was sorely disappointed; it was the only chance of actual action he ever got. He did not blame anybody. Gentleness was characteristic of him – but what strength of spirit there was behind that gentleness!

This failure roused in me a fury against our own incompetence and want of thoroughness. If we could not do better than this we ought to get out and let others try. We could not afford failures; a few of them and morale would crack. That fatalistic swansong of defeat would infect us again, and we would add just another futile chapter to the long story. With those who said 'hard luck' I was impatient and could not agree. I believed the fault was in ourselves; we needed more thoroughness, more forethought, more attention to detail, and more hard thinking and hard work. There was nothing wrong with the men; every one of them called on had turned out, although each man knew there was the possibility that he might not return. From that point onwards, it became for me more and more a job of work. We had forged a weapon of sorts; it had possibilities as well as limitations; we must learn how to use it effectively. Nothing, either intellectual laziness or physical discomfort, must be allowed to frustrate us.

One minor result was that every subsequent expedition in which I took part, I planned the route myself, sat next to the driver with a shaded flash lamp and a map on my knees, and gave my whole attention to keeping the car (or the two, or three, or six cars), on the planned route. Ballyquirk was my last experience of going astray.

Almost invariably on these journeys we drove without lights. We had four or five drivers who were marvellous at night. Jim's brother Miah, was I think the best.

The tendency to play tricks and have a bit of fun never wholly deserted us. Though this is out of chronological order, a later incident comes to my mind. It was the night we went out for the first attack on Inchigeela barracks,[25] a winter's night, cold and dark with driving snow showers. There were six of us in the car – Jim Grey driving, I next to him, Dom [Dominic] Sullivan outside me, Seán O'Hegarty, Joe O'Connor, and Dan Donovan in the back. We were nearing our destination without having passed through a village or a town. No one in the car except myself had the haziest notion of where we were, but at that stage of our development no one ever bothered to ask me if we were alright, it being assumed that we would arrive. Jim was giving all his attention to keeping the car out of the dykes of the narrow roads. In a whisper, Dom suggested to Jim and myself that we should stop and pretend that we had gone astray – with the idea of raising the ire of Seán O'Hegarty. We stopped. I concentrated on the map while Dom apologetically confided to Seán that I had got lost. He automatically erupted into vituperative blasphemy, to the great delight of all concerned. In a minute or so he checked himself and peremptorily demanded of me what the hell had gone wrong. I could not maintain the joke any longer and when he saw it he became yet more furious. Although any of us would have gladly put our bodies between him and a bullet, we would not forego our privilege of pulling his leg. We were the few; the great majority of officers and men stood in awe of him.

Partly as a result of experience in the MacNeilus and Ballyquirk incidents, and partly out of our ignorance of enemy organization and sources of strength, I became more and more impressed by the need for putting the collection and evaluation of information on some organized basis. We had then nothing more than a few individual men in the General Post Office who brought up an occasional copy of the police message in cipher – messages that we were not always able to decode. I thought we needed a basic organization in every Company and Battalion, with men specially detailed to study the area and its possibilities from the Intelligence point of view, as well as a wide development of such sources as Post Offices and Telephone Exchanges.

For a time no Brigade officer except myself was very enthusiastic about such a service. But by then I had a very free hand and went ahead cautiously. Tomás was well aware that I would always consult him on new departures and would never out-step his authority. One result was that when, later on, everyone realized the value of the service because it produced results, it was decided that I should continue in control of what I had built up. Thus I had added to my work as Brigade Adjutant the additional post of Brigade Intelligence Officer; both of these I held until I went to the Division to the same two posts in April, 1921. There is amongst my papers a talk I gave to the [Irish] Army and LDF [Local Defence Force] officers during the Emergency.[26]

Part of O'Donoghue's lecture explains the essential elements of guerrilla warfare intelligence:

It is generally admitted that the IRA had a competent Intelligence Service in the pre-Truce period, and that the efficiency of that service contributed in a substantial way to the success of its military operations. This efficiency was due to neither chance nor to the exclusive abilities of any one man. It was due to three things: First, to a keen appreciation on the part of GHQ at the time of the value of Intelligence; second, to the efficient organization and exploitation of sources and information; and third, to the fact that every member of the Defence Forces at that time – and to a large extent every loyal citizen also – regarded it as a para- mount and personal duty, promptly and at all times, to pass on to those in authority every item of enemy information that resulted from his constant watchfulness. And of these three contributory sources, the last one was by far most important.

This gives an idea of how the basic organization was built up and what it was designed to do, so there is no need to cover the same ground here. The Quinlisk case was the first real test of it.

A former British soldier, Timothy Quinlisk had joined Casement's Brigade during the First World War while a prisoner-of-war in Germany.[27] Afterwards, he became a paid agent of the British Secret Service, with orders to infiltrate the IRA in Dublin and track down Michael Collins. His efforts ultimately failed when Collins' Intelligence officers suspected Quinlisk of being a traitor. Eager to be rid of him, the Dublin officers told Quinlisk that Collins was hiding out in Cork. Quinlisk then journeyed to Cork city and tried to infiltrate the IRA there. However, the Cork Volunteers were likewise leery of Quinlisk and thought he could be working for the British. Though suspicious, they had no proof that he was a spy.[28]

At that time O'Donoghue's network was intercepting and deciphering coded telegrams to the RIC headquarters in Cork. In one evening's intercepted message, the head of the British Secret Service in Dublin Castle told Cork police to expect a letter for a man named 'Sullivan' in the next police post. O'Donoghue suspected that 'Sullivan' was the same dubious character nosing around Cork Volunteer circles.

To what I said in the talk I should add that GHQ had not told us Quinlisk may come to Cork. In fact there was no regular Intelligence contact between the Brigade and GHQ at that time. Collins and I, each without the knowledge of the other, were trying to build up something similar, but with this difference. I had put down a basic organization in the Companies and Battalions but had made no progress in the espionage aspect at that stage, where he had practically no basic organization, but had made very considerable progress on the more valuable espionage aspect. Working in Dublin, and with contacts in London, his opportunities in this regard were much more extensive than mine. Out of the Quinlisk case there arose a comparing of notes and a mutual co-operation and close contact that proved valuable.[29]

My personal connection with the case may perhaps be expanded a little. It was late that night when I got back to Wallaces', and after midnight before I had the messages deciphered. Everybody had gone except Tomás. When I suggested that we should collect the police mail in the morning he agreed and said he would call to Tom Crofts[30] on his way home, get Tom to mobilize one other man, and meet me at the South Mall at 7.15 in the morning. I said that I would get Matt Ryan and that four of us would be ample.

Tom and I took the lad with the dispatch case. We had turned him round and told him to march up the South Mall before he found his tongue. We did not want him to have any chance of having a good look at us. He had gone some distance in a dazed way when he said the silly sort of thing a man will say in this kind of sudden stress. 'Give me back the bag,' he said in a strong Northern accent. The few passers-by who had taken in what was happening, stopped to watch Tom and I walking behind the policeman with guns in our hands. I have never forgotten Tom's half-grim half-jocular reply – 'If you don't keep going and keep your mouth shut what you'll get will be an additional hole in your arse.' When we came to the next street corner we told him to keep going and not to look back. I can still see his set shoulders as he moved up the Mall. He was red-headed and a six-footer.

We scattered. I took the dispatch case to the public lavatory at Emmet Place, cut out the lock, and stuffed the dispatches into my pockets. Leaving the case there, I went home. There was a fairly big quantity of correspondence. I sorted through the envelopes looking for the small one which I anticipated would contain the special message. There was no trace of it. Had I left it in the case, or dropped it in Emmet Place or on the way home after all our trouble? With mounting alarm I began to tear open the sealed envelopes and take a quick look through their contents. To my great relief I found the small envelope enclosed with some other matter in a large one. I was at work as usual at 9.00 a.m. but it was an anxious day. Quinlisk had to be collected before the police could get to him. He was.

On 19 February 1920, city Volunteers met with Quinlisk and offered to show him a weapons cache. When the party arrived at an empty lot on the city's outskirts, the Volunteers shot him. They then pinned a note on the corpse warning Cork citizens of the penalty for spying. Timothy Quinlisk became Cork city's first fatality in the War of Independence.

It is so common a practice in other countries to buy information that I had better say I never had one single penny to disburse for Intelligence purposes during the whole of the Tan War, and that no single individual of the thousands who helped in this work expected any payment. In fact we never had any real money. The two pence and three pence scraped up from the men weekly were our only real source of revenue. It was not until March of 1921 that GHQ commenced to supply us with a monthly sum sufficient to give £3.00. a week to a small number of officers who had left far better employment to take up whole-time service. Never surely was a fight for freedom financed as this one.

Perhaps this is as good a place as any to say what my personal feelings were to the soldiers and police opposed to us. Except occasionally, in the case of some particular reprehensible outrage by the Auxiliaries or Black and Tans, I never felt any burning hatred of them individually or collectively. I often wondered what that violent hatred in some of our men sprang from, and questioned if there was not some cold, unnatural streak in myself. I hated passionately the conquest which the forces of occupation represented; I hated, passionately and painfully, the terrible thing that conquest had done to the minds of our people, but against the men who were the instruments of conquest I could not feel any bitter hatred. For a few of them I felt genuine admiration because they were soldiers activated by a sense of duty, doing that duty as they saw it without viciousness or excess. The more my Intelligence work enabled me to read their minds, the more familiar I became with their responsibilities, problems, and diffi culties, the more the possibility of any violent hatred of them as persons vanished. That frame of mind made it sad to see men die in so unworthy a cause.[31]

The reference to the Quinlisk case is slightly out of chronological order – the date was February 1920 – but I have included it here because of its association with our early efforts to build up an Intelligence service.

O'Donoghue created an effective intelligence network in Cork city.[32] He targeted the three components of British communication – mail, telephones, and telegraph. In each of those offices in Cork, he found reliable Republican men and women willing to help. Around them he built special intelligence teams, which opened letters, tapped phone lines, and intercepted and decoded telegrams. These compartmental-ized sections then forwarded the information to O'Donoghue's full-time six-man intelligence staff for compilation and analysis.[33]

The British and local population recognized the IRA's efforts in these areas. The British Army 6th Division later lamented, 'all methods of communication, except wireless telegraph' were at the mercy of a staff composed of 'ardent rebels'. IRA control of the mails was particularly obvious. One Cork loyalist complained of the IRA, 'they open and examine all my letters'. Another loyalist corresponding with 6th Division commander General Strickland said, 'I did not write my name or address lest my letter would be opened and I would be a marked man.' In the fall of 1920, British Army intelligence officers tried to discredit the new Lord Mayor Donal 'Og' O'Callaghan by sending disinformation about him through the Cork Post, assuming the letter would be opened and the contents shared with the IRA. (It was, though O'Donoghue did not fall for the ruse.)[34]

A second tool in O'Donoghue's network was the well-organized Cork Volunteer apparatus. O'Donoghue encouraged every Volunteer to act as an intelligence asset in his home area and place of work, and to forward all military information to their unit intelligence officer. He also ordered each local company in Cork (sixteen in the city alone) to appoint four capable and active intelligence officers.[35] These company intelligence officers possessed a firm understanding of their neighbourhood, from the location of British posts to the identity of local touts and hostile Irish loyalists. Strangers in the area could be scrutinized and suspicious people followed. Intelligence officers closely monitored conversations and mail of known British agents or supporters, and could call on the assistance of fellow Volunteers when needed. They maintained a constant watch over police barracks and military headquarters, taking note of all visitors. Volunteer strength at this time was 2,000, in a city of 76,000, so the IRA possessed the necessary manpower to keep much of the city under surveillance. Each of those Volunteers could collect additional information from their own circle of friends and family. That information was compiled by company intelligence officers, and then submitted in reports to Battalion intelligence officers, who forwarded them to O'Donoghue's Brigade Intelligence staff for further study.

In addition to the Volunteers, O'Donoghue was bolstered by the Cork Cumann na mBan and Fianna boy scouts. Ten active branches of the

Cumann stretched across the city and its members provided essential assistance to local intelligence efforts. Like the Volunteers, the Cumann na mBan members were transformed into information gatherers. A loyalist complained of their activities, 'The Sinn Féin boy and girl scouts are everywhere, watching the people and listening to them when they happen to converse in the street.'[36]

Finally, O'Donoghue relied on the help of local citizens to help the Volunteers. His intelligence officers recruited sympathetic civilians working in sensitive positions around the city. The railway station, civic clubs, and hotels were considered especially important. Cork Volunteer commander Connie Neenan remembered, 'We had staff in every hotel. You could not enter Cork at that time without us knowing all the details about you.' Domestic servants were tapped for information while shop clerks around the city pumped unsuspecting British personnel. Even local police passed along news and warnings. Scraps of information trickled in from all over town. 6th Division Headquarters warned its officers, 'The rebel spies are everywhere.' Volunteer Eamonn Enright recalled fondly, 'The people were very good in the Tan War.'[37]

During his army intelligence lecture twenty years after the War of Independence, O'Donoghue told an anecdote that illustrated the strength of his Cork network. Florrie was receiving assistance from a sympathetic RIC clerk named Michael Costello. Every evening after curfew, O'Donoghue slipped into the policeman's home to retrieve confidential information, including the RIC code cipher. Within a few weeks, an IRA company intelligence officer requested O'Donoghue's permission to kill a civilian who had been observed meeting secretly with a police officer. O'Donoghue checked the address and discovered that it was Costello's home and that Florrie himself was the subject of the execution request. Apparently Costello's residence had been under observation for a year and O'Donoghue's visits were quickly detected. (Costello's role as an informant had been kept secret from the local Volunteer company.)[38]

## NOTES AND REFERENCES

1   For details of the Irish Conscription Crisis, see George Dangerfield, *The Damnable Question*, pp. 264–304; R.F. Foster, *Modern Ireland*, 486–93; J.J. Lee, *Ireland*, pp. 23–4; Sheila Lawlor, *Britain and Ireland 1914–1923* (Dublin: Gill and Macmillan, 1983), pp. 20–27; Dorothy Macardle, *The Irish Republic* (Dublin: The Irish Press, 1951), pp. 247–57; Nicholas Mansergh, *Unresolved Question*, pp. 107–11; Joseph O'Brien, *William O'Brien and the Course of Irish Politics 1881–1918* (Berkeley, CA: University of California Press, 1976), pp. 212–24, and 233–5; and Adrian Gregory '"You Might as Well Recruit Germans": British Public Opinion and the Decision to Conscript the Irish in 1918' in Adrian Gregory and Senia

Paseta (eds) *Ireland and the Great War* (Manchester: Manchester University Press, 2002), pp. 113–32.

2    Nora Wallace served as Brigade Communications Officer. Wallaces' Shop remained the IRA's headquarters until it was closed by military order in May 1921 (See the *Cork Constitution*, 18 May 1921).

3    Dominic Sullivan was a prominent brigade officer.

4    Father Dominic O'Connor, a Capuchin priest, served as Cork No. 1 Brigade Chaplain.

5    Florrie was his family's only son.

6    MacCurtain was struck down by the 'Spanish Flu', the great influenza epidemic that killed millions in Europe and the United States. See O'Donoghue, *Tomás MacCurtain*, p. 144.

7    O'Donoghue's version of the escape appears in *Tomás MacCurtain*, as well as *Sworn to Be Free, The Complete Book of IRA Jail Breaks* (Tralee: Anvil Books, 1971), and *Rebel Cork's Fighting Story* (Tralee: Anvil Books, 1961), the latter two books edited by O'Donoghue. He first told the jailbreak story on national radio in 1936, which served as his debut as a historian.

8    Fred Murray was a founder of the Volunteer movement in Cork city and had been imprisoned a number of times. He was the uncle of Patrick 'Pa' Murray, who was one of the most competent officers in the Cork No. 1 Brigade.

9    Sinn Féin Hall, frequently used for meetings by the Volunteers.

10   *Cork Examiner*, 12 November 1918.

11   After the burning of Cork city by Crown forces in December 1920, Cork's Catholic Bishop, Daniel Cohalan, denounced both the IRA and British forces. He ordered the following message read at every mass in his diocese: 'Besides the sinfulness of the acts from their opposition to the law of God, anyone, be he a subject of this diocese or an extern, who, within the diocese of Cork shall organize or take part in ambushes or kidnapping, or shall otherwise be guilty of murder or attempted murder, shall incur, by the very fact, the censure of excommunication.' See the *Cork Examiner* and *Cork Constitution*, 13 December 1920.

12   For background on Sinn Féin's triumph in the 1918 General Election, see D. George Boyce, *Nationalism in Ireland* (London: Routledge, 1985), pp. 315–22; Joseph Curran, *The Birth of the Irish Free State* (Alabama: University of Alabama Press, 1980), pp. 19–22; George Dangerfield, *The Damnable Question*, pp. 298–304; R.F. Foster, *Modern Ireland*, pp. 490–93; Tom Garvin, *The Evolution of Irish Nationalist Politics* (Dublin: Gill and Macmillan, 1981), pp. 114–22; Joe Lee, *Ireland*, pp. 39–41; and Joseph O'Brien, *William O'Brien*, pp. 39–41.

13   *Cork Constitution*, 16 December 1918.

14   For some details, see Joost Augusteijn, *From Public Defiance to Guerrilla Warfare*; Arthur Mitchell, 'Alternative Government: "Exit Britannia," The Formation of the Irish National State, 1918–1921' in Augusteijn (ed.), *The Irish Revolution, 1913–1923* (New York: Palgrave, 2002), pp. 70–84; and Arthur Mitchell's *Revolutionary Government in Ireland* (Dublin: Gill and Macmillan, 1995).

15   While de Róiste and Walsh founded the Irish Volunteers in Cork and led the city's Gaelic revival, neither would be considered zealous Republicans. Both voted for the Anglo–Irish Treaty in 1922 (despite death threats from Seán O'Hegarty and Dan 'Sandow' Donovan). J.J. Walsh headed the Cork GAA, fought in the 1916 Rising in Dublin, and had his death sentence commuted. After his release from prison in 1917, Walsh spent the next four years focused on the Dáil, in between jail terms. Liam de Róiste had been president of the

Cork Gaelic League and was a champion of the Irish language. A devout Catholic, he questioned the morality of Cork's guerrilla war. In 1921, drunk Black and Tans tried to assassinate de Róiste, but instead killed a Catholic priest lodging in his home. Additional details can be found in J.J. Walsh, *Recollections of a Rebel* (Tralee: The Kerryman, 1944), and Fearghal McGarry, *Irish Politics and the Spanish Civil War* (Cork: Cork University Press, 1999).

16     Prominent GHQ officers in Dublin. They had the following titles: Chief of Staff, Richard Mulcahy; Director of Intelligence, Michael Collins; Adjutant-General, Gearóid O'Sullivan; Dublin Brigade OC, Dick McKee; and Dublin Brigade Vice OC, Peadar Clancy.

17     Mulcahy feuded with Seán O'Hegarty and held no great love for O'Donoghue. See Risteárd Mulcahy's, *Richard Mulcahy, A Family Memoir* (Dublin: Aurelian Press, 1999).

18     This absence contributed to the rift between IRA country units and GHQ, which proved disastrous in the march towards Civil War. Country units, including the Cork brigades, often clashed with GHQ, which provided little logistical or financial support but insisted on maintaining its authority. Many of GHQ's orders and criticisms did not reflect the conditions in the country, and it frequently disrupted actions planned by active Brigades. Often ordered to Dublin at considerable risk, country officers resented GHQ officers' unwillingness to reciprocate by visiting those important commands. This gave the impression of a double standard. Visiting country officers also frequently commented on the comfortable living conditions displayed by Dublin staff. Their lifestyle contrasted with the country officers', who mostly existed in poverty and material misery.

19     'Pickings' in the sense that Varien could pick and choose which Volunteer operations to join. If he was met on the street by a colleague and asked to participate in a Volunteer activity, Varien could refuse by displaying his gun as evidence that he was already employed on another secret operation (even if he was not).

20     Peter Hart's *The IRA and Its Enemies* (pp. 79, 240–41, 246, 247) emphasizes the tension between the Volunteers and the IRB in Cork city. Hart argues that Seán O'Hegarty led an 'irregular' squad of IRB men that acted as an 'underground' body, outside the command of the Cork No. 1 Brigade. I believe Hart overstates the case. Rather than an IRB 'gang' operating unilaterally, I believe the situation in Cork was one of individual Volunteer companies acting on their own to secure weapons and control their own areas. While IRB men frequently organized and led non-sanctioned sorties in Cork (such as the arms raid Florrie describes), they seem to have acted on behalf of individual Volunteer companies rather than the IRB. That is an important distinction. Non-sanctioned 'wildcat' actions of this type were common throughout the Volunteer movement. Local units frequently failed to report intended actions to superiors, for fear the proposal would be rejected or that the captured weapons might be shared with other units. For example, as O'Donoghue writes, the Cork No. 1 Brigade stopped informing GHQ of its operational plans in mid-1920. O'Donoghue angrily refuted the same charges of an 'alleged ill-disciplined element' within the Cork city IRA, written in response to Seamus Malone's book *B'jhiu an Braon Fola [Blood on the Flag]* (Ballincollig: Tower Books, 1996), on which Hart bases some of his argument. See Ms. 31,293, NLI for a convincing rebuttal of Malone's account by Florrie O'Donoghue, Donal O'Donoghue, and Liam O'Brien. The IRB probably played a role squeezing moderate officers out of the Cork city

Volunteer organization. Such an effort would explain Florrie's rapid rise to the Brigade leadership. In addition, according to Pa Murray, the city IRB arranged the election of IRB men to quartermaster posts in the city's Volunteer companies, placing them in charge of local arms. That policy is understandable in light of the 1916 Rising, when MacCurtain and MacSwiney surrendered Volunteer weapons to the British. See Pa Murray's BMH Statement, for details of the IRB's quartermaster policy.

21    For another example of the Capuchin Order's aversion to controversy, see chapter 5 for the fate of Cork Capuchin Father Dominic O'Connor.

22    The Cork No. 2 Brigade is often referred to as the North Cork Brigade. Similarly, the Cork No. 3 Brigade is also called the West Cork Brigade.

23    Built for use in the First World War.

24    Dan 'Sandow' Donovan later commanded the First Battalion and the Cork No. 1 Brigade Flying Column.

25    This was actually the second IRA attack on Inchigeela Barracks, but the first where Brigade officers participated. The Brigade Staff organized the assault and built a bomb to blow a hold in the side of the police barracks, which would then be stormed by local Volunteers. On the night of 8 March 1920, IRA units cut all the roads leading to Inchigeela and surrounded the building. However, the Volunteers withdrew after the bomb failed to explode. The local Volunteers tried a third attempt on 23 May, but the plan miscarried and was abandoned without a shot being fired. See Donal Cronin's 'Ballingeary Volunteers 1920' in *Ballingeary Historical Society Journal*, 1997, p. 33.

26    This presentation is an excellent introduction to guerrilla war intelligence. See Ms. 31,443, NLI.

27    The German Army allowed Sir Roger Casement to recruit his 'brigade' from Irish prisoners of war in Germany. The Casement Brigade was intended for deployment in Ireland during a rebellion or German invasion, but never left Germany because only about fifty soldiers joined the unit.

28    For details of the Quinlisk spy case, see P. Béaslaí, *Michael Collins and the Making of a New Ireland*, Vol. I (Dublin: Phoenix Publishing, 1926), p. 393 (the passage includes a captured letter from Quinlisk to Dublin Castle); D. Nelligan, *A Spy in the Castle* (Dublin: McGibbon and Kee, 1968), p. 60; F. O'Donoghue's 'Military Intelligence Lecture', p. 23, Ms. 31,443, NLI; O'Donoghue, *Tomás MacCurtain*, p. 60; O'Donoghue in the O'Malley Notebooks, UCD; the *Cork Examiner*, 20 February 1920; Mick Murphy's BMH Statement; and Company Captain J. O'Dwyer's account, A0535 XV, Military Archives. There was some suspicion that Quinlisk acted on behalf of the British Secret Service while he served with Roger Casement's Brigade in Germany. Casement apparently considered Quinlisk a rogue and wrote, 'The men are now, I believe, all against him and say he's a traitor.' Historian Andreas Roth says the charges, 'cannot, however, be verified'. See Andreas Roth '"The German Soldier is not Tactful" Sir Roger Casement and the Irish Brigade in Germany During the First World War', *Irish Sword*, Winter 1995, Vol. XXII, No. 89, pp. 318, 323, 331. See also Geoffrey de C. Parmiter, *Roger Casement* (London: Arthur Barker, 1936).

29    Collins' characterization in recent years as a super spymaster seems over-stated. The Quinlisk case indicates the parochial nature of Collins' network. In that episode his Dublin subordinates failed to notify their Cork colleagues that they had deliberately directed a British spy to Cork. In Collins' correspondence with O'Donoghue from this period, Collins displays ignorance about key information from Cork, such as when he asked Florrie whether he had ever heard of an RIC

Head Constable who had figured very prominently in the MacCurtain Inquest (see Collins to O'Donoghue, 25 August 1920; and 30 July 1920, Ms. 31,192, NLI). While Collins skillfully directed his own spy network in Dublin, on a national level he basically encouraged local IRA intelligence officers and forwarded them relevant information, rather than directly managing their efforts. Outside of Dublin, Collins was a cheerleader rather than a micro-manager who planned each assassination and cultivated every IRA spy in Ireland. Much of Collins' reputation came from Collins himself, since he had a habit of boasting. (His nickname 'The Big Fellow' was given to him by fellow prisoners at Frongoch Prison Camp, who thought Collins possessed an inflated opinion of himself.) Florrie notes above that there was little systematic and centralized intelligence structure in the Volunteer organization, and that up to this time Collins had not maintained regular contact with Cork on intelligence matters. In the intelligence sphere, O'Donoghue seems to have regarded Collins as a peer rather than superior, and the records of their collaboration supports that view.

30   Tom Crofts was a Cork city IRA leader who subsequently commanded its Active Service Unit.

31   O'Donoghue was particularly impressed by Major Compton-Smyth, a decorated British intelligence officer who was captured near Blarney while disguised as a fisherman. O'Donoghue interrogated Compton-Smyth before the latter's execution in Blarney in the spring of 1921, and remembered him as a 'fine type'. Compton-Smyth wrote of singing songs with his captors, whom he considered 'mistaken idealists rather than a murder gang', and left his watch to the officer who executed him, 'to mark the fact that I bear him no malice for carrying out what he sincerely believes is his duty'. See O'Donoghue in the O'Malley Notebooks, UCD; and the report of the Cork Quarterly Session in the *Cork Constitution*, 17 October 1921.

32   For a more complete examination of O'Donoghue's intelligence network, see my thesis *Informers, Intelligence and the 'Anti-Sinn Féin Society': The Anglo-Irish War in Cork City, 1920-1921*, which can be found at Boole Library, University College, Cork.

33   Members of the Brigade intelligence staff received a small salary, which was a rare occurrence in the IRA. For details, see the Intelligence Squad list and Collins' letter to O'Donoghue, 8 March 1921, Ms. 31,401, NLI; O'Donoghue in the O'Malley Notebooks, UCD; Robert Aherne's BMH Statement; and captured correspondence between the Cork No. 1 Brigade and GHQ, published in the British Army pamphlet 'The Irish Republican Army' (p. 363) found in the Strickland Papers, IWM.

34   See the division's official *History of the 6th Division in Ireland*, p. 49, a copy of which is found in the General E.P. Strickland Papers, Imperial War Museum; a letter to the *Church Times*, reprinted in the *Weekly Summary*, 11 February 1921; and a letter to Gen. Strickland from an anonymous loyalist, dated 24 January 1921, Strickland Papers, IWM. The Donal Óg disinformation attempt is covered in the *History of the 6th Division in Ireland*, p. 49. Michael Collins refers to the episode in his letter to Florrie O'Donoghue, dated 14 April 1921, Ms. 31,192, NLI.

35   See Appendix A for the full order. This is a fascinating document.

36   Letter to Strickland from an anonymous Loyalist, 24 January 1921, Strickland Papers, IWM.

37   For Neenan's quote, see U. MacEoin *Survivors* (Dublin: Argenta Publications, 1980), p. 240. The 6th Division order comes from the 'Summary of Important

Orders to 17th Infantry Brigade from HQ 6th Division', GS 12/106, Strickland Papers, IWM. That booklet was assembled by Brigade-Major Bernard Montgomery of El Alamein fame. Eamonn Enright's statement can be found in the O'Malley Notebooks, UCD.

38   From O'Donoghue's intelligence lecture, Ms. 31,443, NLI. O'Donoghue did not name Costello during the lecture, but identified him during his conversation with Ernie O'Malley. T. Ryle Dwyer reports that at the end of 1920, Costello was transferred to County Kerry with the rank of special crimes sergeant. O'Donoghue put Costello in touch with Kerry No. 1 Brigade Intelligence Officer, Tim Kennedy, and Costello supplied him with RIC cipher keys. See O'Donoghue in the O'Malley Notebooks, UCD; and Dwyer, *Tans, Terror and Troubles, Kerry's Real Fighting Story 1913–23* (Cork: Mercier, 2001), p. 261.

# 4

# 'A CAMPAIGN AGAINST PUBLIC ORDER'

## Florence O'Donoghue

1919 was on the whole a year of happy activity for me. Events in that period remain much more clearly in my memory than do those of the strained and crowded days of 1920 and 1921. It was a year of increasing tension and of a new orientation of the public mind to the struggle of freedom. Clashes with the occupation forces became more frequent. There were more arrests, police and military raids, trials, refusals to recognize Courts, protests and demands for political treatment in prisons, hunger strikes, and a general stiffening of national resistance. Carefully compiled records for that year give these figures – seven persons murdered by the occupation forces; twenty-two deported; 382 armed assaults on civilians; 12,589 raids on private houses; 963 arrests; 777 sentences; 364 proclamations and prohibitions; and 26 news-papers suppressed.

I continued to visit the country Battalions on Sundays, sometimes alone, sometimes with other officers. On one of these visits Tom Crofts and I went out on a Saturday night to the Eighth Battalion and stayed with Patrick O'Sullivan's family at Kilnamartyra.[1] Patrick was the Battalion Commandant and his father the principal teacher at the local National school. They had a special pew in the church, the first below the altar rails on the Gospel side. We went to Mass with some of the family on Sunday morning and sat in this pew with them. The PP [parish priest] came out of the sacristy before Mass and took a good look at us. Evidently making up his mind that we were engaged in the same foolish and dangerous business as Patrick, he devoted his sermon to warning the young men of the parish against being led astray by strangers, cocking a glaring eye at us now and again. 'No one,' he said, 'knows who they are; no one knows where they came from, and no one knows where they are going.' He was by no means unique in his attitude to us at the time. Incidentally, it was the first and last time I ever saw a priest come off the altar during Mass and take up the collection himself.

To provide Jim Grey with cover and opportunities in his job as Brigade Transport officer, we helped him get going on his own in a small garage practically outside the gate of the [Victoria] military barracks. His brother Miah, also a mechanic, went into it with him, and by some process which is not too clear to me they attached themselves a third member of the firm, Jack Cody, a rangy, fearless eighteen-years-old lad with a shock of fair hair and a good tenor voice. He was the second best driver I ever knew and he had about as much sense as a hen.

In due course a signboard appeared over the garage – 'Grey Brothers & Cody, Automobile Engineers and Mechanical Experts'. They were mighty pleased with this. To build up an innocent reputation for them so that they would not be suspect, we encouraged them to keep away from Volunteer association. So well did they do this that Jim was later able to obtain an official police permit to carry a revolver, on the ground that he needed it to protect his business and his person against the possibility of raids by the IRA.[2] Although they were fair mechanics, they were poor businessmen. Yet they did manage to acquire some ordinary customers and in time some repair work from the military barracks. That eased our transport problems because they could always produce for a night journey some customer's car left in for servicing. But they wanted to do better than this. They wanted to be able to provide any required number of cars on any night at short notice. So they became expert locksmiths, set about procuring keys that would open any garage in the city, and in time were able to take a car where ever they wanted and put it back in its garage before the place opened up in the morning.[3]

Not satisfied with this, they wanted a car that would be our own property and available at all times. This is how they got it. One day they had no work and were downtown. They saw a Ford car break down in Patrick Street and went to the assistance of the owner who turned out to be a cattle dealer from Dungarvan. Whatever line of salesmanship they used on the poor man, he agreed to leave them the car for repair and to return for it on the following Saturday. I forget what the damage was – back axle, I think – but anyhow it needed to be put in the fire. Jim and Miah had tackled the job, as Cody was missing. While it was warming up they went out next door for a few pints, met a few transport NCOs from the barracks, and forgot all about the job. When they returned, it was ruined and a new axle (if it was an axle) had to be provided. They had no money and they began to think fast.

They decided to steal the required part out of the barracks. Jim went in to reconnoitre, came back and reported that there was no hope of stealing the part, but that there was a sporting chance of stealing a Ford van out of which they could get the part. There was a lorry inside marked out to them for repair. If, while the Transport NCO was at dinner, they hitched the van on to the lorry, there was a chance that the Military policeman on duty on the gate would pass them out on the docket for the truck. If it failed they could plead a slight mistake. It worked; they brought out the van hitched to the truck.

Cody was mobilized and they spent a feverish night taking the van to pieces and disposing of the parts. The cattle dealer got his car on Saturday. We bought whatever the damaged part had been; out of some dump the boys resurrected an ancient Ford body, built it on to the van chassis and we had our first car. It had a splendid engine, no hood or windscreen, and when driving Cody used to ease his feet by putting them out, one on either side of the steering wheel where the windscreen should have been.[4] All three of them took on the job of teaching me how to drive and do simple repairs.

A curious thing about Jim, who had (so to speak) been reared on petrol, was that he had an overpowering ambition to own a horse. Somehow or other he realized his ambition and bought a horse. Stabled in the garage, the problem of feeding was got over for a time by taking the animal out to crop the grass on the sides of Ballyvolane road. But when his ribs began to look like coming through his skin, other measures had to be taken. Over the garage the owner had oats loose in a loft. An auger hole bored up through the garage roof, and a bag filled with oats, with a cork put in the hole until further supplies were required, solved the problem for a time. Inevitably, when the owner found a lot of his oats missing, suspicions were aroused and Jim made a reluctant parting with his horse.

Lest I should give the impression that in their disregard of the Seventh Commandment these men were typical of the Volunteer Organization as a whole, let me say that they were not. The great majority were decent, honest, God-fearing men, a great many of them deeply religious, a few of them saints. If here and there some of the best were lax in one way or another – well, that is how it was and I must not pretend to represent them as being otherwise.

I hate firearms. That may be a queer confession for one to make who had been for two periods of his life some kind of soldier, but it is true. Absence of any mechanical aptitude may account in part for my lack of interest in weapons. Arms were essential to what we were doing and some proficiency in their use had to be acquired. I did not reach the status of owning a rifle until 1921. In the early days none were available; after 1919 there was nothing one could do with a rifle in the city. A revolver or automatic was a handier and more portable weapon. From an initial chubby Bulldog, whose calibre I have forgotten, I graduated to a Smith & Wesson .38, an American Army pattern .44 automatic, and a .45 Webley, to a lovely German Parabellum which

Seán got through IRB sources and gave me.[5] And thereby hangs a tale – but it comes later.

There was no question of the importation of arms in any quantity at that time. Odd weapons and small supplies of ammunition were coming in through the crews of trading vessels. Almost the only other source of supply was purchase from individual soldiers. I remember one of our lads coming to me one day in the shop to say that there were three Connaught Rangers in a pub nearby who wanted to desert.[6] They had their rifles with them but no ammunition. They wanted £2.0.0 each and three complete sets of civilian clothes. The cash was not difficult to procure; three sets of clothing and shoes were a tougher problem. Eventually we got the stuff together and the three lads began to change. Everything was going well until one of them discovered that the pants we had provided were too big. The deal was held up until we procured a better fitting one. I remember thinking at the time that if the average British soldier was of the same standard as these Connaught Rangers they were not such formidable opponents as we thought.[7] I often wondered what became of them. We never saw them subsequently.

An organization such as had been built up at that time cannot maintain a static existence. It has to progress or it will crumble. 1919, particularly from the summer onwards, brought us face to face with that fact. Training had begun to pall; more and more men wanted action. Much has been written in late years crediting the origin of guerrilla warfare with one Brigade or another, or even dating it to ideas discussed in pre-Rising days. My personal conviction is that it was not a preconceived policy planned by GHQ or any Brigade. It was certainly not a predetermined or planned policy in our case, in the sense that we visualized it completely in advance, as a series of steps that would result in the development of it in the particular form that emerged. We made no such plans. That is not to say that there was no planning. Far from it. There was careful planning of each successive step, but it was only when that step had been taken that the possibility of the next step became evident.

The three factors which in my recollection influenced the manner in which the struggle developed in our Brigade were – first, the natural and widespread urge to resist the ever growing measure of repression taken by the authorities (arrests, deportations, raids, searches, proclamations, and suppressions); second, the imperative need for arms; and third, the necessity for action of some kind under the disciplined control if the organization was to be kept intact. The first factor became increasingly evident as the year progressed; its logical consequence was the second. We had a few small successes earlier, the

Grammar School raid in September 1917, Bealagleanna in July 1918.[8] In other Brigades in the south there had been actions; Soloheadbeg in January 1919, Araglin Barracks in April, the fight at Knocklong in May, Rathclarin in July, and the first attack on military as distinct from police in Fermoy in September.[9] In all of these except Knocklong the acquisition of arms was the main object.[10]

After a round of visits to the Battalions by Tomás and myself, a Brigade Council meeting was held about September at which all the Battalion Commandants were present. The question of action was fully discussed and a decision was made to seek GHQ sanction for attacks on police barracks. In the country Battalions these were the obvious targets for initial efforts. It could be hoped that some badly needed arms would be secured. If the buildings were destroyed after capture, it was unlikely that suitable alternative accommodation for police could be found locally, and areas would thus be cleared of the menace of hostile observation. Large numbers of men could be employed in the blocking of roads and other protective duties, thus giving the greatest possible number of them something active and dangerous to do. Plans were made for simultaneous attacks on three barracks in the same night – the most our limited arms would enable us to undertake with any degree of safety. GHQ refused to sanction the project, giving as a reason that it might prejudice an action they had planned. This was the attack on Lord French.[11] A month or so later GHQ asked for Volunteers from the Brigade for an operation under GHQ control, which we understood to be an effort to shoot members of the British cabinet. We were all opposed to sending men out of the Brigade area. Tomás went to Dublin and eventually in December got sanction to our own proposal. The attacks were fixed for the night of 2 January 1920.

The three police barracks selected for attack were Ballygarvan, Kilmurray, and Carrigtwohill. The arms of the adjoining Battalions were pooled to enable the Second, Fourth, and Seventh [Battalions] to carry out the attacks. There was no Volunteer organization in the Ballygarvan district at this time, but it was within six miles of the city. Its selection was influenced partly by the fact that the police there were believed to be less alert than elsewhere; and partly for the purpose of giving one of the two city Battalions an opportunity of participating in the first Brigade operation.

The Second Battalion on the south side of the city and nearest the objective was detailed for the attack. A few nights before the date fixed, the OC of the Second, Seán O'Sullivan, reported that having inspected the position with some of his officers they were of the opinion that the barracks could not be taken with the available arms. It was plain enough that he was not prepared to make a serious effort and was awed by the responsibility for possible casualties. His officers had taken the line of least resistance in agreeing with him. He was allowed to resign. It was too late, however, to reorganize an attack on the fixed date and it was decided to let the other two go ahead.

Carrigtwohill barracks was captured with all its arms and ammunition after a fight – the first in Ireland to be taken since Tom Ashe took Ashbourne in 1916. Kilmurray successfully resisted the efforts of the Seventh Battalion on that occasion. No Brigade officers took part in either of these attacks. That was a mistake on our part. It would have been good for the morale if some of us had taken a hand, and it would have been valuable experience for later efforts. However, we rectified our error by active participation at Inchigeela, Carrigadrohid, and Blarney.[12]

These attacks produced prompt reaction, though not of the kind we had anticipated. A number of the more isolated and weakly garrisoned barracks were closed down, including Ballygarvan. Thus began a policy on the part of the occupation forces that continued throughout the struggle – the closing down of small posts and concentration of their forces in fewer and larger buildings. It had a good effect on our morale. Men saw the visible effect of aggressive policy; they saw that the police made no serious effort to locate or arrest those responsible for the attacks. Some Battalion areas were almost entirely cleared of police, giving us a consequent freedom of action and movement that were very valuable.

Moreover, the enemy was losing his most valuable source of information over a large part of the county. The RIC was a very efficient organization for its purpose and it was an indispensable instrument of British policy in Ireland. In any country district there was really nothing worth knowing about the local population that the police did not know. British policy in Ireland had been a continuity for 300 years. The Imperial rulers who devised and administered that policy were astute enough to realize that the basis of its continued existence was an accurate knowledge of the mind of the people, and in the light of that knowledge the taking of such action (either by purchase, intimidation or removal), as would secure the elimination of the elements that menaced its security. Since the inception of the force, the authorities had relied upon it for the continued provision of that essential information.

I wondered how the British would try to repair the loss the withdrawal of the police represented for them. I was sceptical of popular ideas about spies. I think it had become habitual with me by this time to keep looking at the facts and trying to see all of them. Perhaps I had become so immersed in the practical realities that the candle of vision burned only dimly, because I remember taking myself to task occasionally after meeting one of the political people and being treated to soaring conceptions of victory, freedom, prosperity, and a new heaven upon earth. But the facts continued to dominate. I knew more than the political people did the precariousness of our position as an armed force, and I was convinced if that was broken everything else went down in disaster.

Looking at the facts I could not see spies being successful against the tight organization we then had. By this time everybody of any consequence knew everybody else in the Brigade, in the adjoining Brigades, and at GHQ. We were not accepting anybody at his own valuation. The man who could horn in successfully would need to be a genius. Traitors and informers were a more dangerous possibility. I dare say we were all subconsciously sensitive to the havoc worked by these wretches in former national movements. Ours was remarkably free of this stain. In a Brigade of eight thousand men we had during the whole course of the struggle only one solitary case of a Volunteer turning informer, and in his case it was the result of pressure put upon him while a prisoner. The lives of seven of his comrades were lost because of his crime. He gave information that enabled the British to raid the place where they were sleeping at Ballycannon, just outside the city. They were surrounded while asleep and murdered before they had a chance to resist. The British smuggled the informer to America subsequently, but we traced him. At a time when every man and every shilling was needed, we went to the trouble and expense of sending three men after him to America. He was shot in New York.[13]

As the basic Intelligence service began to function with some efficiency, and as men became trained to appreciate the kind of information that was of value to us, we began to get a clear picture of the British organizations opposed to us. Though considerable and enlightening, this information was limited to what could be gained through observation. We had not yet tapped any sources, other than the Cork GPO telegraph office, which would enable us to see something of the enemy from the inside. We had listed the strength and arms of all police barracks; we had some information on the personnel and security measures in most cases, and the information was kept up to date. Of the military organizations we knew little beyond rough estimates of strengths.

We began to see that the civil population might be put into three categories – first, those who would help us as far as they could, and they were the majority; second, those who would stand aloof either through indifference or fear; and third, the minority who would help our enemies.[14] For the acquisition of information we organized a wide variety of contacts designed to make the maximum use of those who would help, particularly where they were favourably placed for the purpose.

On the counter-Intelligence aspect we found that the minority who would aid the enemy could be divided into two distinct classes – the members of England's faithful garrison of civilians; and the mercenary touts and pimps, usually local and native. The first were by far the more potentially dangerous. They were not merely hostile, they were anti-Irish and regarded themselves as honoured in any service they could do for England. They were in the main intelligent observers, they had wide business and social contacts, and the Masonic cement kept them well integrated. The second class, contemptible and unprincipled, were men of such limited range and ability that their value to the enemy must have been slight. We put some of them out of action for their proved guilt, as a stern warning to others and to let their paymasters know that we were aware of their activities.

The absence of any facilities for the detention of prisoners over a long period made it impossible to deal effectively with the doubtful cases. In practice there was no alternative between execution and complete immunity. That made it imperative to obtain the clearest proof of guilt before a man was executed. Except in the Quinlisk case, and in that of O'Connor to which I will come later, this was never an easy matter. I felt it to be a personal moral responsibility to secure it in every case before sanction for execution was given. Frequently we deferred action over and over again where there was reasonable doubt; in most of these cases we never took any action at all. In the tense atmosphere of late 1920, when Seán O'Hegarty was Brigade OC, I remember him on one occasion getting impatient at my careful presentation of the evidence pro and con in one case, and exploding, 'Kill the bastard – what good is he anyway!' I knew of course that was not an order and that particular gentleman went free.

During the War of Independence, the Volunteers executed at least twenty-seven suspected informers in Cork city. Like O'Donoghue, city IRA veterans claimed everyone executed was a confirmed spy, but today there is no way of establishing guilt in many of those cases. It should be noted, however, that O'Donoghue's intelligence network displayed the competence and skill required to uncover civilian spies operating in the city.

The shooting of suspected informers intimidated other civilians who were inclined to pass on information to the Crown forces. Later the British Army would complain about the failure of civilians to help them locate their underground enemy in Cork.[15] Without reliable information, the Crown forces struck blindly at the Volunteers, who were able to sidestep the blows and remain intact as a fighting force.

Certain policemen in the city made themselves particularly obnoxious by their aggressiveness towards us. It was decided to shoot two of them – Sergeant Ferris and Constable Murtagh. Relays of pairs of men who had volunteered for the job searched the streets at night for an opportunity of meeting these men in circumstances where they could be dealt with. It was on one of these patrols that I came to experience panic and to understand its frightening effects. On a bitterly cold February night, Matt Ryan and I had been on duty in the centre of the city since eight o'clock. About 11.00 p.m., when we were thinking of abandoning the quest for that night, we decided to try a last turn on the Grand Parade. We had noted previously that about that time policemen sometimes left Tuckey Street Barracks on their way to their headquarters on Union Quay. A minute or two after we had stood in a doorway on the far side of the Parade from Tuckey St., we saw three policemen come out and walk diagonally across the wide street towards us. One of them was Ferris. We decided to attack.

With revolvers half drawn out of our overcoat pockets we waited. As the three policemen neared the footpath on our side I glanced round. What I saw caused a sudden feeling of what I can only describe as blind panic. Twelve or fourteen police were coming from behind us towards the three. They were close upon us, burly and enormous in greatcoats, all armed. In our concentration of attention on the smaller group we had not seen them approach. Somehow I warned Matt. We stood half turned towards each other as if in friendly conversation. There was no conversation; I was incapable of uttering a word. I can understand the phrase, 'rooted to the spot'. I was. If I had been capable of running I am sure I would have done so. The fact that we did not move probably saved us. The police took no notice of us. The large group, which had evidently come to escort Ferris, turned round and the whole party moved off towards Union Quay.

It was about a month later, 10 March, when Tom Crofts and I made a pair one night and came quite unexpectedly face to face with Ferris and District Inspector MacDonagh, both in civilian clothes and unescorted, on the Southern Road. This time (nor ever again, thank God) there was no feeling of panic. Guns were out and the first shots fired in a matter of seconds. I had the Parabellum Seán had given me. Suddenly, after two rounds it jammed and no wrestling of mine with it in the dark could get another round into the breach. One at least of the police had been as quick on the draw as we were, and though both were on the ground one was firing at us. Tom had emptied his gun and there was no more we could do.[16] We got away.

I had lost my hat, shot off I think, and I discovered that a bullet had gone through my clothes and grazed my side under the left arm. At that time it would have attracted attention to go about without headgear, and the inevitable bit of amusement was provided when we held up the first male citizen we met and took his cap off him. He yelled murder! It was filthy and too small for me. We got into Tom's brother's shop in the North Main Street and examined my Parabellum. A round was jammed nose up in the breach. That was one of our troubles always, wrong ammunition and bad ammunition. Tom hadn't a scratch, for which I was deeply thankful. Ferris was transferred immediately after the attack to somewhere in the North, where he was safely out of our reach, but at least we had eliminated his local efforts.[17]

The attempted assassination raised tensions in the city. The *Cork Examiner* called it 'another sensational shooting affair', while Cork's Catholic Archbishop Cohalan denounced the IRA assailants from the pulpit, warning, 'a campaign against the police is a campaign against public order'. Later that evening, parties of police assaulted Republicans around town, wrecking Sinn Féin halls and private residences in reprisal. However, they failed to identify their colleagues' attackers.[18]

Despite much advice to the contrary, I continued to work in the shop up to March 1920. The main reason was that my sisters would have found it hard to keep the house without my earnings. I had no money saved, and I did not see where any was to come from if I gave up my employment. My youngest sister, Margaret, had come to Cork, leaving only the second youngest, Lizzie, at home with my parents. There were then only very meagre funds available to us, and I had a reluctance, amounting to stubborn determination, not to avail of them except in some desperate necessity. In the event, neither of my sisters nor myself ever received a shilling from these funds during the whole period of trouble.

I was reluctant too to leave Michael Nolan. Others had come and gone, some relatives, some strangers, but I had been with him from the beginning. Although we disagreed on some things, and although he could be bad tempered when he had drink taken, he was essentially decent and occasionally generous. He had always treated me well, notwithstanding his disapproval of my activities outside business hours. I felt he would have difficulty in replacing me. He had. But when Tomás MacCurtain was murdered in March, the whole situation was changed for all of us and a new phase opened. I worked my last day in the shop on the 19th.

## NOTES AND REFERENCES

1   Patrick O'Sullivan and his brother Mick (Michael O'Suileabháin) were prominent members of the Brigade Flying Column. Their photo can be seen in photo 6 in the plate section.

2   District Inspector Swanzy signed the gun permit, and Grey gave the pistol to Tomás MacCurtain. After MacCurtain's death, the gun was smuggled to Lisburn for the Swanzy's assassination. Seán Culhane used it to fire the first shot into Swanzy. See Culhane in the O'Malley Notebooks, UCD; and Culhane's BMH statement. One of the other Swanzy assassins verified Culhane's use of MacCurtain's gun in the killing. See Roger McCorley's undated letter to O'Donoghue, Ms. 31,313, NLI. Additional correspondence relating to the assassination can be found in those papers.

3   Since private homes in the city typically were built without a car garage, cars were often housed in a few privately operated garages.

4   Cars of the era usually had an accelerator lever on the steering wheel.

5   The German-made Parabellum was a favourite IRA pistol. The semi-automatic was an early version of the German Army's WWII sidearm, popularly known as the Luger.

6   The Connaught Rangers were members of a British Army regiment recruited from the Irish province of Connaught.

7   In addition to the Connaught Rangers, the British Army raised eight other Irish Regiments during this period: the Dublin Fusiliers, the Leinster Regiment, the Royal Irish Regiment, the Irish Fusiliers, the Irish Rifles, the Irish Guards, the Inniskilling Fusiliers, and the Munster Fusiliers. The British Army was wary of deploying Irish regiments against the IRA, and did not use them during the Anglo-Irish conflict. There were also concerns about the loyalty of Irishmen serving in non-Irish units attached to the British Army's 6th Division. See Staff Captain 6th Division to all Officers Commanding, 9 November 1920; and GHQ Ireland to OC 6th Division, 12 June 1920. Both orders are found in A/0341, DDA. British fears about Irish troops were confirmed in late June 1920, when a battalion of the Connaught Rangers in India mutinied over British repression in Ireland. A group of 300 protesting soldiers raised the tricolour over Wellington Barracks in Jullunder and refused to respond to their officers. They eventually surrendered a few days later. However, at a small hill garrison in Solon (200 miles away), fifty mutineers attacked their post arsenal to seize weapons, and two were killed in the fight. Afterwards, a total of thirty mutineers were sentenced to death, though only one was executed. For details see Anthony Babington, *The Devil to Pay, The Mutiny of the Connaught Rangers, India, July 1920* (London: Leo Cooper, 1991); and Connor Reilly 'Conor Francis O'Brien, Connaught Ranger 1895–1969', *Irish Sword*, Summer 2001, Vol. XXII, No. 87, pp. 328–32.

8   The Cork Grammar School raid was a burglary carried out by city Volunteers led by Dan Donovan and Roibeárd Langford. They secured forty-seven rifles stored by the British Army for an officers' training course at the school. (See O'Donoghue, *Tomás MacCurtain*, p. 133; and Langford's account in a letter to O'Donoghue, Ms. 31,423, NLI.) At Bealagleanna, a party of seven Cork Volunteers held up two members of the RIC on a road near Ballingeary.

Ordered to surrender their arms, the police refused and a scuffle ensued, resulting in the shooting of Constable Butler. The policeman survived. See O'Donoghue, *Tomás MacCurtain*, p. 141 for details.

9    O'Donoghue here refers to a number of violent clashes between Volunteers and Crown forces in 1919. All these episodes took place in either County Cork or County Tipperary.

10   South Tipperary Volunteers led by Dan Breen, Seán Hogan, and Seán Treacy held up a wagon of gelignite in Soloheadbeg and shot dead the two policemen guarding it. A few months later at Knocklong train station, Breen and Treacy rescued their arrested colleague Seán Hogan as police transported him. In a wild and bloody shootout, two RIC guards were killed and four Volunteers wounded. Members of the Cork No. 3 Brigade jumped a British Army patrol at Rathclarin, near Kilbrittain, and seized five rifles. At the Araglin police barracks, Cork No. 2 Brigade Volunteers commanded by Michael Fitzgerald overcame the single RIC sentry (the other police were at church), and captured six rifles. At Fermoy, Cork No. 2 Brigade Volunteers led by Liam Lynch attacked fifteen British soldiers attending church. Using clubs, the Volunteers disarmed the soldiers, though one private was killed and three wounded in the assault. O'Donoghue provides details of the latter two episodes in his book *No Other Law* (Dublin: Anvil Books, 1986).

11   Members of Michael Collins' 'Squad' ambushed the new Governor-General of Ireland (and former commander of the British Expedition Force in France), near his official residence at Ashtowne, Dublin. The Volunteers concentrated their fire on the wrong vehicle of French's convoy, and Viscount French escaped unharmed. In the fusillade a Dublin Volunteer named Martin Savage died and Tipperary's Dan Breen was seriously wounded. There had been a number of earlier attempts on French's life, including one in which Tomás MacCurtain (in Dublin for a meeting) joined the assailants. The following year, members of the Cork No. 1 Brigade's Fourth Battalion narrowly missed shooting French during a visit to Cobh.

12   The latter two RIC barrack attacks will be discussed in Chapter Five.

13   O'Donoghue here describes the case of Patrick 'Croxy' O'Connor (also known as Connor), a former British soldier who won the French Croix de Guerre for bravery during the First World War. A native of Cork city, O'Connor served as a machine gunner with the Cork No. 1 Brigade column at the Coolavokig ambush and was captured shortly afterwards. Some Volunteers made the unproven accusation that O'Connor deliberately jammed his machine gun during the ambush, but there was some indication O'Connor had earlier been a paid British informer. O'Connor subsequently divulged the hiding place of six Cork city men who served with him in the brigade column (rather than the seven O'Donoghue claims). Crown forces killed the Volunteers at Clogheen (in an episode also known as the 'Kerry Pike murders'), probably after they were in military custody. British Intelligence relocated O'Connor to New York City, but a Cork woman there recognized him and notified the Cork No. 1 Brigade. The Brigade sent Pa Murray and two Volunteers to New York and they shot down O'Connor outside Central Park on 13 April 1922. Miraculously, despite being wounded three times in the body and once in the face, O'Connor survived the attack, though it is unclear if he ever recovered. See Stan Barry, Dan Corkery, Dan Healy, Raymond Kennedy, Mick Leahy, Pat Margetts, Florrie O'Donoghue, and Mick O'Sullivan in the O'Malley Notebooks, UCD; a Captured letter of Captain Kelly, Ms. 31,228, NLI; Collins to O'Donoghue, 5 April 1921, Ms. 31,228,

NLI; *The History of the 6th Division in Ireland*, p. 55, Strickland Papers, IWM; correspondence between O'Donoghue, Pa Murray, and Moss Twomey about the New York trip, Ms. 31,296, NLI; the BMH statement of Daniel Healey (which tells the full story of the New York operation); and the *New York Times* 14, 15, and 17 April 1922. The date of the shooting comes from Mary O'Leary's MA thesis 'Social Change in Currykippane, 1885–1935', University College, Cork, forwarded to me by Tom O'Neill.

14    British forces agreed with this rough division of the Irish population. In a lecture on military intelligence during the Anglo-Irish war, Colonel French of the Hampshire Regiment (stationed in Cork city) told a gathering of staff officers, '5/6 of the population is either actively or passively opposed to us' (7/16, Foulkes Papers, Liddell Hart Centre for Military Archives, King's College, London). The Irish Command likewise stated, 'The bulk of the people were our enemies and were therefore far more incorruptible than has been the case in former Irish movements.' In Cork city, the population was hostile, explained the official history. 'The inhabitants are mainly of the lower orders and were on the whole bitterly opposed to the Crown forces, the proportion of loyal people being very small.' See Peter Hart *British Intelligence in Ireland, 1920–1921, The Final Reports* (Cork: Cork University Press, 2002), pp. 47 and 39. Information dried up further after the shooting of suspected civilian informers. The 6th Division official history remarked, 'Civilians who had previously given information were now unwilling to run further risks, and refused to assist the troops or police in this matter.' (*History of the 6th Division in Ireland*, p. 29, Strickland Papers, IWM). The Irish Command's official history agreed, 'The terror created was such that all who had been given information previously were silenced.' (Hart, *British Intelligence in Ireland*, p. 28). Brigadier-General F.P. Crozier, who commanded the Auxiliary Cadets, later declared, 'It was foolish for "loyalists" to "talk" in Ireland in 1920 and 1921. It was madness to "inform".' See Crozier, *Word to Gandhi* (London: Williams and Norgate, 1927), p. 53.

15    See *History of the 6th Division in Ireland*, p. 29, Strickland Papers, IWM.

16    The *Cork Examiner* reported that Sergeant Ferris emptied his revolver at his two assailants. An innocent pedestrian was seriously wounded in the shootout, probably by a shot fired by Crofts. See the *Cork Examiner*, 11 March 1920.

17    Sergeant Ferris was transferred to Springfield Barracks, Belfast and promoted to District Inspector. There, IRA officers believed Ferris became involved with an unofficial RIC reprisal campaign against Belfast Republicans. On 3 May 1921, IRA gunmen shot Ferris three times (twice in the back and once in the head), but once again Ferris miraculously survived. See Jim McDermott, *Northern Divisions* (Belfast: BTP Publications, 2001), pp. 50, 77, and 80.

18    The shooting of District Inspector MacDonagh was national news and contributed to the growing tension in Cork that culminated in the assassination of Tomás MacCurtain. In response to the MacDonagh assault, Cork police raided and wrecked two Sinn Féin halls and three homes, including that of reluctant Volunteer commandant Seán O'Sullivan. District Inspector Swanzy commanded one of the destructive police parties. His name will reappear in Chapter 5. The night of the shooting, some police officers broke out of barracks apparently to assassinate unnamed Sinn Féin politicians as a reprisal for the MacDonagh shooting. However, Swanzy convinced the men to return to their station. See the *Cork Weekly News*, 10 April 1920; and the *Cork Examiner*, 11, 13, and 15 March 1920.

# 5

# 'A HARD, PALPABLE REALITY'

## Florence O'Donoghue

On the night of 19 March 1920, city IRA Volunteers shot and killed RIC Constable Joseph Murtagh on Pope's Quay in Cork.[1] Two hours later, a party of police with blackened faces invaded Tomás MacCurtain's home and shot down the young Lord Mayor as he opened his bedroom door.

I was asleep at No. 55 North Main Street when Michael Barrett called about 3.00 a.m., woke me up with persistent knocking, and told me that Tomás had been shot dead at his home by police. I had parted with him at Wallace's about four hours previously, and I hurried to Blackpool and looked on his quiet, dead face. All the bullets had been fired at his body, and except for a wound on one finger he was not visibly disfigured. His poor wife was in a state of collapse; the house was filled with the wailing of his young children, and Father Dominic in his brown Franciscan habit who had arrived just ahead of me, was doing his best to console them. Terry came and then Seán, and there was much to be done.

The three of us worked until the second night following almost without a break. Then Dr Tadg Murphy, almost by force, carried me off to his place and put me in his own bed.[2] In the meantime, I had been present at the post mortem and had watched the doctors in their professional detachment do what was necessary to trace the course of the bullets and locate them. I knew it was necessary but it seemed sacrilege. Afterwards when they had bound it together again with endless rolls of bandages, we put his uniform on Tomás's body. We had taken him to the City Hall where, in an open coffin, he lay in state. Although I had been up all the previous night and part of the one preceding it, I found it hard to sleep. When I did I had a nightmare. I thought the coffin, which we had placed on high trestles in the City Hall, was slipping off and there was no one to prevent it from crashing on the ground. I woke up in a sweat of anxiety.

The killing of Lord Mayor Tomás MacCurtain was a pivotal moment in the Anglo-Irish conflict. The slaying headlined newspapers around the world and garnered much sympathy for the Irish cause. It also signalled Britain's violent new policy for ending the insurgency. IRA Chief of Staff Richard Mulcahy later remarked, 'The MacCurtain assassination could be said to have opened the period of Crown force reprisals known as "the terror" which continued until July 1921.'[3]

MacCurtain's funeral was the largest in Cork city's history. Schools, offices, and businesses shut for the day of mourning and black bunting hung over buildings and monuments. Civic, commercial, and religious bodies from around the country joined the funeral procession. The mile-long cortege contained an estimated 10,000 marchers and took one-and-a-half hours to pass any one spot. Approximately 100,000 people (a crowd larger than the city's population) watched the procession to St Finbarr's Cemetery. All contemporary observers agree that it was a stunning and moving display.[4]

Florence O'Donoghue, Joe O'Connor, Seán O'Hegarty, and Terence MacSwiney served as pallbearers. Amid their grief they were already planning vengeance.

There is no need to say anything of the funeral as a spectacle or as a tribute to the dead man. We had done a good job of organization. The Brigade Staff in uniform marched immediately behind the hearse in the funeral; we shouldered the coffin in and out of the City Hall, in and out of the Cathedral, and at the graveside. We did that deliberately after consultation, believing that the time for further concealment was ended. And that no matter what the cost, the event called for an open avowal by us of our positions of responsibility.

I remember the day after the funeral very well. I went to the City Hall to meet Terry. His face was grey with weariness, only in his ice blue eyes was there any animation, and the inevitable cigarette looked as incongruous as ever in his sensitive mouth. 'Well, Florrie,' he said, 'what are we to do now?' I said, and it was hardly a question, 'You will take Tomás's place as Brigade Commandant.' Quietly he said, 'Yes, Florrie, I will take Tomás's place.' 'The next thing to do,' I suggested, 'is to get Seán O'Hegarty back as Vice Commandant.' 'Do you think he would come back,' he asked. I replied that I believed he would. 'Will you ask him, Florrie?' I agreed and no more was said about the matter. I have mentioned earlier that Seán had gone back to the ranks after the row over IRB control.

I went to Seán that night and spoke my mind very freely. I told him that it was now his plain duty to resume his post as Vice OC of the Brigade. Whatever difficulties existed, it was not a time when the Brigade could afford to be without the guidance of his strong hand and clear mind. I told him that I believed that every officer and man in the Brigade who was genuinely anxious for an active forward policy would welcome his return. He did not need much persuasion, only he was anxious that it should be generally acceptable and that there would not be opposition. I knew we could carry it easily and told him so. GHQ ratified the appointment without question.

On 31 March 1920, Terence MacSwiney succeeded MacCurtain as Lord Mayor. His acceptance speech sums up the IRA's ethos, and would be quoted often during his hunger strike the following autumn. '... I wish to point out again the secret of our strength and the assurance of our final victory. This contest of ours is not on our side a rivalry of vengeance, but one of endurance – it is not they who inflict most, but they who can suffer most – will conquer – though we do not abrogate our function to demand and see that evil-doers and murderers are punished for their crimes.'[5]

As the Volunteers and police played lethal games of hide-and-seek, a pattern of guerrilla war began to emerge in Cork city. Local IRA units made aggressive assaults on Crown forces. Civilian informers started to fear for their lives. Increasing numbers of Volunteers adopted a war mentality. The decision to kill was made with less hesitation.

The British tried to fight fire with fire. In the month of March 1920, the first RIC reinforcements recruited in Britain appeared on Irish streets. A uniform shortage forced the new constables to wear combinations of military khaki and Irish police bottle-green clothing. The Irish public nicknamed the new police 'Black and Tans'. Mostly unemployed veterans of the First World War, the Black and Tans were violent and poorly disciplined. Feared and hated in Ireland, they soon became infamous abroad.

The Corporation elected Terry Lord Mayor in succession to Tomás. He took his Municipal responsibilities very seriously. He was TD for the mid-Cork constituency as well, and because of his frequent periods of detention in the previous years, his knowledge of the Brigade was not, and could not have been, as intimate as was that of his predecessor. Consequently, although he did a lot of work, and was in fact a complete slave to it from March until his arrest in August, and although we kept him fully informed, nevertheless the bulk of the work fell on Seán, Joe O'Connor, and myself.

Now a period of action was beginning, different in its characters and demands to the preparatory years we had been through, a venture into uncharted territory, where many new problems and difficulties were added to the old ones. So far as policy was concerned, all GHQ could do was to indicate its general lines in the broadest way, and ban certain kinds of activity. The extent to which that policy was put into effect depended almost entirely on the vision and exertions of the local units. Frequently it depended on a very few men. This is the explanation of the lack of uniformity in the fight throughout the country. Where there was progressively expanding activity in an area, one always found a man, or a small group of men, who were its mainspring and inspiration.

A Brigade was, however, a compact unit, responsive to control and direction by its officers, and this resulted very generally in developments by Brigades. We in Cork No. 1 were fortunate in the variety of our personnel and resources. We had the city and all that a city's resources imply in a contest such as ours, but our main strength was in the country, over the sixty-mile stretch from the sea at Youghal to the Kerry borders. As I felt it then, the Brigade had developed a distinct character. It was a live and vital organism, sometimes touchy and sensitive, but with a hard core of steadfastness and a willingness to work and fight. It had a fundamental unity of objective, ambition, and method that made possible much local initiative. There was fine courage, much manliness, ardent devotion to the cause, the idealism of citizen soldiers, and a discipline that must have been unique. In contrast to the activities of the earlier period (sincere, finely inspired, and exhilarating though they were), the struggle was now on another plane. It had acquired a hard, palpable reality.[6]

By the summer of 1920, British suppression of IRA activities forced many Volunteers to go 'on the run'. Wanted by police, it was no longer safe for the militants to sleep in their own beds or appear at their workplaces. Freed of home and work obligations, the fugitives now dedicated themselves full-time to the IRA. Their evolution into professional revolutionaries quickened the pace of the insurgency throughout Ireland.

In the country, many of those on the run carried arms to resist arrest. These armed men frequently banded together for mutual protection and support. They became the nucleus of the IRA's 'flying columns', groups of guerrillas who travelled around the countryside striking at vulnerable Crown forces. The threat of IRA ambush compelled the British to concentrate their units in secure locations and to travel only in large numbers. This cleared the police and army from even more locales, allowing the IRA to assert their authority in the vacated areas.

Turmoil and instability in Ireland was turning into a full-blown guerrilla war.

On commencing whole-time duty I had to decide whether or not I would follow the example of other city men who had gone on the run and take to the country, or whether I would remain in the city. The city was the natural centre and focal point in the Brigade, and from no other point could the routine work of my two departments be handled so conveniently. The country was safer of course, but I had seen some good men go out into safe areas only to stagnate. We had that problem earlier. I decided to stay in the city.

The personal problem of finance was quickly solved; GHQ made a small allowance available to the few of us on whole-time duty. One of the many slanders upon us at the time was that the extreme element in the movement comprised a gang of unemployed desperadoes, who were being well paid in German gold to murder and loot. In fact every whole-time officer and man in our Brigade had come out of employment to give his whole time to the work. It was the same in most other Brigades. This was the first time that any of us had been made any allowance. The number so sustained at any time up to the Truce, in a Brigade of eight thousand officers and men, did not exceed fifteen.[7] I personally valued the regular payment (small though it was) very highly, not alone because it relieved my mind of anxiety for the welfare of my sisters, but also because there was an assurance of continuity as long as I was alive.

That seemed at the time to be at best only a short span. I had no real belief that I would survive the conflict. I thought that inevitably the day would come for each of us; we would be eliminated one by one; we were too few and too poorly armed against so many. While accepting that, I did not have the positive conviction some men had that they would be killed. Charlie Hurley comes to mind; he was so utterly sure of it that I have no doubt it helped him when the day came. He died well.[8]

On the decision to remain in the city, two things became necessary – a place in which to work and a place to sleep. The second presented no difficulties because lists had been made in all city Companies of houses whose occupants were prepared to provide a bed when called on. In the first month I did not stay long in any one place. There could be no question of payment, and I felt that any prolonged stay would be an imposition on people often not too well off. After a month, arrangements were made for Terry and I to share a double bed at Hurley's, 15 Sundays Well Road, and we stayed there, except when he was out of town, up to the date of his last arrest in August.

This arrangement was in part protection for him. Since the murder of Tomás we had kept an armed Volunteer, Christy MacSweeney (one of the MacNeilus rescuers), continuously engaged as an unobtrusive armed guard on him in the daytime. I took over this duty at night. Mr and Mrs Hurley were more than kind to us. We would arrive often late, and let ourselves in quietly, hoping not to disturb them. But there never was a night that we were not intercepted by the good woman who was sure to have supper waiting for us.

The Hurleys appeared to be well off. Certainly the house had every comfort. It was neat to the point of fastidiousness. There was a strip of immaculately white, flower-bordered oilcloth covering with mathematical exactitude the centre of the stair carpet. Terry used to make jokes about what Mrs Hurley would do to us if we went in with muddy boots.

He could be very charming. I remember the first night we went there as complete strangers. Mr Hurley was not there and Mrs Hurley was formally polite and considerate, but without a trace that I could detect of enthusiasm for us or our mad projects. Presiding over the tea-pot, she enquired, 'one or two, Mr MacSwiney?' 'Two, ma'am,' he replied, 'I'll put in the other two myself.' The ice was broken; we could all be easy and natural from that moment. I think she was a little in awe of him at first. Never at any time did she attempt to discuss his work, and I often wondered if she suspected we were armed or thought about what a wreck would have been made of her lovely home if it was raided for us. She took the risk calmly and bravely, typical of the good people who sheltered us.

Although the neighbourhood was so highly respectable that it was not one in which we were likely to be looked for, our enemies having the curious idea that the 'respectable' element in the population could be ruled out of participation in our villainies, we always left early in order to avoid attracting attention. Yet, no matter at what time we got up our hostess was ready with a smiling face and breakfast. I never saw a maid in the house.

Terry was a great talker. We often sat up late or continued the discussion in bed. An idiosyncrasy that I think may be indicative of his nervous tension at the time was that he would never sit down to take off or put on his boots. He would lace or unlace one standing on the other leg in the middle of the floor. To fill in the time between leaving Hurley's and that at which he could appear at the City Hall (usually 10 a.m.), we would go either to his home at Belgrave Place or to mine at North Main Street. Study of the routine of our opponents led us to believe that the raids at this hour in the morning were very improbable.

Terry had a .38 automatic of which he took great care. At this time each morning he would unload it to ease the magazine spring. One morning, going along Wellington Road towards Terry's home, a hurrying man in civilian clothes came round the corner form York Hill and almost collided with us. There was a swift glance of mutual recognition and he hurried on – District Inspector Swanzy, the man primarily responsible for the murder of Tomás. He was no doubt going from King Street Police Barracks [now MacCurtain Street] where he had spent the night to his flat on St Patrick's Hill. He appeared to be even more of a fugitive than we were. We could have shot him on that deserted road, but the Inquest was still going on and the whole effect of the verdict would have been lost. Soon afterwards he was transferred to Lisburn, and although it took months to trace him he was shot dead there by men from the Brigade.

The MacCurtain Inquest proved a major embarrassment to the British Government and led to the suppression of civilian coroners' juries in Ireland. During three weeks of testimony before a packed hall, witnesses offered considerable circumstantial evidence that local police had assassinated the Lord Mayor.[9] The Cork Coroner's Jury returned a verdict of wilful murder against British Prime Minister David Lloyd-George, Ireland's Viceroy Lord French, Irish Chief Secretary Ian MacPherson, District Inspector Swanzy, and 'unknown members of the Royal Irish Constabulary'.

During this period, the Cork No. 1 Brigade worked to avenge the death of Tomás MacCurtain. On 11 May 1920, it tracked the two policemen thought to have fired the shots that killed MacCurtain. Volunteers led by Pa Murray boarded a streetcar carrying Constable Daniel Harrington and Sergeant Denis Garvey, and shot and killed them.[10] Two months later, Volunteers tried to blow up the King Street Barracks, where MacCurtain's killers were seen to return after the killing. The explosion did not work properly (a common problem with the Brigade's home-made bombs) and no police officers were seriously hurt. However, the blast wrecked the building interior, resulting in its evacuation and ultimate destruction a few nights later in a fire set by Volunteers.[11] But the main object of the Brigade officers' revenge remained their long-time nemesis District Inspector Oswald Swanzy, who they believed had planned MacCurtain's killing.[12]

Shortly after the MacCurtain Inquest, the RIC transferred Swanzy out of Cork for his own protection.[13] The Cork No. 1 Brigade leaders did not know where to find Swanzy, but kept their eyes open for possible clues. A couple of months later, O'Donoghue's intelligence colleague Seán Culhane received word that Swanzy's belongings were being removed from his Cork home and shipped to his new location. Culhane contacted a Volunteer working in the train station luggage department and found Swanzy's bags hidden under a false name, destined for an address in Lisburn, Northern Ireland. One of Michael Collins' Belfast agents (an RIC sergeant named Matt McCarthy) then confirmed Swanzy's location in Lisburn. Florrie O'Donoghue and Seán Culhane travelled to Dublin to request permission to assassinate the District Inspector. They met with Michael Collins, Richard Mulcahy, and Dáil Defence Minister Cathal Brugha, and secured Brugha's permission, which was needed to proceed. The Brigade sent two Cork city men, Seán Culhane and Dick Murphy, to Belfast where they contacted the Belfast Brigade under the command of Joe McKelvey. Belfast officers arranged the operation.

On the early afternoon of Sunday, 22 August 1920, Seán Culhane and Dick Murphy, along with Belfast Volunteers Roger McCorley and George Fox, waited for District Inspector Oswald Swanzy outside the Church of Ireland in Lisburn. When the District Inspector emerged from church services, the Volunteers followed him for a block, then shot him down. Culhane fired first using Tomás MacCurtain's own gun, which had been smuggled to Lisburn for the purpose. Enraged bystanders tried to capture the killers, who had to fire warning shots to clear a path through the crowd. The assassins escaped, and hours later the Corkmen boarded a train to Dublin.

In response to the shooting, Protestant mobs attacked Lisburn's Catholic population. Houses were sacked and businesses burned, but local police did little to check the violence. During three days of riots, about 100 premises were destroyed and most of the Catholic population were forced to flee the city. Order was finally restored by regular British troops, who enforced a strict curfew. Passing through Lisburn on the Dublin train, Culhane and Murphy watched the flames of burning Catholic homes.[14]

By the summer of 1920, IRA attacks against British forces had increased throughout Ireland, especially in active counties like Cork, Tipperary, and Limerick. The Royal Irish Constabulary, the backbone of the British Administration in Ireland, was in headlong retreat. Police resignations soared and morale plummeted. Many constables became passive, refusing to expose themselves to isolated assassination or ambush. Hundreds of small and vulnerable police posts were abandoned around the country, leaving much of the cities and countryside free of police scrutiny. At Easter 1920 (the fourth anniversary of the Easter Rising), about three hundred of these abandoned barracks were burned around the country, including a number in Cork city.

As the RIC disappeared off the streets, the Volunteers (now known as the Irish Republican Army) filled the power vacuum.

In Cork city, violent clashes, ambushes, and assassinations grew more frequent. In July, a brawl between ex-servicemen and British soldiers turned into a full-scale riot. British troops fired into a crowd of civilians, killing two and wounding twenty.[15] Military authorities declared a curfew for the city that remained in effect for the duration of the conflict. The same week, Brigade officers assassinated RIC Divisional

Commissioner Gerald Smyth while he sat in the Cork Conservative Club, the bastion of British Unionism in the city.[16] During July alone, city police report being fired on eight times.[17] In September, Volunteers led by Florrie O'Donoghue and Seán O'Hegarty narrowly missed assassinating the British 6th Division commander General Strickland as he drove up Patrick Street in Cork. (They managed to wound his driver.)[18] In October, city Volunteers ambushed a military lorry on Barrack Street, inflicting four British casualties.

The British Government searched for a resolution to the disorder. For an imperial power, a political settlement based on full Irish independence remained out of the question. Prime Minister David Lloyd-George vowed to forcibly re-establish British rule of law in Ireland. The British Army garrison was reinforced, and armed troops began to scour the country. The Government recruited more British replacements for the depleted RIC and created an elite police fighting force called the Auxiliary Cadets, composed of former British military officers. The new police were given a free hand by the British Government.

Auxiliary Cadets, RIC constables, and British soldiers patrolled the streets of Cork, creating an atmosphere of military occupation. The city population learned to live with random British hold-ups, long queues through checkpoints, and speeding lorries of police shooting into the air. The sounds of gunfire and explosions became common. In the face of continued IRA attacks, the Auxiliary Cadets issued ominous threats to local civic leaders and prominent Sinn Féin officials. An unofficial reprisal campaign took shape.

Provoked by the IRA's guerrilla attacks, the Crown forces resorted to a counter-campaign of arson and murder. Coercion tactics turned the civilian population against the British, which only worsened the security situation. They also caused international and domestic furore. While Britain had frequently used violence to repress disturbances in its far-flung empire (and was at that very time dropping mustard gas on Iraqi civilians protesting their country's occupation by Britain), coercion was politically unsustainable in a place like Ireland. Europeans proved to have a significantly lower threshold for colonial brutality when it was used against fellow Europeans.

The IRA and its civilian supporters were not deterred by the appearance of aggressive Black and Tans or professional British soldiers. Illegal activities moved deeper underground and more Volunteers went on the run throughout the city. Fortunately for them, the British reinforcements were unfamiliar with the area and could not distinguish wanted men from innocent civilians. IRA commanders moved about unarmed, disguised as clerks and labourers. They remained largely undetected while directing the ongoing guerrilla campaign.

The first office I had was in Patrick Street, in the flat of two brothers named Martin. They were Dublin men, one of them married, and as they were both Volunteers it was not the best place to be. I stayed there only long enough to look round for a suitable office. After a few short spells, one on the opposite side of the street and one in Douglas Street, I found what I required in a block of commercial offices in Cook Street. On various visits to Dublin I had seen how the GHQ officers utilized offices in commercial localities and assumed the cover of some legitimate business. Cork was so much smaller that at first I doubted the effectiveness of such an arrangement but decided to try it.

So I became George Egan, a representative of Dripsey Woolen Mills, with an office in a building almost entirely occupied by commercial agents. So wide awake a body must have been well aware that I was spurious, but never by so much as a questioning look did one of them let it appear. We had by then reached the stage where the average citizen had learned to ignore and keep his mouth shut about what he saw and did not understand. Against a raid based on information this kind of cover was worthless. I had the feeling, well justified by events, that we were safe against deliberate treachery, but it was essential to guard against the indiscriminate raiding then becoming general. I did not neglect the thoroughness of detail that would make the cover convincing in the event of a raid.

I had samples, order books, and the usual accumulation of odds and ends normal in such an office. The presence of the typewriter and typewriting materials could be plausibly justified. I had numerous envelopes addressed to me in my fictitious name that had never passed through the post, but had been stamped on different dates by our own men in the Central Post Office. I had the firm's official cards with my fictitious name printed on them, and if enquiry had been made the firm would have acknowledged me as genuine. I had a home address where the same answer would have been given to any enquiry. Few knew of the existence of the office; no one came there except Joe O'Connor at rare intervals, and a messenger about whom I must say something later. Seán [O'Hegarty] never came near the place; we met at Wallaces' or elsewhere. I took pains to make the deception as watertight and copper-fastened as possible.

In the event it all proved unnecessary; I was never raided. One morning when I had been there for some time, I thought the bluff would be put to the test. Joe O'Connor had just dropped in when the block was surrounded and a house-to-house search started. We bundled up our arms and documents, put them in the prepared hiding place and waited. Nothing happened. After a couple of hours whistles were blown, and to our astonishment we saw the party gathering to their lorries and moving off. We found out later that some soldiers had looked in on the floor below us, walked round in a casual way, asked a few harmless questions, and left. Probably they reported having searched the building, though they did not come up to our floor. Police or Auxiliaries would have been more thorough.

Although I have not an exact date, I am reasonably sure it was in April 1920 that we had the first serious disagreement with GHQ over a proposed action. GHQ was not in a position to supply arms to us or to any other Brigades, except in the minutest quantities. Since the previous November our attention had turned more and more towards acquiring the badly needed arms through attacks on police. Plans for attacks on barracks were still in the making, and the city Battalions worked out a proposal for a simultaneous attack on a given night on all the police patrols in the city. Police still patrolled in groups of five or six, all armed with .45 Webley revolvers. We reckoned the attack could net us fifty or sixty weapons with a fair supply of ammunition.

We asked for GHQ sanction but it was refused. P.S. O'Hegarty has written an account of what he knew of this matter, but it is not accurate.[19] After some correspondence, in which we reiterated our request for sanction, GHQ asked that some one be sent up to discuss the proposal. I do not now remember why, but I was sent. I saw the Adjutant-General, Gearóid O'Sullivan first. He was non-committal and sent me to Collins. Collins hedged, for the first and last time in my experience of him, but we had a very useful talk on Intelligence that was the basis of all our close co-operation in this work up to the Truce. On our proposal, he said that Mulcahy and Cathal Brugha would have to be convinced and that I had better see Mulcahy first.[20] Mulcahy took me to his own house for lunch (at least I presume it was his own house because he introduced me to Mrs Mulcahy), and talked to me long and earnestly about the Army getting itself into a position from which only the politicians could extricate it. The general tenor of his attitude was that he feared we in Cork wanted to go too fast, that we were naturally looking for revenge on Tomás' murderers, and that this action would involve large casualties on both sides.

I told him, as I had told the others, what was foremost in our minds was the acquisition of arms. I did not deny that there may be casualties on both sides, but I thought quite honestly they would be slight. Good timing and swift action would ensure that the police groups were overwhelmed before they could make any great show of resistance. We had ample manpower and could mobilize enough weapons for the action. He was unconvinced and said he would arrange an interview with the Minister for Defence for me next morning.

In his office at Lawlors [Hotel] I saw Cathal Brugha next morning. It was my first experience of that rock-like, imperturbable little man. When he had heard me out silently, he said 'no' very emphatically and would not discuss the matter. I must have been very insistent, because at the end of my one-sided argument he said, apparently on impulse, that he would give me a note to [Arthur] Griffith, who was acting President, and if I could convince Griffith he would sanction our proposal. I could tell Griffith that.[21]

I met Griffith for the first time that evening in the office of the paper he was then editing – *Nationality*, I think. He listened to me very patiently and asked a number of questions, mainly on the possibility of casualties. Then he got up and began to pace up and down the office silently, chewing his moustache, stopping now and then to rock himself backward and forward on his heels and toes. Pacing stolidly again, he swung suddenly towards the chair where I was sitting, his pince-nez glinting in the evening light, a grim, stocky figure. He exploded rather then said, 'No! You can't do it.' I dare say I was on the point of explosion myself, because I replied, 'We can do it; what I haven't yet heard is a convincing reason why we will not be allowed to do it.' 'Because the people would not stand for it,' he shot at me. There was no more to be said.

Thinking over my failure coming home in the train, I could not dismiss the recurring thought that my experience was a most curious way of making a GHQ decision. If Mulcahy could go home to lunch and Brugha could be in his firm's office, there seemed to be no insuperable obstacle to a Staff meeting. Collins had taken me for a meal in a city restaurant, with Geroid and Tom Cullen,[22] as he always did when I was in Dublin. None of them appeared to be in imminent danger of arrest. Had the final decision on our project been made before I went to Dublin, and was I merely the fool who was sent further? If so, why? P.S. O'Hegarty's version, which I did not hear for many years afterwards, was that on a visit to Cork he went to see Terry [MacSwiney], and that Terry had advised him to leave the city. Pressed for a reason, Terry said that this job may be coming off. P.S. went straight to Griffith and had it forbidden.[23] At the time of my interview with Griffith (and on reflection later), I was and remain convinced that he knew nothing of the project before I gave him an outline of it. It may be that P.S. was in Cork during the few days I was in Dublin, and that Terry, believing I would get sanction, had told him, incautiously, what was proposed. If that is so, anything P.S. said to Griffith related only to a matter on which he had already made his decision.

But what I thought most about was Griffith's, 'The people would not stand for it.' I asked myself if this was true, and the answer was that I did not know and that there seemed to be no way of knowing for certain, except to put the matter to the test. The people had not revolted over Bealagleanna, Fermoy, Soloheadbeg, or Knocklong. Unless GHQ had a serious intention of developing the fight, we in Cork were making fools of ourselves. I did understand that we needed over-all direction, that we needed cohesion and uniformity in the development of the struggle, and I had no predisposition to indiscipline. Nevertheless, I thought no progress would be made unless some area gave a lead in larger and sustained actions. Moreover, I had close contact with our own officers and many of the rank and file; I was sensitive to their temper and spirit; I knew they wanted to fight and I believed we had come to the point where if we did not go forward we would inevitably go back.

The upshot was that this particular project was never carried into effect, but that we went on with smaller actions, without looking for any sanction as far as I remember. Some police were shot on Lower Road in May.[24] On 1 June the barracks at Blarney was attacked and destroyed and on the 10th Carrigadrohid was attacked and left uninhabitable. I was at both of these actions. All barracks had by this time been put into a state of defence with steel shutters, sand bags, and barbed wire protection and were immune to rifle or shotgun fire. Other means of attacking them had to be improvised.

Blarney barracks was a house attached to a licensed premises. The plan was to blow a breach in the dividing wall with explosives and rush the barracks through the breach. We had a small quantity of gun cotton and our Engineer at the time, Des Dowling, assured us that it was sufficient to blow a substantial hole. It was made up in a wooden case. We took it out in one of the ten or twelve cars and vans used to take the city men to the scene. We drove up to the pub door. At the moment one of the police was outside the barbed wire and the barrack door was open. If we had left our gun cotton in the car and rushed the barracks we would have taken it without firing a shot, but we were all too much engrossed with keeping to the plan which had been so carefully worked out to grasp the unexpected opportunity.

So we took our gun cotton inside the pub and Dowling placed it midway in the dividing wall. What he or we did not know was that just at this point on the opposite side of the wall in the barracks there was a cross wall with two corner fireplaces and chimneys, and consequently a pretty solid block of masonry. The explosion practically wrecked the pub and blinded us with dust and debris, but it did not make a breach in the wall. We had shot our bolt and had to leave it at that. There could be no question here of a long fight. We were only six miles from the strong military forces at both Cork and Ballincollig. We had a couple of hundred men from the First, Second, and Sixth Battalions out on the road blocking and protecting. In fact this was the one reason for the selection of Blarney – it gave an opportunity of turning out a very large number of men on various duties. But we were not anxious that any of them should become casualties. We had left open one route over bye-roads to get our ten or twelve cars and vans back to the city, and in this Jim Grey's transport section did a very efficient job. We did not lose a man or weapon, although the whole area was swarming with military before we got back into the city. The result was not quite as bad as we feared. The barracks was so badly damaged it had to be evacuated.[25]

Carrigadrohid was a different proposition. Dan Donovan and I had a look at it following a report from the Seventh Battalion. It was attached to another house that projected further forward than the barracks, with the result that a small gable window on the top floor overlooked the barrack roof. We both agreed that this was the most accessible point to attack. Plans were made to burn out the building through a hole made in the roof underneath this window. The family in the house next door were reported to be hostile. The other gable of their house had a bedroom window overlooking the roadway.

On the night of the attack – a black dark, June night – the party which went out from the city, including Seán O'Hegarty, Joe O'Connor, Dan Donovan, the two Greys, and five or six others, waded across the Lee at a point some distance east of the village, and were led by a local guide through a small wood and over some fields to the vicinity of the barracks. The Seventh Battalion men were waiting, Dan Corkery, the Commandant in charge. As far as I remember it was Charlie Brown[26] who went with me up the ladder to the gable window on the roadside to persuade the occupants to leave their beds quietly, come down the ladder, and leave us in possession of their house. This was managed without alarming the barrack, although we were working in the dark and did not allow the three occupants of the house to put on any lights. They were abusive but kept reasonably quiet after we had assured them that the minimum damage would be done to their premises, that we would not hurry them unduly, and that they could take with them any valuables they wished.

The last to go down was the youngest – a girl in her early twenties I thought, though seen only dimly. I was then in the same. At the top of the ladder she turned to me and said, 'Keep away from that window,' pointing to the one through which we proposed to make the attack. When Seán and Dan Corkery came up I told them what she had said, and it was decided to barricade the window and make the attack instead through the roof of the back bedroom, which was level with the barrack roof. That we did, and hours later, before leaving we took down the mattresses and other things we had piled against the gable window to find them riddled with bullet holes. I do not know how it was possible for the police to fire at this window, but evidently they had seen its potential danger and were able to cover it in some way. That girl probably saved some lives that night.

In this case the cause of our failure to compel the police to surrender was that the supply of paraffin became exhausted before the building was completely uninhabitable – although it was evacuated the next day. We lost whatever arms we would have got if the police surrendered, because in the position of Carrigadrohid in relation to strong British posts, we could, with the road blocking protection which had been done, have continued the fight until daylight. I had attended a Seventh Battalion Council meeting the previous night to check their plans, and I remembered afterwards with remorse that I had too easily accepted an assurance that two barrels of paraffin were at a shop near at hand and that they would be brought to the scene. It turned out that there was in fact less than one barrel. We learned the hard way.

Many years afterwards I was told of an incident that happened on the night of the attack. Four or five shotgun men had been put in position behind a low wall covering the front of the barracks with instructions to fire an occasional shot at the loop holes in the steel shutters after the roof attack commenced. This fire could be effective only to the extent it drew the police to answer it and so distract some of them from concentrating on the roof. Our men would also cover the police if they emerged through the front door of the building.

One of the shotgun men was Denis O'Mahony of Macroom, a keen sportsman and angler, and later a fellow rate collector and companion of mine on a few Kerry and Galway fishing holidays. He was at the end of the line. At the other end a shotgun man, from the moment the attack opened, kept blazing away at the barracks as fast as he could load and fire. This waste of good ammunition was too much for Denny's sporting instincts. He crawled down to the over-enthusiastic shotgun man and found he did not know him. 'Where are you from?' he asked. 'Bawnmore,' the lad replied. 'Any cock up there?' was the next question. 'A few, sometimes.' 'Well for the Lord's sake, save a few cartridges for them.'

I fear that I have been prolix in my review of events up to this point, but from now on this must be a merely personal narrative. It is neither necessary, nor would it be possible within the limits which I must set for myself, to give any adequate account of the activities of even one Brigade. You will understand that my own experiences can represent no more than a tiny fraction of the general effort of the next two years.

These years were lived under such continuous strain and so heavily overloaded with work, that it is not surprising to find memory able to recall only the events that then made the deepest and most searing impressions. Most of the minor day-to-day problems are completely lost. I intend to use the slight contemporary records that exist for the purpose of checking dates only, and to rely on what memory retains of personal experiences.

The most important feature of the next phase is my meeting with your mother and its results. As far as I know there are now few extant records of our Intelligence work, and unless the GHQ Intelligence files that Collins kept are still in existence, or unless anything is subsequently disclosed from British sources, the story must of necessity depend on what she and I can remember and recall. We will try to set it down not fully, because so much is irretrievably lost, but honestly, without exaggeration, evasion, or distortion.

## NOTES AND REFERENCES

1   Peter Hart writes that the killing of Constable Murtagh was the work of 'the wild men of the IRB' and not authorized by Tomás MacCurtain (See Hart, *The IRA and Its Enemies*, p. 79). I disagree. There is some evidence to support Hart's conclusion, including the fact that when MacCurtain phoned the Cork Infirmary to check on Murtagh's condition, he offered his condolences. O'Donoghue's papers include a letter from Volunteer Cornelius Kelleher who heard second-hand that MacCurtain said he would make the killers 'pay the piper' for 'shooting police on their own'. (The note is found in Ms. 31,430, NLI.) However, as O'Donoghue states above, the Brigade had already targeted Constable Murtagh (and Sgt Ferris) weeks earlier, for being 'particularly aggressive and obnoxious towards us'. That would indicate that MacCurtain previously approved the shooting of Constable Murtagh. In his BMH statement, Pa Murray supported O'Donoghue's view, testifying that Murtagh's two killers, Christy MacSweeney and J.J. O'Connell (who were both serving under Murray), acted 'on instructions from the brigade'. Murray stated that 'Detective' Murtagh had used 'extreme methods' on a captured Volunteer named Martin Condon, while being held in Victoria Barracks, which explains the decision. Hart believes Murtagh was killed because 'he was a policeman and an easy target' (ibid.). In *Police Casualties in Ireland, 1919–1922* (Cork: Mercier Press, 2000), Richard Abbott states that Murtagh was 'by all accounts... an inoffensive officer' (p. 64). O'Donoghue's and Pa Murray's versions question those assertions.

2   Sixty years later, O'Donoghue recounted this kindness while speaking at the dedication of a memorial to Dr Murphy. See O'Donoghue's material related to the Tadg Murphy Memorial, Ms. 31,444, NLI.

3   For the Mulcahy quote, see P7b/188, UCD. While writing about MacCurtain's death (*Tomás MacCurtain*, p. 170; and 'Tomás MacCurtain, First Lord Mayor of Cork' in *Rebel Cork's Fighting Story*, pp. 55–68), O'Donoghue argues that MacCurtain's death was not a direct reprisal for the shooting of Constable Murtagh, but rather an RIC assassination that happened to occur on the same

evening as Murtagh's killing. He cites the large number of police that had to be organized, disguised, and posted at various positions to seal off MacCurtain's home from the neighbourhood. This complex deployment would have been almost impossible to co-ordinate in the ninety minutes between the killing of Murtagh and the start of the operation to shoot MacCurtain. Disguised police had also fired shots at Sinn Féin Alderman Stockley earlier in the week (*Cork Examiner* 19 March 1920), and seem to have tried to kill Sinn Féin Alderman Seán O'Sullivan following the shooting of District Inspector MacDonagh the previous week. (See the testimony of Constable MacCarthy in the Report of the Tomás MacCurtain Inquest, Public Records Office, CO 904/47, repeated in the *Cork Weekly News* 10 April 1920.) That would indicate a police counter-assassination policy already in place. While O'Donoghue raises good points, it seems too much of a coincidence that MacCurtain's killing occurred only two hours after the shooting of a Cork policeman. The most likely explanation is that the local RIC had earlier plotted to assassinate MacCurtain if another policeman was shot in the city (probably in response to the shooting of District Inspector MacDonagh by O'Donoghue and Tom Crofts). The police then put their plan into action upon hearing of Constable Murtagh's killing.

4   For local reaction to the MacCurtain killing, see the *Cork Examiner, Cork Constitution, Cork Weekly News,* and the *Dublin Times* for the week of 20 to 27 March 1920.

5   Quoted from Mitchell and Ó Snodaigh's *Irish Political Documents, 1916–1949* (Dublin: Irish Academic Press, 1989), p. 71.

6   I would argue that the Cork No. 1 Brigade boasted the finest leadership cadre found in any individual IRA unit outside of Dublin. The Brigade enjoyed charismatic commanders in Tomás MacCurtain, Terry MacSwiney, and Seán O'Hegarty. The Brigade staff included O'Donoghue and the capable Joe O'Connor (who rose to become the Anti-Treaty IRA's Quartermaster-General). At the Battalion commander level in the city there were four outstanding characters, Dan Donovan (who became Brigade OC in 1922), Tom Crofts (OC First Southern Division, 1922–23), Mick Murphy, and Connie Neenan. Pa Murray, OC of the city's Active Service Unit, had one of the IRA's best fighting records, and in 1922 took over as OC Britain for the Anti-Treaty forces. O'Donoghue's deputy, Seán Culhane, proved a brave and effective intelligence officer at the brigade and division level. Cobh's Michael Leahy led the vital Genoa Arms Purchase, succeeded O'Hegarty as OC Cork No. 1 Brigade, and later acted as OC of the Anti-Treaty's Overseas Purchases. His Fourth Battalion colleague Seán Hyde served on the IRA Executive in 1923. Also deserving mention are four leaders in the Brigade's battalions, Leo Murphy, Patrick O'Sullivan, Charlie Brown, and Dan Corkery.

7   Few other areas of the country received such a stipend, which caused some accusations from other units that Michael Collins favoured the Cork Brigades. Considering the miniscule amount of money distributed to the country units and the failure of GHQ to import significant amounts of weapons, the question remains as to what happened to the millions raised in Ireland and overseas by the Republican movement. Though Collins' biographers depict him as a financial wizard, it seems remarkable that so little of the Minister of Finance's funds made their way into the hands of the IRA. Members of the IRA's country units frequently described their poverty and dependence on the charity of their local supporters, many of whom were themselves impoverished. Republican finances during the War of Independence remain a relatively unexplored, yet

important research area for scholars of the period.

8    On 19 March 1921, the Cork No. 3 Brigade OC Charlie Hurley died in a shootout with British troops who raided the West Cork farmhouse where he was hiding.

9    For details, see the MacCurtain Inquest, CO 904/47, PRO.

10   For the Garvey and Harrington killings, see Dan Healy's BMH statement; Roibeárd Langford's Pension Statement, CAI; Anne MacSwiney to O'Donoghue, Ms. 31,282 (2); and Pa Murray's BMH statement, which explains his role as leader of the assassination squad that killed the two policemen. The RIC reported that both officers received threatening letters the week before their assassination. See the County Inspector Report for May (Cork City and East Riding), CO/904/112, PRO.

11   The *Cork Constitution* said of the barracks attack, 'For cool daring and brazen audacity, nothing could exceed the outrage perpetrated.' See the *Cork Constitution* 1, 10, 11, and 12 July 1920; Mick Murphy's BMH Statement; and 'Activities – Cork City', list compiled by Florence O'Donoghue, Ms. 31,301, NLI.

12   In April 1920, Terence MacSwiney wrote a letter that accused Swanzy of direct responsibility. See Terence MacSwiney to Lady Arnot, 24/4/20, Ms. 31,163. Though O'Donoghue later stated that he was unsure of the exact identities of the RIC triggermen in the MacCurtain assassination (see him in the O'Malley Notebooks, UCD), he never expressed a doubt that Swanzy played a key role organizing the killing. For more details, see Ms. 31,313, NLI.

13   RIC Inspector-General's Monthly Confidential Report for August 1920, CO/904/112, PRO.

14   See Ms. 31,313 NLI for O'Donoghue's research into the Swanzy assassination compiled for an unfinished article. It includes correspondence from some of the participants, as well as his own recollections. See also Seán Culhane in the O'Malley Notebooks, UCD; and Culhane's BMH statement. Newspaper accounts in the *Irish Times*, *Cork Examiner*, and *Cork Constitution* for the week following 22 August describe the Loyalist mob violence in detail. The RIC County Inspector Report for August (Down) CO/904/112, PRO, supports newspaper accounts that the Lisburn RIC basically stayed off the streets during the unrest, and even released detained Loyalist rioters after a mob threatened to storm the Lisburn barracks. The Lisburn RIC's failure to arrest or inflict casualties on the rioters indicates that it acquiesced in the anti-Catholic violence.

15   For details of the Cork city riot, see the *Irish Times*, 19 and 20 July 1920. British soldiers killed a local ex-serviceman, sparking the unrest. Days later 5,000 members of the Cork Branch of the Irish Federation of Demobilized Sailors and Soldiers marched at his funeral as a protest (*Cork Weekly News*, 24 July 1920). The British Army reported that as a result of the riot, 'very bitter feelings existed between the Crown Forces and the civil population in Cork for sometime afterwards' (*History of the 6th Division in Ireland*, p. 45, Strickland Papers, IWM).

16   Smyth was a much-decorated Lt Colonel who lost his arm in the First World War. He had gained prominence by encouraging RIC constables to use counter-terrorism against the Republicans, sparking the 'Listowel Mutiny'. The Listowel incident was not a true mutiny, but rather a tense stand-off between Smyth and Irish constables already aroused by police union complaints about pay and poor working conditions. Constable Jeremiah Mee (the police union ringleader) and four colleagues resigned from the force in protest. Mee later toured the United States on behalf of Sinn Féin. Anthony Gaughan's *The Memoirs of Constable Jeremiah Mee* (Dublin: Anvil Books, 1975) provides the full background of this

episode. Cork newspaper coverage of Smyth's inflammatory remarks prompted the Brigade's response. Seán Culhane organized the assassination, using a waiter informant who notified him of Smyth's presence in the club. The IRA party included Seán Culhane, Dan Donovan, and Pa Murray. County Inspector Craig was wounded, though Culhane later said that no one but he shot at the unrecognized officer. In a precursor to the Swanzy assassination, Protestant Loyalists attacked Catholics in Smyth's native Banbridge, after they heard of the killing. Some anti-Catholic disturbances also broke out in Lisburn. (For details see the *Irish Times*, 24 and 26 July 1920.) There is a popular story that one of Smyth's assassins shouted as he fired, 'Your orders were to shoot on sight. You are in sight right now.' However, I have not come across any witness who actually heard such an utterance. Culhane seemed to contradict the story by stating in his BMH statement, 'We opened fire simultaneously, without any preliminaries.' For details, see Seán Culhane's, Daniel Healy's, and Pa Murray's BMH statements; Seán Culhane in the O'Malley Notebooks, UCD; the *Cork Examiner*, 20 and 21 July 1920; and the *Irish Times*, 17, 19, 20, and 21 July 1920. Some of Smyth's controversial police memoranda can be found in Abbott, *Police Casualties in Ireland*, pp. 99–103.

17    RIC County Inspector Report for July (Cork City and East Riding), CO 904/112, PRO.

18    Some sources claim the Brigade intended to kidnap Strickland and hold him hostage in exchange for the release of hunger-striker Terence MacSwiney, but the intention is not clear. O'Donoghue was present at the attack, but probably didn't fire at the general. Armed Volunteers had been posted in ambush positions for a number of days, which was a hardship due to their work obligations. While O'Donoghue and Seán O'Hegarty stood on a street corner debating whether to continue the deployment, Strickland's car sped past the inattentive Volunteers. The ambush party managed to open fire on the car, but the speeding vehicle proved a difficult target. They succeeded in wounding the car driver, but had to endure return pistol fire from the car's occupants, including Strickland and Captain Kelly. The episode prompted O'Donoghue to write to GHQ for funds to establish a full-time Active Service Unit and Intelligence Staff in the city. Richard Mulcahy and Cathal Brugha rejected the scheme, though the following March O'Donoghue was finally awarded £20 for the weekly upkeep of a six-man intelligence team. He and a few of the Brigade officers also received a £4 weekly stipend. These details come from captured correspondence between the Brigade and IRA GHQ, published in the British Army pamphlet 'The Irish Republican Army', p. 363, Strickland Papers, IWM. See also the *Cork Examiner*, 25 September 1920; *History of the 6ʰ Division in Ireland*, Appendix III, and General Strickland's diary entry for 24 September 1920, Strickland Papers, IWM.

19    O'Hegarty wrote of the plan, 'The proposal seemed to me to be fiendish and indefensible and inadvisable from any point of view, and it still seems so to me.' See O'Hegarty, *The Victory of Sinn Féin* (Dublin: Talbot, 1924), p. 46.

20    Richard Mulcahy was the IRA Chief of Staff, serving under Dáil Defence Minister, Cathal Brugha.

21    The founder of Sinn Féin, Arthur Griffith acted as Dáil President during the absence of Eamon de Valera, who was raising funds in America.

22    Tom Cullen was one of Michael Collins' top intelligence officers.

23    In *The Irish Revolution and its Aftermath* (Dublin: Irish Academic Press, 2003), p. 76, Francis Costello identifies the P.S. O'Hegarty passage as a proposal to

assassinate Cork Bishop Cohalan. He is incorrect. Moirín Chavasse wrote in her book *Terence MacSwiney* (Dublin: Clonmore and Reynolds, 1961), p. 213, that during an interview with P.S. O'Hegarty about the episode, he told her he believed the Brigade intended to shoot all the Cork policemen, rather than simply disarm them. That clarifies and explains his objections. Chavasse's description of the plan jibes with O'Donoghue's version (that the Brigade intended to disarm the police), which isn't surprising since he and Seán O'Hegarty provided her with that information. With regard to Francis Costello's claim, while there was considerable Republican outrage at Bishop Cohalan after he excommunicated the local Volunteers in December 1920, to my knowledge the Cork No. 1 Brigade did not consider assassinating the bishop. O'Donoghue dates the proposed curfew patrol ambush operation as April 1920, which was eight months before the Bishop's Excommunication order. In addition, during this period Cohalan earned some Republican kudos for his strong denouncement of the slaying of Tomás MacCurtain and his naming of District Inspector Swanzy as MacCurtain's killer (see Cohalon's letter to the *Times*, 20 August 1920).

24 As previously noted, these two policemen were Garvey and Harrington, killed for their role in the MacCurtain killing.

25 Years later, Cork veterans spoke of the Blarney attack with the fondness of a youthful prank, laughing at their ineptitude. Writing to O'Donoghue in 1961, Pa Murray recalled the moments after the explosion, as he watched a stunned Dan Donovan trying to fix his hat, which had been ripped to shreds by the blast. 'I also remember Connie [Neenan] standing in the room, dejected and sullen. "We must do something", was his cry, "we cannot go away in this way." I remember holding a bomb (German) which was believed to be a gas bomb, and wondering whether I should let it go or not. Someone sensibly said, "Do it if you want to gas us all." I remember yourself and I could almost read your thoughts – You were a sad man and you were so busy with your thoughts that you could hardly say a word or make a decision.' Murray to O'Donoghue, 6 July 1961, Ms. 31,301, NLI.

26 Charlie Brown, Adjutant of the Seventh Battalion, Cork No. 1 Brigade.

# 6

## 'MOTHER'S STORY'

### Josephine O'Donoghue

My parents were Henry James and Bridget McCoy. They were married in Kenmare on 9 January 1876. I was the youngest of a family of ten, four of whom died in infancy. The survivors were Alice (Nancy), Margaret, Kathleen, Cecily, James and myself Mary Josephine. I was born at Adare, Co. Limerick on 10 September 1891.

My mother was an only child, an O'Sullivan, born at Bonane, Kenmare, Co. Kerry. Both her parents having died young, she was reared by her aunt Mrs Bridget Hennessey. The Hennessey's had a wine and spirit and a bakery business in Kenmare and on completion of her education my mother assisted in the business until her marriage. My father, born at Pallaskenry, Co. Limerick, was a member of the Royal Irish Constabulary, stationed at Rosscarbery at the time of his marriage. He served at Drinagh and Millstreet Co. Cork, and later at Arklow, Co. Wicklow, Kildare, Waterford, and Adare. His promotion to Head Constable became effective on 1 January 1891 when at Adare, and in that year he was transferred to Limerick, the last station in which he served.

It was a hard life for my mother with a large young family and frequent removals from one station to another. I do not think my father was ever quite happy in the force. My mother told me of an occasion when he was one of a party of police at an eviction during the Land War when an order was given for fire to be opened on the crowd which had gathered. He refused to obey the order, saying that he was the son of a farmer himself and would not fire on his own people. He was probably a Sergeant at the time because the disciplinary action taken against him was that he was reduced in rank and transferred from the station in which he was then serving.

He must have been a competent and capable man of more than average ability to have overcome the set-back of a reduction in rank and reached the status of first class Head Constable in less then twenty years' service. He was then in line for promotion to District or County Inspector. Very few Catholics at that time ever reached these ranks. After some years in Limerick he found that the prospects of further promotion were very remote and he decided to retire from the force on pension. That would be about 1902 or 1903. After his retirement General Doran, then commanding the British military forces in Cork, offered him some kind of confidential intelligence post that he did not accept.

We came to Cork, first to Copley Place, where we had as neighbours Mrs O'Hegarty and her two sons Patrick and Seán [Sinn Féin leader P.S. and Cork No. 1 Brigade OC Seán]. Some few years later we moved to 2 Rockboro Terrace, Old Blackrock Road and for a time we had as neighbours there Terence MacSwiney and his sisters when they lived in Arundel Terrace. After coming to Cork I attended SS Peter's and Paul's National School, and later was a pupil at St Aloysius Pension School, St Marie's of the Isle. After leaving St Aloysius I took a commercial course in Shorthand and Typing, passing all the examinations in due course, and at the same time studied music under a German teacher, Mr Birrell. I passed with honours in four pianoforte examinations. I was the leader in singing at school and on one occasion I sang for the Bishop of Cork at a school concert. The song was 'Green Isle of Erin'. The nuns wished me to have voice training and suggested going to the School of Music for a test. There I sang 'When all was Young' and was awarded a scholarship. I never took it up – my father decided against the idea – but later I sang at concerts in the Catholic Young Men's Society Hall in Castle Street and at the City Hall.

My Sister Cecily had married an Englishman, Alfred Hore, an engineer, who was then Manager of the Electric Tramway Company at Llanelli, South Wales, where they lived. As Cecily was expecting her second child and needed help, I decided to go to her. My mother, who was then in poor health, did not like the decision, but realizing that I was not happy at home agreed to my going.

Alfred Hore was a convert and a very good friend to me, one for whom I had the greatest admiration and the highest regard. He was like a father to me. After I had been with them for some time in 1911 he decided to resign his post in Llanelli and go into the timber business in Manaos, Brazil. Cecily and the two children, Fred and Clara, returned to the old home at Rockboro Terrace in Cork.

Coleridge Marchment was an occasional visitor to my sister's home at Llanelli and there I made his acquaintance. He was born at Salisbury and was then a travelling salesman. His correct name was Coleridge Brown, but he had changed his surname to Marchment after his business had gone bankrupt. After my sister returned to Ireland I took up a position as a governess to an only child at Newport Mon., where I was very happy except for the loneliness for home which was distressing. How I'd long to hear Shandon Bells, hear the merriment of the ladies of the Coal Quay, take a walk to Blackrock, or hear the chime of the City Hall clock. Yet I did not wish to return home.

At Newport, Coleridge visited me occasionally and informed me that he was taking instruction and intended to become a Catholic. He said he found great consolation in the Faith. Some time after he was received into the Catholic Church I accepted his proposal of marriage and we were married in the Parish Church, Llanelli. He did not tell his parents of the marriage at the time, and I did not tell mine. We lived in Llanelli with an elderly couple whose only daughter was an epileptic.

Very soon I found that my allowance for housekeeping was inadequate and so found employment as a shorthand typist with a solicitor, Mr Spicknell, in the town. Expecting my first child I held on to my post as long as possible. As the event approached, it became a source of great worry and anxiety to me that neither my husband's people nor my own knew of the position or of the plight I was in. My health suffered and I had to resign my post with Mr Spicknell. Eventually a doctor was called and my baby was born before its due time, on 23 November 1913. He was baptized Coleridge Marchment after his father.

Leaving me and the baby in the care of an elderly lady and the district nurse, my husband decided to go to Cadoxton[1] and tell his people that he had become a Catholic, had married, and was the father of a son. Anxiously I waited his return, only to be disappointed to find that he had found it too difficult to tell them. Later, constant reminders to my husband that I wished to meet his people seemed to have no effect whatever.

When Reggie was a few months old a letter came from home to say that my mother was dying. I decided to go and see her. The ordeal of leaving so young a child in the care of an elderly lady was a frightening thought on my mind all the time. Nervous and upset as I was, I feared to tell my mother that I was married. She died on 27 March 1914 without knowing. After the funeral I returned to Wales.

Some time after the outbreak of the war in August 1914, my husband was called up for army service and he then decided to acquaint his parents of our marriage. We were then invited to come and live with them for the duration of the war, an invitation I had to accept but which I felt was not a good arrangement. I had to resign my post at Llanelli, which I had resumed, and break up my home. In reply to a letter which I wrote to my father and Cecily telling them of my marriage and that I had a young son, my father replied inviting us to

come and visit him and saying that he was in poor health. On arrival
in Cork we found that he was in hospital and was disappointed that we
had not brought the baby with us.

Living with the Brown family at Cadoxton was an unhappy
experience in which I had many difficulties and hardships. My husband's eldest sister Maud was a teacher, a very dominating character
who took control of the whole household. Mrs Perry, a younger sister
who had no children, lived in the house, and gradually I felt that my
little son was being taken over entirely by her.

I decided to find another post and I engaged a girl to look after
Reggie in the daytime during my absence. I got employment with a
firm of solicitors, Morgan, Bruce, and Nicholls, in Pontypridd. It
meant leaving Cadoxton early every morning, taking a train to Cardiff
and then to Pontypridd. I held this post until shortly after the birth of
my second child.

Alfred Hore was home from Brazil on a holiday in the summer of
1916 and came to visit me. Seeing how unhappy I was and the state of
my health, he insisted that I should return to Ireland with him. He had
taken a house at Island View, Knockaverry, Youghal, [County Cork]
where Cecily and their two children were then living. There I had
every care and attention, and there Gerald was born on 2 August 1916.
My husband, then in army training at Catterick Camp, got compassion
leave and came to Youghal bringing Reggie with him. Although I was
far from well, we returned to Cadoxton with the two children.

At Cadoxton I was informed that my husband had written two
letters, one to me and one to his parents, which were being held by
their solicitor and were to be opened in the event of his death in the
war. It was hoped that he would come back himself and destroy both
letters. During my absence in Ireland my sister-in-law had gone to visit
him at Catterick Camp, but I was never told what transpired at this
visit.

Living with my husband's parents and their two daughters was a
constant strain. They were hostile to Catholics and did not wish a
Catholic in the house, neither did they want the children to be
brought up in the faith. More and more Mrs Perry was exerting her
influence on Reggie, gradually the atmosphere became impossible,
and domestic relations were often strained. My health suffered and I
wrote to Alfred for advice. Before he returned to Manaos, he came to
see me and suggested that I should return to Cork with the two
children and take over the old home at Rockboro Terrace of which
Cecily still retained the tenancy.

When I told my people-in-law that I was going back to Cork the
grandparents were very upset and begged me to leave Reggie with

them for a while. After a lot of persuasion, and most unwillingly, I unfortunately agreed to this. When I arrived in Cork with Gerald my father, with more foresight than I had, warned me that I would have difficulty getting Reggie back. He did not live to see the difficulty I did have. He died on 5 October 1916.

When I took over the tenancy of No. 2 Rockboro Terrace, Cecily went to live in her house at Island View, Youghal. Alfred was then in Manaos. Kathleen was with me except for periods when she was away nursing. I took in two boarders and took on a few pupils for piano lessons. On medical advice I had to give up these sources of income after a while, as I was not in a fit state of health to continue. Cecily agreed to take care of Gerald and I decided to look for employment in Cork.

I got an appointment as secretary to Dr A.W. Winder, Ll. D, then in charge of the British Red Cross Society's office at South Mall. I was happy in this post but after a short time Dr Winder resigned. Before doing so he recommended me to Major Cooper, who was then in charge of the Ministry of Pensions office in Cork with an office in the City Hall. I worked with Major Cooper until he resigned following the death of his son in action in France. He had urged me to apply for what would be a better position with the military at Cork Barracks. He thought that with my experience and references I would have no difficulty in getting placed.

At this time I was constantly worried by requests from the Browns for more money for Reggie's upkeep, and even more concerned with the fear that he was not getting any Catholic teachings and was in an atmosphere hostile to it. I was anxious to get him back and have the two children together. I wrote several times offering to go over and bring him back. My husband had clearly and definitely expressed in his writing that he wished the children should be brought up as Catholics and, from my experience of the Browns when living with them, I feared that his wishes would not be carried out if Reggie remained under their control and influence. I thought too that the best place for the child was with his mother.

While evading a positive refusal of my request the Browns did everything they could to persuade me to leave Reggie with them; in fact they wanted me to bring Gerald over also. I began to realize that they had no intention of parting with Reggie.

In August 1917, rumours began to circulate in Great Britain and Ireland of a terrible British military offensive underway in the Ypres Salient in Flanders. 'A benchmark of unsurpassed horror', this Third Battle of Ypres (also known as Passchendaele) proved to be the British Army's lowest point in a war of low points. Poor leadership and obsolete tactics sent wave after wave of British divisions into an atrocious killing ground. Heavy artillery shelling, incessant rain, and a high water table turned the battlefield into a morass. Thousands of soldiers literally drowned in the mud.

During the three-month offensive, the British suffered 70,000 dead and 200,000 wounded, and won only a few miles of territory. The British Army had been used up with virtually nothing to show for its sacrifice. 110,000 of the British casualties occurred in October, after most strategists considered the campaign a failure.

British Field Marshal Sir Douglas Haig ignored the urgings of his subordinates to stop the offensive, and continued to throw fresh troops into new attacks. On 30 October 1917, he ordered units of the Fifth Army over the top. Mud and German fire stopped them in their tracks. The assault yielded 2,000 casualties and gained no ground, inducing in one historian, 'a sense of inexpressible melancholy'. Among the dead lay Private Coleridge Marchment, 4th Battalion, Yorkshire Regiment (Princess of Wales' Own).[2]

On 30 October 1917, I received official notification from the War Office that my husband had been killed in action in France. When I recovered from the shock I became seriously alarmed about Reggie and realized that I was going to have great difficulty in getting him back. After consulting a few friends I was advised to see the Bishop of Cork, Dr Cohalan, and put the matter to him. He lived then at South Terrace [Cork city]. His view was that the only remedy open to me was a legal one and that an action in the Courts was the only way in which I could pursue it. He sent me to his own solicitor, William Murphy, South Mall. Mr Murphy got the case taken up by a firm of solicitors in London, Smith, Randell, Dodds & Brockett, of 9 John Street, Bedford Row, WC 1.[3] In this way I was drawn into taking my case to the English Law Courts, but the hearing did not take place until 26 July 1918.

Meanwhile, in December 1917 I had taken Major Cooper's advice and applied for a post as a clerk in the Registry office of the 6th Division. Hours of duty were longer than they are nowadays, 9.00 a.m. to 6.00 p.m. Was it not for the generous one and a half hours allowed for lunch, I could not have managed the double journey home and back each day on foot – which was the only way in which I could get to the barracks then. The 9.00 a.m. start in the winter was hard enough.

During the 1919–1921 period there were roughly 40,000 British soldiers in Ireland.[4] Initially these troops were organized into three divisions, the 5th Division (Northern Ireland and the Midlands), the 6th Division

(Munster), and the Dublin Military District (a division-strength formation).[5]

The 6th Division was the largest division in Ireland, composed of 15,000 troops and twenty of the fifty-one British Army battalions stationed in the country. Headquartered in Victoria Barracks in Cork city and commanded by General E.P. Strickland, the 6th Division eventually controlled all British Army units in counties Clare, Cork, Kerry, Limerick, Tipperary and Waterford. [Later Kilkenny and Wexford were added to the area.] Unit deployments, operation orders, and military intelligence all emanated from the Division Headquarters.

Victoria Barracks (now Michael Collins Barracks) sits atop bluffs overlooking the city centre. During Jo's time the headquarters buildings would have contained hundreds of civilian employees and military staff. The headquarters and city was guarded by a garrison of 2,000 men from the 2nd (Battalion) Ox & Bucks Regiment and the 2nd (Battalion) Hampshire Regiment.[6]

Very soon I was transferred to the typists pool and worked there in a very pleasant atmosphere. After a few months I was promoted to the position of forewoman over a staff of twenty-five female clerks and typists. I was then the youngest war widow on the staff. This position, which I held until I resigned in 1921, gave me in addition to control of the female staff, a post in the Division Sergeant Major's office and the duty of acting as relief for him in his absence. It gave me also control of material from the typing pool and its distributions to the offices of the members of the Divisional Staff. In this way I had access to all the offices including that of the Divisional Commander, Major General E.P. Strickland. All Army Council instructions, Divisional and other orders, as well as routine correspondence passed through my hands. All the female staff were obliged to join the Women's Army Auxiliary Corps, and we wore uniform up to the end of 1919 when the Corps was disbanded.

The correspondence from my people-in-law in Wales continually called for more money for Reggie's upkeep, although I had at their request transferred to them the Ministry of Pensions allowance for him.[7] I was trying to save something from my earnings to meet the costs of the law case, and eventually I had to supplement these savings by borrowing £30.0.0. from the Munster and Leinster Bank. It took me a long time to repay the loan.

The London solicitors asked for testimonials from persons of standing who knew me. Several friends in Cork were most helpful in this matter, especially Mr Gamble, NT [national teacher], Sundays Well. I got testimonials from clergy, doctors, JPs, teachers, nurses, and the police. I was given compassion leave from the barracks to go to London for the hearing of the case. Cecily came with me and we stayed with some Irish friends who were most kind to us. They got two reporters from Catholic papers to attend the court and report the case. I'll never forget the sea crossing; we had a narrow escape from being sunk by a German submarine.[8] In London the Zeppelin [air] raids were still taking place and on one occasion we had to take shelter in the Underground during a raid.[9]

The case came for a hearing before Judge McCardie in London on 26 July 1918. He gave a decision against me. It was a prejudiced decision. McCardie was possibly even then not normal mentally; a short time afterwards he committed suicide.

> The custody case seemed to have hinged on the letter Coleridge Marchment Brown left with his solicitor during his last home leave. In it, he asked that the children be raised in the Protestant faith under the guidance of his family. According to her above statement, Jo was not aware of the contents of this letter until after Coleridge's death. The climax of the hearing occurred when Judge McCardie ordered four-and-a-half-year-old Reggie Brown to take the stand. The judge asked the boy whether he wished to remain with the Marchment family or go with his mother. Reggie said he would prefer to stay with the Marchments (specifically his aunt, Mrs Perry), which apparently was good enough for Judge McCardie.
>
> As Jo enjoyed suitable employment and could provide Reggie with a stable home environment in Cork, it seems likely that anti-Catholic sentiments played a crucial role in Judge McCardie's decision.

The case was then taken up by Rev. George B. Hudson of the Birmingham Diocesan Rescue Society, Coleshill, Birmingham, for an opinion as to the advisability of an appeal. In the following November Father Hudson wrote to me enclosing a copy of the opinion. His legal advisers saw no hope in an appeal, but recommended that I should make good and constant my right to visit the child. In any case I did not have the money to go with an appeal. Every legal avenue appeared to be closed.

> In later years, Jo told her daughters that during this period she became deeply depressed over the loss of Reggie. She recalled one occasion when she walked along the banks of the River Lee in Cork city and considered throwing herself into the river.

The position remained so until the summer of 1919 when I was in

Youghal on holidays. No one living in Cork at that time could fail to be aware to some extent of the struggle that was developing between the British authorities and the Irish people, then led by Sinn Féin and the Irish Volunteers. Apart from what I read and saw in the streets, one aspect of it came under my notice every day in my work at the barracks. Prisoners were brought in, correspondence was concerned largely with Volunteer activities, and the Intelligence staff of the Division under Captain Kelly were very busy.[10]

My sympathies were then with the Volunteers and I felt that I could and should help them. How best to do that, how best to make a reliable contact with them was the problem. A false step could be disastrous for me. I did not know anybody connected with the movement in Cork well enough to feel safe in making an approach on so delicate a matter. It was while I was in Youghal that summer that the problem was partly and not too satisfactorily solved. Someone put me in touch with Michael Walsh who was afterwards Town Clerk of Youghal, and who we believed had some connection with the movement.[11] I spoke to him and offered my services. They were availed of by him only to a limited extent, some contacts with prisoners and some messages not of great importance. After my return from holidays I felt that I was losing even this unsatisfactory contact. And then something happened which I can regard only as Providential.

I had been receiving many abusive letters from the Browns with constant demands for money for the child's clothes, for dental treatment, for one thing or another, even for an article he broke or damaged in the house, even though they had got his Ministry of Pensions allowance. One day a letter came that upset me very much. After coming home from work I took Gerald in the go-car and went into town to the Holy Trinity Church. I went to Our Lady's Altar and begged her to help me. An old Capuchin brother tending the altar saw me in tears. He came over and asked me if I was in trouble; I said I was. He suggested that I should come round to the Friary and he would get one of the priests who would console me.

I did not then know the name of the priest who came to me in the little bare room in the Friary. Afterwards I found that he was Father Dominic, and he was, though I did not know it, Chaplain to the Cork No. 1 Brigade of the IRA and later Chaplain to Lord Mayor MacCurtain and MacSwiney. How else than Providential can one regard the fact that it was he who was on duty that evening, and that a disquieting letter should have driven me into Holy Trinity at the moment when that understanding lay brother was attending the altar? I poured out my troubles to Father Dominic. He was most sympathetic and helpful, and at the end of our conversation said with reassuring confidence, 'I will get your child back for you.' On my request to be put in touch with the IRA, he asked me to give him something by which I could identify whoever would call on me. I took a slip of paper and wrote on it the capital letter 'G' and gave it back to him. It was Gerald's initial and I hoped through it to get my two boys together again.

Father Dominic must have acted promptly because one evening a few days later a young man, who did not give me his name but said he had come from the IRA, called to see me. He had with him the slip of paper I had given to Father Dominic. I told him of my contacts with Michael Walsh, of my position at the military barracks, and of my willingness to help in the national struggle in any way I could. I think it was some time later, when we had each gained the confidence of the other, that he told me he was Florence O'Donoghue, then Adjutant and Intelligence Officer of Cork No. 1 Brigade IRA. It was a little later too that I mentioned the problem of Reggie and asked if the IRA could help me to get him back. I said, however, that I would not expect them to do anything until I proved that I could be of some assistance to them.

We discovered later that this was not the first time we had met. I had on one occasion gone to purchase something for my father at the shop in Castle Street where he worked, but that first brief contact, though remembered, meant little to either of us. The first evening at Rockboro Terrace we made the arrangements under which I worked as Intelligence agent for the Cork No. 1 Brigade from then until the Truce of July 1921.

I realized that the task then given me by the Brigade, in contrast to my contact with Michael Walsh, was a much more difficult and dangerous one, and that the information I could supply would be of considerable value to them. It was impressed on me that I was in an exceptionally favourable position to acquire and transmit the kind of information most badly needed, and that as the British 6th Division covered Munster and a few other counties this information would be valuable not alone to Cork No. 1 but to other Brigades and to the GHQ of the IRA.[12] Two essential elements in the arrangement were continuity and precautions against being caught. I should take the most extreme care in all my intelligence activities to ensure that I did not come under the slightest suspicion from the British authorities. Only in this way would it be possible to maintain an extended service. The risks that I would have to take, and the dangers from possible pitfalls and traps in so unusual a situation as mine, were not overlooked either by me or by the Brigade.

No one else was to be put in touch with me except on the case of most urgent necessity, and then only Joe O'Connor, a brother of

Father Dominic's, who was then the Brigade Quartermaster. Only Florrie, Joe, and the Brigade Commandant were to be made aware of my activities. Visits to Rockboro by Florrie had to be limited to the absolute minimum (the city churches were a more frequent though less satisfactory meeting place) and every possible precaution had to be taken to ensure that no indication of a contact existed which could arouse the suspicions of the police or military authorities. In the existing state of tenseness and alertness on both sides in the struggle at the time, there were a hundred ways in which some little incident or bit of gossip could, even innocently, uncover the connection between me and the IRA. Of my family only Kathleen knew of the contact.

Thus began a period of almost two years under constant strain, during which the shadow of possible detection and calamity was never wholly absent. And yet it was a happy period. Each day brought some new task, some new opportunity of helping those who were fighting outside, some call for a decision the consequences of which I could not perhaps foresee. Current documents, particularly those relating to the Intelligence section of the Division, were of course of primary value. When it was possible to bring out copies of them I did so. When it was not possible, I made shorthand notes to whatever extent time and opportunity permitted.

Documents of which a number of copies were made as normal routine were less difficult to procure, and over the whole period I brought out hundreds of these.[13] At other times it seemed to me that nothing less than the original document itself would be credible, and I had to take the risk of bringing it out and getting it back into file the next day.[14] On other occasions material actually made up for the post was taken by me and subsequently put back in the post after it had been opened, read, and resealed by Florrie. As well as bringing out documents and notes, I was of course able to give him up to date information about the composition and personnel of the different sections of the Division Staff, the location and strength of formations, transfers of officers, and many other matters.

The fact that I alone of the Division staff operated for the IRA deprived me of any source of inside help or advice and compelled me to rely solely on myself at all times. Some civilian employees came under suspicion as time went on, and it must have become evident to the military authorities that there was a serious leakage of information. Some were dismissed on suspicion, one was interned, although in fact they had nothing whatever to do with activities such as mine.[15] Florrie told me later that he had a contact in the 17th Brigade [British Army], a man who lasted less than a month before he came under suspicion and had to go on the run.[16] I was able to continue my work without a break and without arousing suspicion until I resigned in July 1921.

About Christmas 1919, Florrie asked me if I would give the Brigade full authority to get Reggie back to Ireland in any way they could. Having by that time proved my worth to them, they were prepared to see what could be done. I agreed but told him that I had no money to defray any expenses that might be involved. He said that he did not think the question of money would arise or cause any difficulty. From then until the following August we discussed it frequently, and although he assured me that the project was being considered and efforts were being made to plan the action to be taken, I began to fear that nothing would come of it. I decided without telling him that I would go and see Terence MacSwiney who was then Lord Mayor.

In endeavouring to get an interview with the Lord Mayor I had to give some reason to his secretary. I told him very briefly about my problem in regard to Reggie and he advised me to go write out a full statement of the case and bring it to City Hall on the night of 12 August, when we would have made an appointment for me with the Lord Mayor. Without consulting anybody I wrote the statement and included in it some account of the work I was doing for the IRA. Telling my sister Kathleen that I was going in to town to see Dr Dalton, I left home in time to be at the City Hall at 8 o'clock. As I was leaving, my next-door neighbour Kate Murphy called me and asked me to read the *Echo* [newspaper] for her. She was old and her eyesight was poor and this was something I did for her almost every evening. The result was that I would have been late for my appointment if I had gone to the City Hall. But I never reached there. On my way, at Rockboro Road, I met a woman I knew who lived there. When I told her I was going into town she begged me not to, saying the City Hall was surrounded by hundreds of troops and that there had been many arrests. I turned back. Terence MacSwiney was arrested there that night, the final arrest that ended in his death on hunger strike in Brixton. And if I had been caught there with the statement I had written on me it would have been the end.

It was soon after MacSwiney's death that Florrie told me arrangements had at last been made for bringing Reggie to Ireland and that he was going over himself for the purpose.

## NOTES AND REFERENCES

1    Cadoxton is a neighbourhood in the town of Barry, which is located eight miles from Cardiff. While Cadoxton is incorporated within Barry, locals consider it a separate village and Jo refers to it as such.

2    Coleridge Marchment's battalion was attached to the British 50th 'Northumbrian' Division. Marchment's remains can be found in the Tyne Cot Memorial, Belgium, along with about 35,000 other British dead. His death identification record comes from the Commonwealth War Graves Commission website, www.cwgc.org. For 'a benchmark of unsurpassed horror', see Nigel Steel and Peter Hart, *Passchendaele, The Sacrificial Ground* (London: Cassell and Co., 2000), p. 317. The quote on the attack of 30 October 1917 comes from Trevor Wilson and Robin Prior, *Passchendaele, The Untold Story* (New Haven: Yale Note Bene Press, 2002), p. 177. To really appreciate the human scope and suffering of the battle, see Lyn MacDonald's excellent *They Called it Passchendaele* (London: Michael Joseph, 1978).

3    There is small irony in Bishop Cohalan's kindness towards Jo, since he later excommunicated Florrie and the Cork Volunteers for their IRA activities in December 1920.

4    Estimates of overall Crown forces strength in Ireland during the conflict stretch from 40,000 to 60,000. I would put the figure at 55,000, with roughly 40,000 soldiers and 15,000 police. These numbers fluctuated throughout the conflict, due to resignations in the RIC and the varying strength of British Army units. The British Army was over-extended during this period because of military occupation duties in Germany, Egypt, Iraq, India, and elsewhere.

5    In January 1921, the British Army's Irish Command reorganized the 5th Division, and created another division (the 1st Division) to police Northern Ireland. The 15th Brigade (formerly with the 5th Division) was attached to the 1st Division, along with the newly-formed Londonderry Brigade. The 1st division deployed ten battalions, while the 5th Division retained nine battalions to cover Western Ireland and the Midlands. The 6th Division numbered twenty battalions, which still outnumbered the combined strength of the 1st and 5th Divisions. See Charles Townsend *The British Campaign in Ireland* (London: Oxford University Press, 1975), pp. 53 and 144.

6    Details about the 6th Division's strength and order of battle can be found in Townsend, *The British Campaign*, pp. 53, 144, and 217–20.

7    Following Coleridge Marchment's death, each of his dependants received a small government pension.

8    German submarines prowled Irish waters during the month of July. On 7 July, the cargo steamer *SS Ben Loman* was sunk thirty miles from Cobh. German u-boats torpedoed the *RMS Carpathia* (of *Titanic* fame) on the Irish east coast on 17 July and the White Star liner *Justicia* off Northern Ireland on 19 July. That same week, the Allies reported sinking two German submarines in Irish waters, one off West Cork.

9    About 600 Londoners died in German air raids during the war. Roughly half the deaths came from Zeppelin airships and the other half from Gotha airplane bombers.

10    Florrie O'Donoghue tried numerous times to assassinate Captain Kelly, but the Ulsterman proved too wily for the Volunteers. Kelly tortured IRA prisoners, which partially accounts for O'Donoghue's order for him to be shot on sight. (See O'Donoghue and Pa Murray in the O'Malley Notebooks, UCD; Tom Hales statement, Donal Hales Papers, CAI; and Pa Murray and Robert Ahern's BMH statements.) The Cork No. 1 Brigade did shoot Kelly's subordinate Lt Green at Waterfall (see p. 144), and during the Truce period secretly executed three others in Macroom, including Lt Keogh (another of Tom Hales' torturers). Hales identified Kelly, Green, and Keogh in his statement, which was smuggled

out of prison in 1920. The Macroom episode is mired in controversy and almost resulted in the ambush of a British Army search party commanded by the 17th Brigade's Major Bernard Montgomery, later known as Field Marshal Viscount Montgomery of El Alamein. For details of the incident, see Nigel Hamilton, *Monty, The Making of a General, 1887–1942* (New York: McGraw Hill Books, 1981), p. 162–63; and Charlie Brown in the O'Malley Notebooks. Roibeárd Langford (Langford Pension Statement, Langford Papers, CAI) wrote that he specifically tracked Lt Keogh in the days before the end of the Truce, which indicates the intelligence officer was known and wanted by the Brigade.

11  He was Adjutant of the very active Youghal Company.

12  As noted previously, the British 6th Division contained 40 per cent of the British Army's strength in Ireland. The Division was responsible for all British forces in counties Clare, Cork, Kerry, Kilkenny, Limerick, Tipperary, Waterford, and Wexford. While there was significant IRA activity in Dublin and other counties (most notably Longford), the bulk of the heavy fighting was carried on in the 6th Division area by Volunteer brigades in Cork, Tipperary, Limerick, and to a lesser extent, Kerry and Clare.

13  Some copies of these documents can be viewed in Florrie's papers, including Ms. 31,223, NLI. See my MA thesis, p. 117, for further details.

14  Florrie told the writer and fellow IRA veteran Ernie O'Malley of one such episode. 'At the end of the Tan War', wrote O'Malley, 'Florrie and a number of officers got out of town every night. They used to go separately to a small cottage so as not to draw attention to themselves. They were, however, observed. An ex-British officer noticed one or some of them, and he gave information. Florrie's wife, [General] Strickland's secretary, saw this note but had no time. She tried to memorise it. Later she got hold of the note and brought it out with her as evidence. The man was arrested, court-martialled, and shot before nightfall. That shook the daylights out of the British.' A similar story appears in O'Donoghue's *Rebel Cork's Fighting Story*, p. 24. This informer was likely Francis MacMahon, who was abducted by the IRA outside the War Pension office and killed secretly on 20 May 1921. Peter Hart (*The IRA and Its Enemies*, p. 298) believes MacMahon was killed for acting as a pension officer, but I think this story offers a more plausible explanation of his death. (For further details, see Seán Culhane's BMH statement; the *Cork Constitution*, 28 May 1921; and the Report of the Cork Quarterly Sessions, *Cork Constitution*, 15 October 1921.)

15  O'Donoghue told the same story to Ernie O'Malley. According to Florrie, while trying to plug the leak the 6th Division intelligence officer Captain Kelly, 'pushed some men out of barracks and others he put in gaol'. See O'Donoghue in the O'Malley Notebooks, UCD.

16  This is probably Con Conroy, an IRA officer employed as a clerk in the Garrison Adjutant's office. In February 1921, Conroy was arrested in a raid on Rahanisky House in Whitechurch along with a number of city Volunteers, including Seán MacSwiney, Terence's brother. While working in Victoria Barracks, Conroy passed on valuable information to the Brigade. In November 1920, he forwarded the travelling details for three suspected British Army intelligence officers, who were subsequently removed from a train in Waterfall and shot by city Volunteers. Conroy also provided information that led to the Brigade's ambush of a British Army lorry in Barrack Street, Cork in October 1920. He had to go on the run in January after the British captured a document that implicated Conroy (this occurred during the raid on Mary Bowles' farm, mentioned in the introduction, p. 6). See Daniel Healy's BMH statement; R.

Langford Pension Statement, Langford Papers, CAI; Mick Murphy in the O'Malley Notebooks, UCD; Murphy's BMH statement; and the *Cork Constitution*, 27 January 1921 and 24 February 1921.

1 Tomás MacCurtain and Terence MacSwiney with Cork No. 1 Brigade officers. Front row (from left): Tadg Barry, Tomás MacCurtain, Pat Higgins; Back row: David Cotter, Seán Murphy, Donal Barrett, Terence MacSwiney, Paddy Trahey. (Source: Cork Public Museum.)

2 Funeral procession of Tomás MacCurtain. Father Dominic O'Connor and Terence MacSwiney lead the IRA contingent in front of MacCurtain's hearse. Uniformed Cork No. 1 Brigade officers Florrie O'Donoghue, Seán O'Hegarty, Joe O'Connor, and Dan 'Sandow' Donovan march ahead of IRA GHQ leaders Dick McKee, Peadar Clancy, and Geróid O'Sullivan. (Source: British Pathé, ITN Archive.)

3 Auxiliary Cadets with armoured car patrol Cork city. Note the revolver held by the 'Auxie' in the foreground. The photo was taken after Cadets burned a large section of Cork city centre in December 1920 as reprisal for an IRA ambush. (Source: British Pathé, ITN Archive.)

4 Josephine Brown O'Donoghue and friends enjoy a day of yachting in the early 1920s. Jo stands second from the right, staring towards the water. (Source: Breda O'Donoghue Lucci.)

5 Father Dominic O'Connor (OFM, CAP) during his exile in Oregon. (Source: Catholic Diocese of Baker, Oregon.)

6 Prominent members of the Cork No. 1 Brigade flying column, in the summer of 1921 (from left): Mick O'Sullivan, Patrick O'Sullivan, and Seán Murray. (Source: Father Patrick Twohig.)

7 First Southern Division IRA Convention delegates, taken in Dublin on 26 March 1922. Group includes most senior IRA leaders from Cork, Kerry, and Waterford. Florrie O'Donoghue is seated in the front row, third from the left, next to Anti-Treaty IRA Chief of Staff Liam Lynch. From left, they include: Front Row: Seán Lehane, Tom Daly, Florrie O'Donoghue, Liam Lynch, Liam Deasy, Seán Moylan, John Joe Rice, Humphrey Murphy; Second Row: Denis Daly, Jimmy O'Mahony, George Power, Mick Murphy, Eugene O'Neil, Seán MacSwiney, Dr Pat O'Sullivan, Jim Murphy, Moss Donegan, Gerry Hannifin; Third Row: Jeremiah Riordan, Mick Crowley, Dan Shinnick, Con Leddy, Con O'Leary, Tom Hales, Jack O'Neil, Seán MacCarthy, Dick Barrett, Andy Cooney; Fourth Row: Tom Ward, John Lordan, Gibbs Ross, Tadgh Brosnan, Dan Mulvihill, Denis MacNeilus; Back Row: Con Casey, Pax Whelan, Tom McEllistrim, Michael Harrington. (Source: National Library of Ireland.)

8 The O'Donoghue family in the late 1930s. Seated (from left): Breda O'Donoghue Lucci, Florence O'Donoghue, Finn Barr O'Donoghue, Josephine O'Donoghue, Margaret O'Donoghue. Standing (from left): Gerald Marchment and Reggie Marchment. Sitting on the floor: Patrick O'Donoghue. (Source: Breda O'Donoghue Lucci.)

9 O'Donoghue speaking at the 1957 commemoration of his former commander, Liam Lynch, in Fermoy. (Source: Father Patrick Twohig.)

10 O'Donoghue relaxes at home with former Cork No. 1 Brigade commander Seán O'Hegarty. (Source: Father Patrick Twohig.)

11 'A long life of devoted love and mutual happiness.' Jo and Florrie in their later years on a fishing holiday. (Source: Breda O'Donoghue Lucci.)

# 7

## 'TO STEAL A CHILD'

### Florence O'Donoghue

In the ordinary course of my intelligence work I heard of Jo for the first time in the summer of 1919. The information came from Michael Walsh who was then Adjutant of the Youghal Company of the Volunteers, and it indicated no more than that he was in touch with her and that she was employed at Cork Military Barracks. Raw to the work as I was, groping in a field in which I had neither experience nor guidance, it is clear to me now that I cannot have realized at first how valuable a contact this would be. Nothing really effective was done at the time to exploit its potential value; nothing more than directing Walsh to maintain the contact and get what information he could.

It was probably in September of that year that, as she has related, she made the contact with Father Dominic, as a result of which an appointment was made for me to see her in Cork. My credential was a slip of paper on which she had written only the capital letter 'G'. I remember very clearly that first autumn evening on which I first went to No. 2 Rockboro Terrace, old Blackrock Road. The initial surprise was to find that 'G' was a young and very lovely girl. I had not expected that.[1] Her sister Kitty was there and when after some general conversation, she left us alone and Jo gave me some account of her position and duties in the Barracks, I realized quickly that she could be of invaluable assistance to us. With that thought came the cognate one that for her it would mean great danger.

Something to this effect I must have said, because I recall how she made light of it and assured me she would use the utmost discretion in her work for us. So began the flow of information which formed so large a content of our total knowledge in the next two years of the main forces opposed to us. We arranged that I would call at Rockboro Terrace not too frequently, and made provision for her to make contact with me if an urgent need to do so arose.

A little later when she had told me something of her personal story, we discussed the matter of getting Reggie back into her custody. For the Volunteer organization as such no action within the law was possible; if we acted at all it would have to be on other lines. The proposal was of course something outside our immediate local control, and was moreover something quite outside our proper functions. So that when I put it to some of the Brigade officers (I do not think it ever went beyond Seán O'Hegarty and Joe O'Connor) it appeared to them to be a matter requiring careful consideration as well as needing the sanction and active help of GHQ.

Nevertheless, the proposal was not turned down, and I began to plan how best we could get Reggie to Ireland. That seemed to me to be the real difficulty. The British authorities were then very active in searching for men and arms coming into the country. Cross channel boats were watched and searched with such vigilance that it was only by the intelligent cooperation of crew members that anything could be got into any port.

The most hopeful idea that emerged was that after taking Reggie from Cadoxton, we should smuggle him aboard one of the small vessels that carried coal cargoes from Cardiff or Barry Dock to ports in the south coast of Ireland. Captain O'Toole of Ballinacurra owned and skippered such a boat, and when approached he very willingly agreed to do his part. He was a friend of Alfred's [Hore]. It was only at that stage that it was possible to present the plan to GHQ with any hope that it would be sanctioned, and to request from them the arrangements of the necessary facilities in Britain. It was to [Michael] Collins I put the proposal and I doubt if it ever went beyond him. In both his capacities as Director of Intelligence and head of the IRB he was in a position to do all that was needed, and he did it.

The IRA in Britain boasted hundreds of Volunteers organized into numerous city companies and battalions in England, Scotland, and Wales. Michael Collins spent his young adulthood in London and maintained close contact with his early Republican colleagues. He considered Britain as his territory and usually organized operations that required assistance from IRA personnel there.

When the question arose of putting the matter into the hands of our men in Britain, I opposed it. From the beginning I said I would go over myself if permitted. Eventually Collins was persuaded that this was the better way. He moved slowly in making the arrangements. Possibly he had his own troubles, but once he became convinced of the value of the military intelligence we were getting from Jo, and I think that was early in 1920, he kept in constant touch with me in regard to progress.

The murder of Tomás MacCurtain in March and its aftermath had the effect of putting every other project into the background for a while. Jo herself became doubtful of our intentions. She could not be blamed for that; she had no contact with anybody but myself, and I did not feel free to tell her more than that we were trying to make arrangements. We were dependent on GHQ for the necessary contacts and assistance in Britain. Our own preparations had to travel at the pace set by them. The anxiety which induced Jo, without my knowledge, to seek an interview with Terence MacSwiney, and from the possible consequences of which she fortunately escaped, came at a time when I was making some progress with the plan.

The Cork City Hall raid that narrowly missed Josephine Brown occurred on the evening of 12 August 1920. Because Terence MacSwiney served as both Lord Mayor and commander of the Cork No. 1 Brigade, the Brigade staff frequently met in his mayoral office. British soldiers became aware of this arrangement and stormed City Hall, capturing a number of top IRA leaders. Terrence MacSwiney was arrested and charged with possessing one of Florrie's police cipher sheets, used to decode intercepted RIC telegrams. Other prisoners included North Cork's Liam Lynch (OC Cork No. 2 Brigade) and the Cork No. 1 Brigade's leadership group of Seán O'Hegarty (Vice OC), Joe O'Connor (Quartermaster), First Battalion OC Dan 'Sandow' Donovan, and Fourth Battalion OC Michael Leahy. Only Florrie O'Donoghue, who had business in Macroom, missed the round-up. (O'Donoghue had been at City Hall earlier that day to meet with Michael Leahy to plan the assassination of an RIC sergeant in Leahy's area.)

Remarkably, the Crown forces tossed away the fruits of one of their most successful operations of the entire war in Cork. Within a week of the arrests, the British freed all the prisoners, with the exception of the Lord Mayor Terence MacSwiney. The only plausible explanation for the release of the Cork IRA brain trust is that the British did not recognize the prominence of their captured prisoners. Such an error illustrates the appalling state of British intelligence in Cork during the summer of 1920.

Court-martialled by the British military, Terence MacSwiney protested the right of Britain to try a citizen of the Irish Republic. He began an epic hunger strike, joining a group of Volunteers in Cork Gaol who were denying themselves food to protest their detention.[2] MacSwiney was moved to Brixton Prison in London, where his struggle attracted international attention and considerable sympathy among the English public. Young, handsome, and articulate, his message of self-sacrifice and dedication to Republican ideals stirred Ireland in a way not seen since the executions of the 1916 Rising leaders. MacSwiney's prolonged demise, along with the death of two fellow Volunteer hunger strikers in Cork Gaol, aroused rage and anguish in Cork city, especially among his

IRA colleagues. Terence MacSwiney's death after 74 days was a water-shed of the Anglo-Irish conflict.

The Cork No. 1 Brigade sought its own justice for MacSwiney. As the Lord Mayor slowly declined, a Brigade assassination team sanctioned by IRA GHQ sailed to England. Hand-picked by Florrie O'Donoghue and Seán O'Hegarty, the Cork Volunteers stalked British Cabinet members around London, including Prime Minister David Lloyd-George and Lord Birkenhead. Reprisal killings of British politicians were cancelled at the last moment, only when it became apparent that they would distract from the considerable public sympathy for MacSwiney.[3]

It was during this troubled period that O'Donoghue planned to travel to Wales to kidnap Reggie Brown.

Then once again MacSwiney's hunger strike and death occupied us to such an extent that there was some further delay. However, about the end of October 1920 I had got from Collins the contacts I required in Britain and letters of instruction to those concerned there. I had also got his and Seán [O'Hegarty]'s approval to going over myself. It was decided to take a driver with me. When we considered which of the Brigade drivers I would take, I asked for Jack Cody. Apart from his ability as a driver and his competence to do running repairs, there were two other reasons for my choice. Although he was young, a bit wild and irresponsible in some ways, he did not drink and he could be depended upon to obey any order I gave him without hesitation or question. Seán agreed.[4]

We left Cork on the direct boat to Liverpool. I do not remember the date, but as I was away altogether about two weeks it must have been early November.[5] Seán walked with me down to the quays, and I thought I sensed in his conversation and in his request to get back as soon as I could a certain note of sadness, perhaps of a question if this was not a final parting. Cody had been told nothing of the mission up to then. There were only a few passengers, and when the boat moved out into the river I took him to quiet spot and told him what we were going to do. His face registered blank amazement. 'To steal a child!' For a moment he looked at me in wide-eyed astonishment and then broke into uproarious laughter. He thought it was the joke of the war.

We got to London the next day, to an address which Collins had supplied but which I have now forgotten. I left Cody there and went to report to Art O'Brien, who was acting somewhat in the capacity of diplomatic representative of the [Irish] Republic in London. This was a mere formality. Art was not aware of the purpose of my visit and it was undesirable from his own point of view that he should be made aware of it. His function was to put me in touch with the OC Britain

[IRA].[6] He envisaged nothing particular in me but did get me in contact with the Volunteer command without delay.

Here I am in difficulty. There were two men present at the few interviews I had which were necessary to make the arrangements in London. One I feel sure was Seán McGrath and the other was either Sam Maguire or Reggie Dunne, who was later executed with Joseph O'Sullivan for the killing of Sir Henry Wilson.[7] All I wanted them to do was to supply a car which Cody would drive. The plan at that stage was to drive to Cardiff; contact there a Mr Terry at Portmanmoor Road, to whom Collins had given me a letter of introduction; to find out if Captain O'Toole was at Barry Dock; and take Reggie there and put him on board the boat, on which I would travel back with him to Ireland while Cody returned the car to London. If it was not possible to contact Captain O'Toole, we would drive back to London with Reggie. I disliked the second alternative and feared we could not escape being discovered if we had to make the long journey to London. But I felt confident that my appointment with Captain O'Toole, then four days away, would materialize and that the car journey would not be necessary.

Difficulties arose from the beginning. No car was to be had. The only solution they could suggest was the purchase of a second-hand car that could be resold when the job was completed. As I did not have enough money to buy a car, Art O'Brien had to be approached for a loan of the price. Understandably, he showed some reluctance when he was not told of the reason of the purchase. Accustomed as I was by then to our own efficient organization at home, I was somewhat annoyed and disappointed with the London people, particularly as they had had long notice in advance that a car would be required. After two days of negotiations I was assured that they had contacted an owner-driver who would be willing to go to Cardiff for a few days. They advised that Cody and I should go on to Cardiff where this man would pick us up. In my anxiety to contact Captain O'Toole and hold him at Barry Dock, I too readily agreed to this advice and Cody and I went to Cardiff by train.

We went to Mr Terry's house at Portmanmoor Road. There we were most kindly received by him, his wife, and family. They were of the greatest assistance to us, and indeed were it not for their invaluable cooperation and advice it is doubtful if we could have succeeded at all in our mission. I went the next day to Barry Dock only to discover to my consternation that Captain O'Toole had sailed the previous night. Once it was loaded, a boat could not remain at anchorage, I found. I felt for the first time that I was facing complete failure. The journey to London with the child in the car could not possibly succeed.

There followed a few days of acute anxiety. Cody and I did not stay more than one night at the same place. We would not risk the danger of drawing any attention to Terry's by staying there. I felt the situation could arise in which we would have to leave Reggie somewhere in Cardiff for a time and this was the only place I knew. Neither did we go about together more than was absolutely necessary. I went alone to Cadoxton to locate the house from the description Jo had given me, and was fortunate in being able to identify it without making any enquiries.

The only information we had from London was that the car would be sent as soon as possible and that we should hold until it arrived. When after a few more days there was still no trace of it, I made what I afterwards realized was a rash and foolish decision. We would go out the road towards Cadoxton, hold up a car, tie up the driver, take the child and head for London. We went out at dusk. By some providential good luck we did not see that night a single car with a driver only, and we walked back to some Cardiff lodging house disappointed and miserable. Next morning when I called to Terry's, there was a letter from London to say that a car would arrive that evening, not from London but from Manchester and that the driver would have instructions.

On the same day Seán Phelan arrived from Liverpool. I had of course never seen him before but had no hesitation in accepting him for what he was – a fine, sincere, well educated lad in his early twenties.[8] He confirmed that the car was coming, and told me also, somewhat to my disappointment, that the driver was not a Volunteer. He was, however, a man who would carry out instructions without question, but would prefer to drive to Manchester rather than London. Arrangements had been made for our reception in Manchester by a namesake of mine, a Kerryman, Patrick O'Donoghue.[9] The driver knew where he lived and would take us there unless we were determined on another course.

Assuming that the car would arrive, I decided that we would go to Cadoxton in a taxi, collect Reggie, and have him in Cardiff ready to leave that night. The three of us got into the first taxi in a rank in the city and told the driver to take us to Cadoxton. Some short distance from the house I told him to stop and wait. Taking Cody with me, I left Seán Phelan with the driver to ensure that he did not move off in our absence. The driver had shown no sign of suspicion up to then. The three of us were armed but no occasion arose to show even a threat of force. I warned Cody on the way to the house that he was not to produce his gun except on my positive order. As numerous subsequent newspaper reports made a dramatic story of the matter, it is as well I should say we did not show any weapons, nor in fact was there any need to, because we met with no real resistance.[10] I may have told Mr Brown we were armed – I do not remember definitely – if I did that was the full extent of any threat to them. We were not disguised in any way.[11]

It was still daylight though duskish. Reggie was present when we went in. I told them we were taking him away, no more, and asked to be given his outdoor clothes and any toys he might like to have with him. I assured them that he would not be harmed and would be taken good care of. We did not hurry them unduly; my main concern was not to make a scene or start the child crying. In fact Reggie was quite unperturbed, and showed no reluctance to come with us. By coincidence it was his birthday, 23 November.[12]

We walked back to the taxi and drove to Cardiff. I stopped the driver some distance from Terry's on Portmanmoor Road, paid him, and we all got out and walked to the house. It was then dark. The house was one of hundreds of the same terrace type in a long road. In reply to their eager questions we told them all that had happened. When I mentioned where we had left the taxi, Mr Terry asked me to describe the exact place. He became alarmed. We had got out of the taxi in front of the police station on Portmanmoor Road. I was a bit alarmed myself, particularly as there was no trace of the car from Manchester. We decided that it would be too dangerous to leave Reggie at Terry's or for any of us to stay there. Mrs Terry went to a friend of theirs named Murphy in a neighbouring street with a request that they would take Reggie and Cody for a few hours until the car arrived. The Murphy family agreed and Kathleen Terry took Reggie round there, coming back later to take Cody. Reluctantly, Seán Phelan and I waited at Terry's. Towards midnight, when the car had not come, one of the girls went round to Murphy's again and asked them to keep Reggie and Cody for the night. I am sorry that I have forgotten the addresses of these good people who were so kind and helpful. Seán Phelan and I went to some lodging in town, and I sent him off very early next morning to Manchester to see what had become of the car.

The next two days strained all our nerves. The car did not come and there was not information of any kind from either London or Manchester. The story appeared in the newspapers, prominently featured in the local ones.[13] The taxi driver had been traced by the police and had given what information he could. That was inevitable anyway and a risk I had undertaken from the start. I thought it was less than the risk that someone would get the number of the waiting car in a quiet place like Cadoxton, and that as a consequence the police everywhere would be on the look out for it while we were trying to make the journey to Manchester. Our one bit of good fortune was that the Murphy family were quite willing to keep Reggie and Cody under their roof as long as was necessary. Fortunately also Reggie gave no trouble at all. He very quickly got on good terms with his ebullient temporary nurse. Cody used his fine voice and his fund of nonsensical stories to keep his charge amused and happy.

It is easy to understand with what relief and thankfulness I greeted the arrival of the car on the evening of the 26th [November].[14] I was ready to retract all the hard things I had said about the London and Manchester people in my joy at seeing it arrive at last. It was an old but road-worthy taxi or public service vehicle, and the owner-driver had thoughtfully provided himself with a store of petrol in tins and a rather bulky assortment of spares sufficient to ensure his independence of garages or filling stations on the road. His forethought delighted me and was the best recommendation he could have brought. When he expressed his willingness to start that night on the journey to Manchester, and did not see any reason why we should not be able to get there, my confidence in him increased. Optimistic for the first time in several days, I felt that once we got out of Cardiff the rest of the job would be successfully completed. I told the driver that Cody and I would do some of the driving if he wished; but although he did allow us to give him a break now and again, he did most of the driving himself and insisted on taking over in passing through cities and towns.

During the long night journey I found that he was a Russian born Bolshevik who had been brought to London as a child, where he had acquired an authentic cockney accent. I got his name – a rather unpronounceable Russian one – but it has escaped my memory. We had to do some stowing of the spare tires and petrol tins in the back seat to make room for Reggie in a position in which he could sleep and for Cody. I sat in front with the driver.

The risk had to be taken of walking Reggie from Murphy's to a point some streets away where, after consultations with Mr Terry, I arranged that the car would stop for a minute so that there would be no waiting by it or by us. One of the Terry girls took Reggie. Cody and I walked separately to the agreed point. All our movements had to be open and as casual as possible in this completely built up area where many persons were always on the streets or at their doors. It still seems something extraordinary to me that no suspicion was ever directed to the Terries or to the Murphies.

All went well. A hasty farewell to our friends and we moved off. Reggie, made comfortable in the back seat, was soon sound asleep and did not wake till we reached Manchester. Apart from the fact that I fell

out of the car at one point, when the driver was slowing down to refill
his tank and I thought he had stopped, we had only one adventure. I
must have been half asleep with a few scratches and a shaking. In the
suburbs at the entrance to some town or city (I did not know the route
and have forgotten the name of the place), we were held up by a
policeman on night duty. He told the driver that he had only three
front lights, apparently an offence then, and he should have had four.
The policeman asked for his driving licence, discovered it had expired
the previous midnight and became more inquisitive. I know we had
agreed upon some story to meet an eventuality of this kind, but again
memory does not recall what it was. One part of this was that Cody and
I would keep silent if at all possible so that our accents would not
betray us.

The driver and the policeman were having a mild argument, only
part of which I could hear clearly as they were both on the road. I did
however catch this from policeman – 'If you go through the town
you'll be pinched.' Then he started to walk round and I began to think
we were in real trouble. Just then the driver stuck his head in to me
and whispered, 'Give me a quid.' When the policeman came round to
him again there was some further talk, and presently the driver was
being given the precise instructions as to the route he should take to
avoid going through town, and, as he told me when we got going
again, meeting the Sergeant who would have pinched him. The
policeman never looked in the back of the car. Neither Cody nor I said
a word.

We reached Paddy O'Donoghue's place in Manchester some time in
the morning, possibly about 9.00 a.m. as shops were beginning to
open. Once again the address had not remained in my memory, but it
was a large comfortable house in a good class suburban district. We got
a true Kerry welcome, and when I settled with the driver we had an
excellent breakfast. Then the good people insisted that Cody and I
should go to bed, assuring us that Reggie would be well cared for.

That night we discussed the remaining problem of getting Reggie to
Ireland. Paddy O'Donoghue was very insistent that we should not
attempt it for some time until the immediate police vigilance had
abated somewhat. We could stay where we were as long as we wished.
Impatient to get back to my work, I did not like this at all. Eventually I
was persuaded that it was wiser to postpone the attempt to take him to
Ireland for a while. It would be a sad end to our efforts if he were taken
from us again because of a too impetuous desire to finish the job.
There was no need for two of us to remain with him in Manchester,
and though I hated the idea of not seeing the job through to the end,
I was persuaded that I should go home and from there make

arrangements for the final stage of his journey. So I returned to Cork. Some weeks later Cody's sister went over and the two of them travelled back with Reggie without mishap.

## FLORRIE'S POSTSCRIPT

When Reggie was safely in Ireland [18 December 1920, according to Florrie's notes], we arranged a meeting with his mother at a house in Blackpool [Cork city]. In doing this a risk had to be taken, because from every point of view it was necessary that she should maintain the position of being unaware of any knowledge of an intention to restore him to her, or of his whereabouts. To bring him home would be inviting more trouble. This was evident from the many enquiries that were made to the police in Cork and to the local newspaper. A good friend in the *Cork Examiner* office, Michael O'Herlihy, kept us fully informed both on the enquiries his paper was receiving, and of police investigations. About this time two Scotland Yard detectives arrived in Cork on the case, but their efforts proved fruitless.[15]

> Reggie was subsequently moved to Alfred and Cecily Hore's household in Youghal, where he remained until the Truce of 1921. Despite the intense newspaper coverage, British officials apparently never suspected IRA involvement in the kidnapping. Jo maintained her innocence and aroused sympathy from some newspaper reporters.
>
> Below are excerpts from a *Western Mail* interview with Josephine Brown, published 4 December 1920.

Mrs Josephine Brown was interviewed at her residence, Rockborough terrace, Blackrock Road (Ireland) by a Western Mail correspondent as to the sensational kidnapping of her little boy, Reginald Marchant [sic] Brown...This was her first intimation that she received of the extraordinary affair.

At first she could not believe the statement, but evidence of the kidnapping having been shown to her, and a report of the occurrence having appeared in this morning's Cork newspapers, which was subsequently read to her, she burst into tears and sobbed.

'Oh, my darling boy! Is he dead or alive? What did they do it for? Why did they kidnap him, a harmless, innocent child?'

Mrs Brown, who is a pretty young woman, aged about 26 years, was married ten years ago to Private Brown, attached to the Duke of Yorke's Regiment...

She said; 'We had two sons born to us. The one who was kidnapped is aged seven years, and the other is just in his fifth year, and is at home with us at present. My husband was a Protestant and I a Catholic. Nevertheless, we both were most united and happy, and extremely devoted to our offspring...'

When news of the death of her husband came, up to which time she lived with his people at Barry, they wanted to claim Reginald and allow her custody of her youngest son. This she thought very unfair, inasmuch as the right of both children should be with the mother, and more particularly so as her husband in his will mentioned that both children should be left in charge of the surviving parent, in whom he had the utmost confidence.

'It is not true,' she exclaimed, 'that Reginald was by his father's will left to his uncle to be brought up in the Protestant faith. There was no such clause mentioned.'

When the judge decreed that for the present it was best for the child to remain with the uncle (which had to be obeyed) Mrs Brown left Wales for Ireland, bringing the youngest boy with her, leaving Reginald with her husband's relations; but in doing so rested somewhat contented at the thought of the little fellow being educated by his aunt, who is a teacher.

'Oh it cannot be true that he is kidnapped, my favourite child! It will break my heart if he is not returned.' ...The thought occurred to her that the distracted state of Ireland might have spread to a part of Wales...

'Why,' she asked, 'did not the Browns in Barry inform me by letter of my child's misfortune? Oh! It's too dreadful to think of.'

...Mrs Brown left with the intention of proceeding to the general commanding the Cork military at the barracks [General Strickland] for his counsel and advice.

## NOTES AND REFERENCES

1   Observers likewise describe Josephine as attractive. A *Western Mail* newspaper correspondent called her a 'pretty young woman'. (*Western Mail*, 4 December 1920). The *South Wales Echo* reported, 'She is said to be a very attractive woman.' (*South Wales Echo*, 2 December 1920). Author Seán O'Callaghan, who interviewed a number of Cork IRA veterans while writing his book *Execution*, described Jo as 'a vivacious, tall, good-looking blonde' (London: Frederick Mueller, 1974 pp. 57–8). Her children agreed that she was outgoing and social. In 1997, I spoke with an elderly gentleman in Cork city, who in his childhood

used to buy sweets from the O'Donoghue's confectionery shop. He remembered Jo as 'handsome' and friendly, with a soft spot for the neighbourhood children.

2    Two Volunteers died on hunger strike in Cork City Gaol. They were Michael Fitzgerald, a Battalion commander from the Cork No. 2 Brigade, and Joseph Murphy, a twenty-two-year-old Volunteer from the city's Second Battalion. Fitzgerald died on 17 October (a week before Terry MacSwiney,) while Murphy lasted seventy-six-days, dying the same day as MacSwiney. At that stage Arthur Griffith and Michael Collins convinced the remaining nine Cork Gaol strikers to end their protest.

3    The assassins were led by 'Pa' Murray and included Florrie's driver Jack Cody. Murray even conducted a dry run on Lord Balfour (former Prime Minister and then Lord President of the Privy Council). Murray tracked Balfour to a speech in Oxford, then approached him and asked for directions to a building. For details of the plot, see Pa Murray's account written for O'Donoghue on 6 January 1959, and Moss Twomey's and Dan Donovan's letters to O'Donoghue (both written in 1959). All the items are found in Ms. 31,296, NLI. Also see Pa Murray's BMH Statement, and Pa Murray and Stan Barry in the O'Malley Notebooks, UCD. In Francis Costello's *Enduring the Most, The Life and Death of Terence MacSwiney* (Dingle: Brandon Books, 1995), p. 161, the author supposes that Pa Murray was dispatched to London to break MacSwiney out of jail. However, the evidence is clear that the IRA intended to avenge MacSwiney through assassination.

4    Cody was in demand as a driver. Pa Murray brought him to Great Britain for the aborted Cabinet assassinations in September. That experience probably factored into O'Donoghue's selection of Cody for the Reggie Brown kidnapping. The previous August, Jack Cody joined the original hit team sent to Lisburn to assassinate District Inspector Swanzy, but was wisely replaced with a Belfast Volunteer driver familiar with the area. After the Civil War, Cody emigrated to South Australia and died there in 1963. See Ms. 31,296, NLI and Seán Culhane's BMH Statement.

5    O'Donoghue incorrectly lists his dates throughout this chapter. The kidnapping occurred on 1 December 1920, so he must have left around the last week of November.

6    This was probably Rory O'Connor, who came over to Britain to organize a sabotage campaign against the country's industrial infrastructure. On 28 November 1920, local IRA Volunteers attacked the Liverpool docks and destroyed nineteen warehouses, causing hundreds of thousands of pounds worth of damage. The close timing of this effort with O'Donoghue's visit may account for the London Volunteers' lack of response to Florrie's requests for a car. O'Connor later headed the Anti-Treaty IRA's militant faction, and he and O'Donoghue clashed on the Anti-Treaty IRA Executive. For details of the British sabotage campaign, see Peter Hart *The IRA at War 1916–1923* (Oxford: Oxford University Press, 2003), pp. 148–59.

7    These men were leaders of the London IRA and key members of Michael Collins' British network.

8    Seán Phelan was a teacher and the son of Irish immigrants living in Liverpool. After a few months, he transferred to the Cork No. 3 Brigade column, and was killed during an ambush of British troops at Upton Rail Station.

9    Patrick O'Donoghue was one of Michael Collins' British IRB contacts and the head of the Manchester Volunteers.

10 For newspaper coverage, see *The Times*, 3 and 7 December 1920; *South Wales Echo*, 2, 3, 4, and 6 December 1920; and *Western Mail* 2, 3, 4, 6, and 9 December 1920. Cork newspapers also covered the affair. See the *Cork Constitution*, 6 December 1920, 6 January 1921; the *Cork Examiner* 3, 6 December 1920; and the *Cork Weekly News* 8 January 1921.

11 The newspaper accounts were indeed dramatic. According to the *South Wales Echo*, four armed men 'with distinct Irish accents' entered the home and pushed a revolver in Mr Brown's face. 'Mr Brown remonstrated with the men, but was told if he did not let them alone they would blow his brains out.' The *Western Mail* offered slightly different dialogue. 'The revolver was pushed into his face, and he was threatened that if he were not quiet "he would be blown to kingdom come".' The *Echo* added another twist, 'when the lad was being taken away he fell on his knees and prayed, and asked to be allowed to remain with his "mam and dad".'

12 Florrie is incorrect. The date of the kidnapping was 1 December 1920.

13 The *South Wales Echo* called it a 'sensational affair', and splashed headlines such as 'HUNT FOR REGGIE BROWN' and 'REGGIE BROWN MYSTERY – HUE & CRY OVER THE KINGDOM'. The *Western Mail* led with the story for a week, and it also appeared with less fanfare in the *Times* of London.

14 The true date was probably 3 December 1920.

15 The *South Wales Echo* reported on 4 December that Scotland Yard detectives interviewed friends of Mrs Brown living in London and were 'interesting themselves in the matter' (*South Wales Echo*, 4 December 1920). By January, Cork newspapers reported that police believed the boy to be in London (*Cork Constitution*, 6 January 1921; and *Cork Weekly News*, 8 January 1921).

# PART II
# TAKING TO THE HILLS

# 8

# LOVE AND TERROR

## John Borgonovo

The weeks before and after the Reggie Brown abduction were bloody ones in Cork city. In November, the Cork No. 1 Brigade acted decisively on its intelligence front. One can surmise that information from Josephine Brown played a role in this move.

Over four weeks, Brigade forces killed a total of six British Army officers suspected of working for military intelligence in Cork. In the middle of November, city Volunteers boarded a train at Waterfall (just outside the city) and held up three British officers dressed in mufti. They pulled the officers out of their compartment, took them to a field, shot them, and secretly buried the bodies. A few days later, Volunteers commanded by O'Donoghue's friend Leo Murphy killed the Manchester Regiment's battalion intelligence officer Captain Hamilton near Ballincollig. Hamilton commuted to his office by motorcycle, so the insurgents stretched a rope across the road and yanked him from his machine. They then shot him on the ground. A couple of weeks earlier, two other British intelligence officers were shot after they were discovered in the Brigade's Seventh Battalion area, searching for information while disguised as tourists. Their accents and queries of locals quickly gave them away. O'Donoghue later saluted the bravery of such efforts, but recognized his opponents' 'boy-scout mentality' that led to such foolhardy ruses.[1]

At the end of November, the Cork city IRA kidnapped five civilians accused of giving information to the British. Volunteers abducted one of them from his hospital bed, removing him before the shocked staff. Two other civilians lived next-door to Josephine Brown, and she notified Florrie O'Donoghue of their clandestine meetings with other suspected informers. In the case of the final two victims, Black and Tans threatened to burn homes and kill 'Sinn Féiners' if the two men were harmed. This did not deter the city Volunteers. They secretly executed all five civilians and buried them on the outskirts of the city.[2]

During the same month, British personnel (probably Auxiliary Cadets) posted notices around the city and in local newspapers threatening to assassinate Republican sympathizers (including members of the clergy) and destroy civilian property if attacks against the police did not cease. They also vowed to shoot any men seen loitering on street corners or walking with their hands in their pockets.[3] In November and December, disguised police killed four city Volunteers in their beds and attempted to assassinate other known IRA activists. During this same period, unidentified members of the Crown forces set fire to a number of Cork homes, businesses, and Sinn Féin Halls.

Already placed a repressive curfew the previous July, Cork city and County fell under Martial Law on 10 December 1920. Under the new regime, citizens found carrying weapons or sheltering wanted men could be executed. On pain of arrest, homeowners had to post on their door a nightly list of everyone sleeping in their house. Civilians living near the location of an ambush could have their home destroyed if they failed to warn Crown forces of the pending attack. The British military could also compel any citizen to perform manual work, such as fixing sabotaged roadways.[4]

The war in City city seemed to come to a climax the following day, when IRA guerrillas ambushed a lorry of Auxiliary Cadets on the outskirts of the city, at an intersection called Dillons Cross. Firing pistols and tossing homemade grenades, the Volunteers killed one Cadet and wounded eleven. The battle occurred only a few hundred yards from Victoria Barracks, so it is likely Josephine Brown heard the firing.[5]

Later that evening, parties of drunken Auxiliary Cadets descended on the Cork city centre. They looted stores, burned homes and businesses, and beat passers-by. Fire fighters trying to control the blaze were fired on and had their hoses cut. The conflagration destroyed much of the city's commercial centre, and separate fires consumed the City Hall and the Carnegie Library. About 100 businesses were destroyed or damaged and an estimated 1500–2000 people were thrown out of work. No Crown forces were disciplined for their role in the reprisal (though the local Auxiliary Cadet company was transferred out of the city shortly thereafter). The Irish Secretary Sir Hamar Greenwood blamed the arson on the Volunteers, while the British Government repressed General Strickland's inquiry into the episode.[6] The episode damaged the British Government's credibility at home and abroad.

The day after the burning of Cork city, Daniel Cohalan, the Catholic Bishop of Cork, tried to end the chaos. He ordered the excommunication of anyone in his diocese involved in arson, murder, or kidnapping.[7] This action was in fact directed at both the IRA and Crown forces, though the blow fell hardest on the former.

In the Cork countryside, mobile bands of IRA guerrillas menaced the Crown forces and their civilian supporters. British forces were rarely seen in many remote areas, often preferring to remain inside their well-protected bases. A systematic IRA road sabotage effort made transportation difficult. The Volunteers constantly dismantled bridges, felled trees, and dug trenches across roadways to hamper British movements.

In the New Year, the IRA campaign continued in Cork city. Two RIC constables were killed and five wounded in an ambush on Parnell Bridge in the city centre in early January.[8] February saw a flurry of IRA executions of suspected civilian spies, seven in twelve days. The Volunteers left messages on the corpses warning of the penalty for collaboration with the British, spreading the sense of terror in Cork city.[9] On 25 February, the Brigade flying column ambushed a strong party of Auxiliaries in West Cork near Coolavokig, inflicting numerous British casualties. Seán O'Hegarty, Sandow Donovan, and a number of city Volunteers participated in the fight. A couple of weeks later, a British raiding party killed six of those Volunteers in the Cork city suburbs, after their hiding place was betrayed by an IRA comrade (an incident Florrie mentioned previously). In the beginning of March, as reprisal for the execution of Cork No. 1 Brigade prisoners in Victoria Barracks, city forces shot over twelve unarmed British soldiers (killing six) in a series of coordinated attacks in the city centre.[10]

Gangs of armed men on both sides hunted the streets for their enemies. IRA assassins attacked informers and British intelligence officers whenever possible. In the evenings after curfew, British intelligence squads (called, without irony, 'the murder gang' by Republicans) prowled the city, raiding homes for wanted Volunteers.[11] Their lorries often carried Irish hostages to deter IRA ambushes. Captured Republicans faced torture in Victoria Barracks and some were 'shot trying to escape'. Seven other Cork No. 1 Brigade Volunteers were executed in Victoria Barracks during this period for carrying weapons. Of the eighteen Cork city Volunteers killed by British forces during the War of Independence, none died in actual combat. All were killed while unarmed during raids on their homes, on the street after being identified, or while in police or military custody.[12] By this time Florrie O'Donoghue was known to British officials by name and would have been a top target of their efforts.[13]

In this dark and dangerous time, Jo and Florrie became romantically involved. They left no record of how their romance developed, but it is not difficult to understand its origins. They collaborated closely and met with each other most evenings. Both were young, attractive, and unattached. More importantly, each was under tremendous pressure and lived daily with the spectre of death hovering over their heads. Because of the confidential nature of their intelligence work, neither could discuss it openly with family or friends. Their intimacy likely sprung from the need to share their experiences with someone who could understand.

The romance remained a secret. Only Seán O'Hegarty, Joe O'Connor, and Kitty McCoy would have been aware of the relationship. Since O'Donoghue was a wanted man, any link to him had to be avoided.

In April 1921, the couple were secretly married at SS Peter's and Paul's Church in Cork city. After the nuptials, Florrie's sisters Nell, Albina, and Margaret eventually learned of the marriage, as did Jo's sisters Kitty and Cecily, and Alfred Hore in Youghal. It was during this time that O'Donoghue moved out of Cork city and 'took to the hills'. His letters to Jo tell the next chapter of their story.

## NOTES AND REFERENCES

1    British officials acknowledged that three of the six officers (Capt. Hamilton, and the two disguised tourists, Lt Brown and Lt Rutherford) were intelligence officers. For details see the 'List of IRA Executions', Military Archives; Charlie Brown and Mick Murphy in the O'Malley Notebooks, UCD; *History of the Sixth Division in Ireland*, pp. 60–61, IWM; *Cork Examiner*, 2 and 24 November 1920 and the *Irish Times*, 22 August 1921. The British Army denied the three officers killed at Waterfall were involved in any intelligence operations. I believe they were intelligence agents, especially as one officer (Lt Green) had been named by Tom Hales as one of the group of Army intelligence officers that tortured him in Victoria Barracks (see Tom Hales Statement, Donal Hales Papers, U64, Cork Archives Institute). The Cork No. 1 Brigade was confident that the Waterfall officers were working on intelligence and went to some trouble tracking and killing them. During the abduction, they also set free a fourth British Army officer travelling with the three men, since he did not appear involved in military intelligence. Josephine Brown and Con Conroy were both in a position to identify the military duties of the three killed men. See my MA thesis pp. 19–24 for additional sources and citations. During this period, two other Auxiliary Cadet intelligence officers were killed while travelling from Macroom to Cork. See Abbott, *Police Casualties in Ireland*, p. 311 for details.

2    Jo lived next door to Fred Blemens, who was shot along with his father James Blemens. (Jo's home on Rockboro Terrace sits in a row of houses adjoining Blackrock Road in Cork.) Both were Protestant Unionists suspected of acting with other loyal citizens to provide information to the British. Mick Murphy and Connie Neenan explain the episode in the O'Malley Notebooks, UCD. Police compelled the *Cork Examiner* to run the threatening notices after the abductions of George Horgan and Tom Downing. I would argue that this action implicated the two as informers. Details and notices can be found in the *Cork Examiner*, 25 and 26 November 1920 and 1 and 10 December 1920; the *Cork Constitution*, 1 December 1920. In 1922 the Cork No. 1 Brigade officially confirmed the fates

of the victims, in written response to queries from the families of the missing (A/0535, MA). Liam de Róiste mentions the disappearances in the de Róiste Diaries, 27 and 28 November 1920, CAI. See also my MA thesis, pp. 25–35.

3   *Cork Examiner*, 10 December 1920. For other threatening notices, see the *Cork Constitution*, 13 October 1920, 24 November 1920 and 1, 12 December 1920; the *Cork Examiner*, 13 October 1920, 27 November 1920, 1 and 10 December 1920; and the *Cork Weekly News*, 18 September 1920. Similar notices appeared elsewhere in Munster during this period, most notably in Tralee.

4   *Cork Constitution*, 13 December 1920, and the *Cork Examiner*, 13 December 1920; Department of Defence Archives, P918 AO413, NLI; Seán Healy letter to O'Dongohue, Ms. 10,915, NLI; and Florence O'Donoghue 'The Sacking of Cork City by the British' in *Rebel Cork's Fighting Story*, p. 120.

5   While the Cork burnings did not match Republican propaganda charges of an entire city destroyed by fire, the scale and violence of the episode remains shocking, even in the context of the War of Independence. For details, see the confidential report to the Irish Secretary, 'Statements on the Incendiarism and Looting in Cork, with Report by Major-General Tudor, Police Advisor', CO/904/150, PRO; the Irish Labour and Trade Union Congress' pamphlet, *Who Burnt Cork City?*, and the *Cork Examiner* and *Cork Constitution* for the week of 12–18 December 1920.

6   Notice of Marital Law, *Cork Examiner*, 12 December 1920.

7   *Cork Constitution* and *Cork Examiner*, 13 December 1920; the full extract can be seen in Ms. 31,148, NLI. Brigade Chaplain Father Dominic O'Connor interpreted the excommunication order with theological creativity. Days after the Bishop's pronouncement, O'Connor advised Florrie O'Donoghue, 'These acts performed by the IV [Irish Volunteers], the army of the Republic, are not only not sinful but are good and meritorious and therefore the excommunication does not affect us. There is no need to worry about it. Let the boys keep going to Mass and Confession and Communion as usual.' Father Dominic did suggest discretion when dealing with the local clergy. 'Just as there is no necessity telling a priest that you went to Mass on Sunday, so there is no necessity to tell him one is in the IRA or that one has taken part in an ambush or kidnapping.' (Brigade Chaplain to Brigade Adjutant, 15 December 1920, Seán Hegarty Papers, UI49, CPM).

8   This was a major clash in the city centre that saw the mobilization of all company officers in the city's Second Battalion. For details see the *Cork Examiner* and *Cork Constitution*, 5 January 1921; RIC Inspector General's Monthly Report for January, CO 904/114, PRO; Mick Murphy's inflated account in his BMH statement; and Florrie O'Donoghue's article and notes on the ambush Ms. 31,301, NLI.

9   My thesis analyzes the February shootings in the context of the wider intelligence war in Cork city, see pp. 36–66 for profiles of the victims and the circumstances surrounding their deaths.

10  Coolavokig was the Brigade's largest fight of the war, engaging sixty IRA riflemen, with another sixty Volunteers armed with shotguns acting as scouts and flankers. After waiting in ambush for eight days, the column attacked a convoy of approximately eighty Auxiliary Cadets in a battle that lasted four hours. At least three Cadets were killed (including the convoy commander) and probably another dozen wounded. The column escaped without casualties. See Pat Lynch's account of the fight in *Rebel Cork's Fighting Story*, pp. 139–45; Dan Corkery, Charlie Brown, Seán Culhane, and Mick O'Sullivan in the O'Malley

Notebooks, UCD; and the *Cork Examiner*, 26 February 1921. Details of the shooting of off-duty British soldiers in the Cork city centre can be found in the *Cork Examiner*, 1 March 1921. Up to that point, the IRA apparently had not targeted unarmed British soldiers in the city.

11    For quotes about British 'murder gangs', see R. Langford's Pension Statement, CAI; Cork No. 1 Brigade Order dated 22 December 1920, Ms. 31,202, NLI; S. Lankford, *The Hope and the Sadness*, p. 260; and Seán MacSwiney's court-martial testimony, *Cork Constitution*, 25 February 1921. A number of killings and attempted assassinations of city Republicans took place in 1920 and 1921. Many of these attempts were made against Sinn Féin politicians. A chapter of my thesis covers this phenomena (pp. 92–101).

12    This list of city fatalities does not include two Volunteers who died on hunger strike (Terence MacSwiney and Joseph Murphy), an unarmed Volunteer shot during the July riot (J.P. O'Brien), a city officer killed by Auxiliaries in Ballyvourney (Christy Lucey), a prisoner shot by a jail sentry (Alderman Tadg Barry), or four others killed in munitions accidents. British forces killed a total of twenty-one of the twenty-seven Cork city Volunteers who died during the War of Independence. See the Cork No. 1 Brigade Casualty Roll, CPM.

13    The British Army's 6th Division's official history identifies O'Donoghue by name and rank (Adjutant, Cork No. 1 Brigade). See *History of the 6th Division in Ireland*, p. 72, Strickland Papers, IWM. Captured correspondence written by O'Donoghue also appears in the 1921 British Army pamphlet 'The Irish Republican Army' (p. 363, Strickland Papers, IWM). These notes implicated O'Donoghue in the 1920 attempted assassination of General Strickland. The British reported a large cache of Brigade papers captured at the Bowles farm in January 1921, and I suspect these papers led to the unveiling of O'Donoghue's identity. (See *History of the 6th Division in Ireland*, p. 70; and Hart, *British Intelligence in Ireland, 1920–1921*, p. 39). Cork No. 1 Brigade documents were also captured with Terence MacSwiney in August 1920 in the City Hall raid. MacSwiney had mentioned O'Donoghue by name in some of his earlier correspondence with Michael Collins, so these papers likewise could have led to O'Donoghue's identification.

# 9

# THE LETTERS OF FLORENCE O'DONOGHUE

## John Borgonovo

Florence O'Donoghue wrote the following letters to his new bride Josephine during the final ten weeks of the Irish War of Independence. During this time, Florrie left Cork city to serve as Adjutant and Intelligence Officer of the IRA's First Southern Division. Jo remained at her job in the Victoria Barracks and continued to pass information to the IRA. On the weekends, she would travel to Youghal to visit her son Reggie, then in hiding with her sister and brother-in-law.

In late February 1921, leaders of the IRA's most active brigades in Cork, Kerry, Tipperary, and Limerick (including Florrie and Seán O'Hegarty) met on their own initiative to coordinate cross-boundary cooperation and gunrunning.[1] This Conference led to a reorganization scheme implemented by IRA GHQ that added a command layer above the IRA brigade level. Groups of brigades in the same region were organized into divisions, under the command of a division staff reporting to GHQ.[2] On 24 April 1921, Munster's top IRA commanders met in Kippagh, North Cork to form the First Southern Division. They elected Liam Lynch (commander of the successful Cork No. 2 Brigade) Division OC, while Florrie O'Donoghue was selected Division Adjutant with the additional role of Intelligence Officer. The high IRB positions held by both men probably figured into their promotion.[3]

With a small staff of about half-a-dozen men, O'Donoghue and Lynch set about building up the First Southern Division structure. The Division area encompassed all the IRA brigades in counties Cork, Kerry, and Waterford, as well as the West Limerick Brigade. Lynch and O'Donoghue established division headquarters in the hills near the Cork/Kerry border. For both security reasons and to avoid overtaxing safe-house owners, the headquarters moved periodically. The Division's longest stay was at the farm of an Irish-speaking family named MacSuibne, near Coolea, in the Cork No. 1 Brigade's Eighth Battalion Area. The local Coolea Volunteer Company provided guards, scouts, and dispatch riders, along with a Cumann na mBan member to help with housekeeping.

Assuming the role of Division Adjutant, O'Donoghue tried to establish regular communications with the disparate units of the First Southern Division. He would have duplicated his efforts in Cork by creating message routes and way-stations throughout Munster. This was a painstaking and exacting task, but necessary for cooperation between units. Quick and efficient communication was particularly important for O'Donoghue's intelligence efforts.

As Division Intelligence Officer, O'Donoghue sought to improve information gathering in each brigade. Many local units had not assigned officers to intelligence duties, so O'Donoghue pressed commanders to fill these vacancies. Having spent the better part of three years as Brigade IO, O'Donoghue tried to impart his knowledge by issuing memoranda detailing methods and strategies for information gathering. He also demanded discipline concerning the compilation of local reports, which he considered the building block of an effective intelligence network.[4] Information flowing to him from various commands was digested and analysed, adding to his understanding of British forces.

O'Donoghue and Liam Lynch planned inspection tours of the various command areas in Cork, Kerry, Waterford, and West Limerick. During their visits they would arbitrate disputes, fill empty leadership positions (many officers had been arrested and killed), and rally hard-pressed commands.

Throughout this time, O'Donoghue served as the effective executive officer of the First Southern Division. His knowledge of IRA conditions and strengths in Munster was likely unrivalled in the country. By the Truce of 1921, he probably had a better grasp of the war situation than any officer in the IRA, including Michael Collins and Richard Mulcahy.

Florrie and Jo's letters to each other were sent via a secure route. They placed their correspondence in a small envelope, which was then sealed into a larger envelope addressed to a cover address and recipient, typically someone thought unconnected to the rebels. IRA couriers (usually teenage boys or Cumann na mBan volunteers) delivered the messages to a 'safe' address. A different IRA courier would be responsible for picking up mail at that safe address and delivering it to the next address in the message chain. (This is the communication system Florrie set up in 1917, which he describes in Chapter 2.) By this fashion, messages travelled hand-to-hand across the countryside. It would usually take about two days for a letter to be delivered from Florrie's location to Jo in Cork city. Jo never received the correspondence at her home, but had to pick them up at a safe house in the city.

The following letters are divided into nine batches. O'Donoghue typically wrote a series of letters, and then sent them to Jo all at once.

This often occurred once a week. Some of the letters include Irish language salutations and sign-offs. These have been translated into English, and are denoted by brackets.

The original letters can be found in O'Donoghue's papers in the National Library.[5]

## BATCH 1

May 3rd, 1921

[Dear sweetheart],
I arrived safely at my final destination this evening without incident. The quarters are just excellent, a great big roomy house, old-fashioned and easy going, and with that tranquil air of quietude about it, which in my mind is always associated with peace and contentful happiness. And you know I am fonder of the quietness of tranquil places than that of the noise and bustle of the busy haunts of men. That is why I always loved a certain quiet house you know in a quiet city road. Just now I am sitting in an armchair with a patchwork cushion like another I know, in a window, and writing on my knee. We have comfort, good food, peace, and safety, and I'm just delighted with everything.

We will be here for three workdays, then we will have some moving round for probably a week, and then back here again. This is to be a sort of base and HQ and resting and recuperation station. It is certainly ideal for the purpose.

I would like if, when you are sending the map, you could also send me the small haversack. It will be very useful, when out for a day or two and it is only necessary to carry a few things. I have absolutely everything else I want.

Well, and how have you been since? I am hoping to get a letter before I leave here. No need to say that every gentle thought that comes sweetly and stays in my mind in these quiet hours is a thought of you. No need to say that every dearest memory which makes reflection pleasant is a memory of you and of all you mean to me. This is as it should be, but it is no less beautiful because of that.

I am wondering if Cissie[6] got my letter yet, and what she will say. If you get a reply from her will you let me know? I sincerely hope for your sake she will not think badly of it. But I'm sure she won't. It has got too dark to write any more tonight, and in any case this will not go until tomorrow – so 'Goodnight'.

May 4th [1921]

Time for a hurried line only this morning. Very busy. Everything is A-1. It would be no harm to send a box of sulphuric ointment in case of necessity. I'm not insinuating that I want to be scratched already, but it's wise to take precautions.[7]

Florrie

## BATCH 2

May 4th, 1921

It has just struck me that if I have time to do so, it would be a good idea to write you a few lines each night, and send them in whenever I can. Always assuming that you can stand the strain of reading these things! This would be in the nature of a passing record of my feelings and movements in these days, and may perhaps be of some little interest later on.

The Staff of the Southern Division is entirely in the shade! The quarters are excellent, the food good (we had fresh meat for dinner yesterday), and the companions merry and cheerful and hardworking. It is pleasant to listen to the lively clatter of three typewriters, and to note the orderly, unconcerned way the business goes forward, as if the enemy were no nearer to us than in England! And then the sweet sunshine of the countryside streams in through the windows, and when you look out one sees a neat flower garden, green branches waving gently against a bold rugged background of purple hills. Birds are singing in the trees, and the clean vigour and keen fresh beauty of the springtime is all about.

We have regular hours of work and take our hours off to use them as we like. For recreation and exercise we have football and the staff is large enough, and young and lively enough, to make the game interesting. I have just come in now after a hard half-hour on the field. It will keep us in good sprinting form at any rate, and that is sometimes very useful!

We have elaborate precautions against surprise, and there is not the remotest possibility of our being surrounded without having warning. This morning at 4.30 a.m. there was a partial alarm. We did not get up, just stayed awake in bed for half an hour, until we were informed there was nothing in it.

This sitting here and talking to you on paper at night is the only relief and care for the loneliness of absence. It reminds me too of the other nights that are among the unforgettable, and perhaps these notes will bring some little pleasure to you in the weary hours. You will understand I know, that I cannot say in them all, or half, that I would wish, that there are many matters I may not even touch on, and these dearest to my heart, owing to the constant danger of their being lost or falling into the wrong hands. I would like to ask about special friends, about Willie and his brother and aunts;[8] but I know you will say as much about these things as you think wise in writing. Mark all my letters 'personal', as my assistants may think them ordinary matter.

That day, Cork newspapers reported an IRA attack in O'Donoghue's hometown of Rathmore. The local Rathmore Company, with some help from North Cork Volunteers, ambushed a party of RIC just outside the village. They used the body of an executed spy (an elderly itinerant named Thomas O'Sullivan who had been seen talking to police), to lure out a police patrol. Eight policemen were killed (six of them Black and Tans from England), the only survivor being an RIC officer who was providing information to the IRA.[9]

We had heard of the Rathmore ambush last night, but had no details until we got the paper this morning. Eight more heroes going home to 'merrie England'! There is also a story that apparitions have been seen at Knocknagree (Nell would know this place)[10] and all the country are going there for cures, etc. Now that I have disposed of the local gossip, I can return to my inconsequential drivel! But, no! It's impossible. I should have told you, we have a piano here, and also – my special pet abomination – a gramophone! The piano is all right, but the other – well, I give it the charity of silence. Just now one of the boys put on one of the Harry Hander's Scotch comics, and who could write with that going on! This is a weakness with one of the lads, so there is nothing for it but to desist. If I continue I'll be only writing in parts of the song, as I nearly wrote in scraps of a conversation one night into a matter of more importance. Do you remember?

May 5th, 1921

Today it has been wild and rainy, and the hill scenery is obliterated in fog. Still we have had a blazing turf fire, and no need to go abroad, therefore we have missed nothing save the evening football exercise. This being a holiday, although not going to Mass, we did not do over much work; so I have been reading de Wet's *Three Years' War* most of the day.[11] Tomorrow at 11.00 a.m. we are to start on our journeying, which will probably occupy a fortnight. But it has been pleasant indeed to sit round the fire and discuss the future and its problems, the past and its memories, and to recount and hear the laughing stories of fights and travels over a province in a twelve-month. And many a modest hero was here shyly telling his exploits in terse words; and wise young heads were set appreciatively to listen. It is a wonderful comradeship this, of men drawn from every walk of life, from the professor to the simple labourer, all united and contented in a noble service. One feels the better for such companionship.

Yet with every little anecdote, with every reference to Cork city – and references were not few, there came into my mind always the thought, the kindly proud thought, that successes which had been gained were due in many cases to someone who was all the world to me. It is now clear to me, when I have been able to see and talk things over with some men, that our assistance has meant more to them than even I had appreciated! Let me now confess, much of the credit was to me! How unjust it seems; but you will be glad to know how you have helped me – helped me indeed in more ways than one – and to feel as I do, that one day these many others whom you have unknowingly helped, and our dear land, will know and appreciate too.

## BATCH 3

May 6th, 1921

We have arrived, wet but safely, at perhaps the most historic spot in Munster – Gougane [Barra] – where Finn Barr taught and prayed, after twelve hours travelling and having covered about thirty miles. It started to rain shortly after we started at 11.00 a.m., and when we halted at Inch [Inchigeela] for dinner and a change of horses, we were a bit wet but quite cheerful. I may say I am already feeling the good effects of the change from the city, being absolutely in the best of form. A rather amusing incident occurred at this house. An old warrior, true-hearted but cranky, was talking to us about things in general just before we left. The woman of the house said she'd hoped we would be all right and safe, and added she was sure we would be, 'as God is good'. To which the old crank answered, 'Sure we know He's good, but God damn it, what can He do, the way things are?'[12]

This set me thinking as we drove along. It seems the fashion in some places to pity us. Now, I rather dislike this; sympathy we should have and every assistance, but pity, no! In reality we are the happiest people in Ireland today; and if some suffer that her freedom may be assured, it is not we but those who sit at home and keep vigil for our coming. The reason is, I suppose, that we are passing on a sacred spiritual tradition, and we are proud and strong in the knowledge that we are insuppressible and indestructible. Ideas never die, they are more powerful than acts or words, and we are the living expression of an idea 'which is older than any Empire, and will outlast every Empire'.[13] There! That's a dogmatic spasm tonight; but I'm a bit tired, and will defer some other things I have to say until mind and body are a little more refreshed.

## BATCH 4

May 8th, 1921

I sent you a letter yesterday morning, which I hope arrived safely. I did not write any notes last night because we had the luck to run into an area where one of our Columns was billeted, and what with the meeting of old friends, and the fact that the houses were crowded and I rather tired, I could do nothing.[14] Night before last we had the pleasure of sleeping in a hotel – and made suitable jokes about peace times etc. – in fact the Craig–de Valera interview was quite appropriate.[15] Yesterday we marched about fifteen miles, over Doughill, Douce, and Shehy mountains into the Dunmanway district. This was five hours journey over very bad country from the point of view of travel, but incomparable in rugged and picturesque mountain scenery. From the top of Douce we had a glorious view of the surrounding hills in all their austere grandeur, of Inchigeela Lakes sparkling in the sunshine to the east, and Bantry Bay stretching out seawards to the west. Seán [O'Hegarty] was with us, and beguiled the way with many a jest and tale told in his own inimitable way. We had with us also a schoolteacher, and Seán in speaking about him later in the day said, 'I met two men today. One of them was a schoolmaster, and the other had no money either'!

We had a strange reception. We walked into a house which we thought was the one we were going to. No one said a word to us – a most amazing thing. But the absolute limit was reached when the man of the house positively identified me as having been in the district with a party of Auxies some time previously! So much for the alleged innocent and harmless looking appearance, which I thought was my proud possession and passport to salvation! When it was clearly demonstrated to him that he was mistaken, it was amusing to see his still doubtful attitude towards me. Pray don't imagine from this that I have cultivated a ferocious or 'murder gang' appearance. If I may venture an opinion, I would say it was the khaki shirt!

Last night we had a meeting, lasting well into the small hours.[16] This morning we had another before starting back for Gougane [Barra].

We came by car and had a glorious drive over little winding ribbons of white roads that crept in and out between the grey rocks and the purple and brown of the heathy rugged hills. We asked a man on the road how far it was to Ballingeary. He answered, 'Oh, 'tis only four mountains.' Quite a new way of measuring distance. I heard a good story, south. A party of military came into a district where our men had been in ambush for them for some days previously. The officer in charge in searching one house asked an old man there if he had seen the Shinners. The old man answered, 'I did then, they were here yesterday, and now that I think of it, 'twas ye they were looking for.' And then as an afterthought, 'Maybe 'twas as good ye didn't meet.'

Well we are back in our hotel again tonight, and Seán has kept us amused all night. We were discussing peace a while ago and he said, referring to the fact that we hadn't seen a paper in three days, 'What will happen is that we'll all wake up some morning to find ourselves members of the civil population, with peace made and our occupation and our power gone. Then I'll go back to the poorhouse, and I suppose you'll start selling collars again.' Quite a cheerful prospect what? Well, I'm for bed, we have a long journey ahead tomorrow – we are going into the 'Kingdom of Kerry'.

As previously mentioned, on 4 May 1921, Volunteers in O'Donoghue's native Rathmore killed eight RIC in an ambush just outside town. In the following days, newspapers reported Rathmore's civilian population nervously anticipating British reprisals. 'A large percentage of people have left the village and business is practically suspended. The Great Southern & Western Railway Company have issued directions to its stations on their line not to accept goods for Rathmore until further orders.' The hammer fell the following day. 'Last evening a special troop train arrived at Rathmore. The military, who were accompanied by police, marched to the scene of Wednesday's ambush, and, as official reprisals, the following farmhouses nearest the scene were burned: Timothy Moynihan, Thos O'Connor,[17] Garret Nagle, and Patrick Donoghue. Rain was falling as the four families were ordered out.'[18]

May 9th [1921]

After a few hours tramp across the mountains to Kilgarvan today, I got Saturday's paper and saw for the first time that our house at home had been burned. Although I anticipated this to some extent, still I got a shock when I saw it. The thought of those fire-blackened ruins of the place where I was born took all the sunshine out of a day that might have been glorious and happy.

Still I must not worry too much over this, only I am so sorry for my aged parents. It is hard enough for them to have the roof burned over their heads at their time of life. It is different for us who are young, and who can face disaster with calm and steady resolution, knowing that we yet will turn it into victory. It is a consolation to me to know that I have done the enemy more damage than they will ever be able to do me or mine; and indeed my actions in the future will lose nothing from the recollection of their cowardice in destroying a house in which there was not even a man of military age. I have written Nell today hoping to get some news of the matter.

Well, to return to the story of my wanderings – and it is becoming a story! In our tramp across the mountains today we had a guide, a shrewd mountainy man, who told us many interesting things of the lore of the wild life of the hills. The birds and animals of the wild were his friends; every rock and stream and headland were familiar to him, and it was delightful to hear him roll off the beautiful soft-sounding Gaelic names of the places as we passed through. At the end of the tramp when we came to the place near Kilgarvan where we were to get a car, we stopped at a house for dinner. Just as we were about to leave again a scout came in to report. He saluted, and told us, 'Four lorries of military on the road between Kenmare and Killarney.' As we had to pass that way we asked what they were doing, and he answered, with just a trace of a smile, 'They are behind there, round a road trench explaining their own misfortune to each other.' This was our first experience of the Kerry scouts, but it struck us rather favourably, and later on we saw that they could be other things as well as humorous. Our next twelve miles in a car was in the nature of a march past. On every vantage point above the road scouts were posted, and we could see their messages passing from hill to hill to ensure our safety. At every cross roads a straight-limbed country boy in his working clothes clicked his heels smartly and saluted as we went past. Everywhere we saw signs of extraordinary efficiency and wonderful organization. It is a never-ending source of wonder to me, and indeed pride too, to note what a splendid organization has been beaten out of this raw material in these last few years. But I know too what toils of brain and body, what patience and courage and loyalty have gone into the work. I can say without exaggeration that I have done my share of the toiling. But we are repaid. No king or prince in Europe could have been treated with the care and honour they bestowed on us. Being a Kerryman, they were proud to make a fuss over me. And I have reason to be proud of them.

When we came to the point at the bottom of Windy Gap where the car could go no further, we found mountain ponies saddled and waiting to take us over the Gap. Behold us then, with knapsacks on our backs, Sam Browne's[19] and revolvers, and rifles across our backs, riding over the pass into the reddening west. It was a glorious evening. We got down to the shore of the Upper Lake, and there found a boat with two sturdy oarsmen ready to take us across to the bottom of the Gap of Dunloe. The lake was smooth as glass, and you may be sure we made suitable comments about the boating on Killarney's lakes with a war on. I will only say that the beauties of this spot have not been exaggerated.[20] We perhaps appreciated it all the more because we had pointed out to us the various places at which poor devils of tourists have to pay for the pleasure. At the bottom of the Gap of Dunloe we found more mountain ponies awaiting us, and we started on the last and most wonderful stage of our journey. I had a rather exciting time. The pony I had was frisky, and the one of my companion rather slow-going. We were somewhat behind the rest of the party, and after a time I drew well ahead of my companion. I tried to get my pony to 'stand and wait' but he wasn't built that way. He proceeded to execute a step dance on the edge of the precipice which runs along the corkscrew road. After that I thought it better to let him go on. Night closed down just as I was getting to the top of the Gap. The scenery was too entirely stupendous in bold and rugged beauty to make any attempt at description by me impossible. Just imagine piles of mighty rock heaved up 2,000 feet above the road at either side, gigantic boulders overhanging at many points, and overhead only a ragged strip of star-lit sky showing between the cliffs. A winding road twisting and turning down this mile-long avenue, and all the time the crashing music of foamy waterfalls to keep one company, made indeed an unforgettable impression. At the bottom I waited for my companion and soon we came to the end of our journey, and also to the most amazing thing of all in this amazing day's journey. It is so wonderful that I will write not one word about it, but will tell you sometime. Also I have a bundle of stories I must tell you when we meet again. And, oh, how I look forward to the day. I write all this nonsense to fill up every minute of my spare time. I'm very tired now though and will write no more tonight.

May 10th, 1921

Today it rained like anything. Meetings and conferences occupied most of the day, but in the evening we moved by car again into West Kerry. The same scouting arrangements impressed us, and we arrived safely but very much soaked. However, after a change of clothes and a feed we felt ourselves again. Nothing exciting today, and as it has been long for me, I'll close. I'm in the very best of form though, and this country work is doing me much good.

May 11th, 1921

After finishing my notes last night we had a further meeting which lasted until 3.00 a.m. Then we got to bed, and made up for the lost sleep by staying there until 12 o'clock today. We were at a very pretty place at the head of Dingle Bay, and the scenery hereabouts is a pleasing contrast to the wild mountain places we have been working through in the past few days. The country is flat and prosperous looking; the brightly-painted ivy-clad farm houses reminding me somewhat of South of England homes. But how different the spirit and mind of the people! Here the kindly, sympathetic, uneffusive welcome of the true Gael awaits you; in every house, rich or poor, we met keen intelligent minds, clean with the sunny freshness of nature. Soft voices these people have, and rugged, faithful, unshakable hearts. In every house one can get good books to read; and although I detest gramophones I forgave some of them because of the excellence of the selection of records.

We are getting ahead splendidly with our work, and indeed faster than we anticipated, and expect to be back by the middle of next week. And then I mean to have a day or two off and run in to see you. I'm just beginning to grow a bit uneasy because I have not heard a single word either from you or Nell, Aggie, or Babe[21] since I came out. However, a mail is due tomorrow morning, and it may bring something. You may be sure I look forward to each post anxiously for news of you, and go through it expectantly and always hopeful.

We moved inland today but only a short distance; here we are to stay until Friday morning – all being well. We will then be finished in Kerry, and will be moving up to the last stage of our journey. I am consoled to know that we are not wasting an hour anywhere.

Fl.

## BATCH 5

May 12th, 1921

This morning we moved again in the Castleisland direction. It was gloriously fine and bracing. Every hedge dew-wet and soft and shimmering green. On every roadside primroses and violets made a riot of delicate colour along the green and mossy banks. The larks sang a carol of peace and sweet contentment overhead, and all the air was filled with the sounds and smells of spring. How I wished that the apparent peace was real, and that you and I were together in the morning sunshine on some open dewy lawn, with the full bright day of our lifetime before us, and our love to light and beautify the world. Vain wishing just now. But some day I promise myself the pleasure and joy of we two visiting these places that I have passed with, sometimes, a lonely heart.

I have had no word from Cork today though the mail came in. I'm wondering if anything could be wrong. I'm not worrying, mind you, only I'd love to get a letter from you. So I'm sending this along now – finishing it up early for the purpose – and I hope it will reach you safely.

I hope to be back in the middle of next week. Needless to say, I'm looking forward. Give my love to all – and may God bless and guard ye.

Fl.

May 13th, 1921

After I had finished and sent off a few day's notes to you last night, we packed up and did a night march to the Co. Limerick border. We came to the decision to move finally, owing to the fact that we had been playing hide and seek with the military since the previous night, otherwise we would have waited till the next morning.

At one time yesterday, three lorries [British] were reported a mile away coming in our direction. I am interested in noting the thrilled feeling which fills the very air of a house when a scout comes in and makes such a dramatic announcement in terse words. Cool, unhurried preparations are made; men, seeing that everything is in order, wait with apparent unconcern, chatting as usual but with every sense alert; the women in the house go on with their every day work as calmly as if the dreaded questions of what fate the next few minutes held was never knocking at their hearts. Truly the people have become immune to war, they have a self-confidence and a courage which is indeed heroic. The tenseness of the waiting was broken in this instance by the unfailing touch of humour which keeps us from growing morose. The next report was that one lorry had fallen into a trench half a mile away. So we calmly proceeded with our work, while the enemy worked frantically to extricate their car and get home before night came on.

Well, we travelled until 4.00 a.m. and then as the dawn was whiten-
ing in the East we put ourselves snugly to bed. We got up again at 2
o'clock and resumed our journey towards the banks of the Shannon
[River]. And here we arrived without incident about 10 o'clock and we
fairly tired withal. Tonight we can see the mouth of the lordly
Shannon, and the lights of the Loop Head on the Clare side flashing
out in the darkness. It is very rich and open country, but I like it not
so well as the more rugged places of Cork and Kerry. 'The savage loves
his native shore.'[22]

May 14th [1921]

Going to bed about 2.00 a.m. did not conduce to early rising today, but
we fairly beat all records by not getting up until 2.30 p.m! However, it
was possible for us to rest as we have no meeting till tomorrow, and
only about nine miles more to travel before we retrace our steps
towards home. Now, we have been dodging an enemy column all day,
in (to us at least) most awful country. Accustomed as we were to
broken and hilly country, this, where there are only eminences of
moor-land, seems as flat as a billiard table. We had to march that nine
miles, except that we doubled [jogged] one half mile across a
particularly flat and dangerous patch. I've had the impression all day
that we are visible for about twenty miles on all sides, but of course it's
imagination. Well, eventually we arrived at our destination, having got
in behind the enemy column into the area they had just left. A
glorious view it is indeed from this little eminence above the Shannon.
A huge saucer-shaped plain, immense in dim blue shade, stretching
away to the foot of the Galtees, the mountains of Clare looking down
from either side, and standing sentinel over the little towns whose
spires shoot up here and there, dotting the plain with points of
brilliance, standing out from the emerald green of fields criss-crossed
with yellow gorse-covered hedges. This is the furthermost point of our
travel, tomorrow evening we start for home, please God, and I'm not
sorry. County Limerick is noted among our men for good quarters. We
struck the best, except than I cannot have the feeling of security here
that I find elsewhere.

May 15th [1921]

Regarding my remarks last night re. Quarters. I noticed another little
difference this morning. While waiting for breakfast, I had a look
round for a book, and had to content my soul in its early morning

asking for light literature, with a battered copy of Mrs Beeton's Cookery Book! Perhaps this was due to the fact that all the girls in the house were old maids, and I suppose it was only natural that cookery should be of first importance! But I smiled when I remembered the assurance of the Billets officer last night when he told us he was putting us in most *comfortable* quarters.[23]

There is nothing wrong with all this forty-two-mile stretch of rich plain, except that its richness and consequent ease of life has made its people a little less sensitive to that beauty and spiritual essence to which the souls of the people have clung with, it seems, a natural instinct in their poverty and their sorrow. In the wild places and the poor the spirit is fiercer, the romantic more apparent, and the keen hard mind more aggressive than here where the luxury has softened men, even if only a little.

Well, our dear friend, the enemy, has been paying special attention to us today, and now, with our work finished, we have tonight worked through his lines. Although he had partly located us and tried to cut us off, we have got through and are resting again in the County Cork on our way home. It has been as exciting a day as I have had for a long time, and at one time things really looked a bit blue. But now we are in a safe retreat and can smile at the attempt which we have no doubt will be made tomorrow morning to catch us in the net, the spreading of which we have seen arrangements being made for the last two days. And so we intend to sleep content, and having done much travelling we feel like resting. One day from home!

May 16th [1921]

Our expectations were realized. The enemy made a sweep at 4.00 a.m. this morning, utilizing his troops as we expected he would. We were, as we had taken good care to be, outside the net; but unfortunately, for some reason not now explained they got one of our best men in this area.[24] However, no use in grumbling.

We are back safely, and our wanderings for the time being finished. My intention was at first to go into town tomorrow, but as I should leave very early in the morning, and it is now very late, I have decided to wait until Wednesday. I have just found that two lots of letters for me are gone around the country after me. I suppose your letters if you sent any are gone in that lot. There is nothing anyhow for me. They may reach here before I leave for town. Anyhow it is only a short time till we meet again and talk one of our old long talks – even into the small hours of the morning. And I suppose Kitty[25] will abuse us as of yore!

May 24<sup>th</sup> [1921]

The attached few sheets were written before I went in to town, but I send them along now as they stand.

Of course, as I told you I got all the letters referred to in the last page before I went in.

Fl.

> Cork city had grown even more dangerous for wanted men like O'Donoghue. Hundreds of British troops patrolled the city, held up pedestrians, and simply interned anyone who aroused their suspicion. Conditions became so bad that many of the city's prominent Volunteer officers sought safety in the hills near Florrie's Division Headquarters. The thousands of Irish prisoners eventually included a number of O'Donoghue's Cork colleagues such as Tom Crofts, Matt Ryan, Seán Culhane, Seán MacSwiney, Sandow Donovan, and Mick Murphy.[26]
>
> In such conditions O'Donoghue's visits to Jo in Cork were very hazardous.

## BATCH 6

May 24<sup>th</sup>, 1921

Although not in the district we had intended to stay, we are settled down very comfortably in our new quarters, and it is even quieter and more remote here than in the other place. I like it very much, but I'm afraid the solitude will be such that we will lose touch altogether with the battling world and the fight going on in our part of it, and be driven in desperation to drink or writing poetry or something equally foolish. However, there is no immediate danger that any such calamity will befall. There is rather more than enough work to keep our minds fully occupied.

Since I came back I have not had time to write a line until today, but that has not prevented my mind from dwelling lovingly on the memory of a few days that were truly beautiful and happy. In the calm hours when no passion stirs, and in this quiet place where nature smiles with the eternal wistfulness of its protecting love, there comes sweetly to my mind that memory of days and places quiet and happy, of every gentle word and act forever inseparably associated with you. And unutterable thoughts, too sweet and gentle for any words to express, surround me with their magic, and weave out dreams of days and things that are to be. It seems to me that you have made splendid and holy the common thing called life, that out of your great love you have built an edifice reaching to heaven, and that to every beautiful thing in this world you have given a new loveliness.

Always your words come back to me, 'Today was beautiful, but it was very sad.' There is a sadness in all great beauty, and in all great love. But is it not a sadness one can bear much better than the changeful warmth of mere passion or the cold feeling of indifference? Yes, a thousand times, yes. And this is changeless and immutable, it will survive sorrow and suffering, it will go through the fires of hell if need be. Let us thank God for our sadness.

May 25th, 1921

Last evening Seán [O'Hegarty] came, and as he was travelling on westward we went a few miles with him for the walk. Before the red sun set, the pensive calm of evening settled down in the dim blue valleys, the purple hills folded us in their strong arms, shutting out the world. All nature seemed sweet and drowsy, blue mist wreathes wandered in the valleys and the distant hills grew indistinct, as if she half-closed her eyes and loosened her hair before going to sleep. A memory came to me of half-closed eyes with bright lights in them, and there was a song in my heart all night for the sad beauty of this world. I was not really lonely I think; this reality was too big and certain, too wonderful and splendid to make my happiness lonely.

Coming back across the mountain in the gathering dusk we came to a brawling mountain stream. And there we started like children again hunting under stones for trout, exploring here and there, shouting out our finds to each other, as carefree for the moment as if we were lads at school again. Wild and romantic nooks there were, which the imagination could easily people with figures of the past, and the setting of many a story cast in the rugged and mysterious precincts of these little-travelled places. How many walked these mountains before in all the years, and what stories they had, what joy and sorrow, what love and grief filled the hearts of those who passed and are no more? Well someday when, 'The warfare's finished, and the victory won, and all the pageant of our triumph done.' I will return to see these hills I love, and tell you there the thoughts, the sweet and gentle thoughts, that would blow into my brain with the soft south wind as it wandered across the heather.

May 27th, 1921

Beloved,
Owing to being very busy I didn't have time to write anything last

night, and this is only a very hurried note. I send you herewith the very few notes written since I came out, and a few written before I went in last time.

I'm not going in this weekend, and do not know about next week until Joe [O'Connor] comes out. We expect him tonight or tomorrow. Will write you again. Hope you will be able to get back from Youghal alright. I see in today's paper that the line is blocked. Those terrible Shinners![27]

I left the pencils in, I think, the table drawer in the hall stand, would you send them out to me, also a pair of the socks I left. By the way, you remember the pocket dictionary which served one Division? If you don't need it, it would now serve another.[28] I'd like to have it for more reasons than one. Are you keeping well? May God send his angels to watch over you and guard you in all your ways.

With all my love,
FL


May 28th, 1921

This is Saturday and Joe has not turned up yet. I hope nothing has happened to him. I had thought to be in town again today but, unfortunately, I have no definite prospect of when I can go in yet. I hope you got back from Youghal alright, and that 'Jerry' came up with you. Give him my love.

We have very good quarters and food here, and I am delighted with it. It is an oasis of quietude hidden away from all the turmoil of the world. There is an old man and woman in the house, splendid, simple characters, and neither of them can speak a single word of English! It is amusing to see us try to hold a conversation. My few words of Irish are bad enough, but the merry youth I told you about, the typewriter thumper,[29] is the pink limit. He does keep us amused. We have a much better service of newspapers etc. here than we had on the other side. We get the [Cork] Examiner every day about 12 o'clock and Independent of the day before at the same time. Washing, etc., is all arranged for, and we intend to stay here till the end of June. By the way, you can send unimportant stuff through the post to me to the address I sent in to Nell for newspapers. Tell her the same.


May 29th, '21

This being Sunday we only did half a day's work, having slept the other half of the day. Nice, isn't it? But there is a sort of cause. Joe arrived at

4.00 a.m. and of course woke us up and we had to discuss all the latest news from Cork and Dublin. This took a long time, consequently the rising was late.

I had been restless for a few days past on account of the uncertainty as to whether I should go to Dublin or not. I was not, indeed, one bit keen on going, but would have been glad to have the excuse to go in to town and see ye all. Well it is settled now for the moment at least, and I can resign myself to the existing circumstances when I know definitely where I stand. I am not to go to Dublin for the present, and not to go at all if it can possibly be avoided. They do not want me to take the risk of going up unless it is absolutely necessary. This is really very kind – everybody is kind to me – and I am duly grateful. If it should be necessary for me to go, I will hear from them at the end of this week or beginning of next. So I have decided, not having a strong tale to spin, not to go in to town this week, but I will try and get off a few days, even if not going to Dublin, in the middle of next week. I hope you won't be as disappointed as I am, but I know you will understand. It is like old times to have Joe here again.[30]

30th May [1921]

I will have an opportunity of sending this on its way in to you early in the morning, so I will just finish up quickly. Will you send me out two ounces of Ruddel's 'Maltan Mixture' tobacco; don't send more as it would only be getting dry. If you can't get 'Maltan' get one ounce of lighter stuff, it will do for the present. I'd like to get too, another small box of cough lozenges, as I have not got quite rid of my cough yet. It's nothing much though.

How did those snaps taken at Blackrock turn out? I'd like to see one. Will you write a few lines if you have time, dear, telling me how you are getting on since, and whether you have took up that position which we discussed.

Herewith £10. I send this in as I am not going myself and you may need it.

May God bless and keep you,
Fl.

May 31st, '21

This morning the OC [Liam Lynch] and Joe moved on a week's tour of inspections and left me in charge of HQ. I should have gone and finished the round I was on before I went in to town last, but Joe is arranging to do my work so that I can remain here. Which is very good of him. I have only my cheerful typist at the moment, but we have so much work that we are unlikely to be lonely. We have just come in from a four mile walk after our day's work.

Seán [O'Hegarty] came across to see us this afternoon, and stayed about an hour.[31] He is in the best of form. Our establishment is likely to be at about its present strength for about a week; and after that, I have a scheme for getting a few days off.

Things pass quietly here. So quiet is everything that I haven't the inspiration of the clash of life which seems to be essential to make me write anything. And in any case, I've almost written myself out in lectures, notes, orders, circulars, etc. The most exciting thing that happens here, is that one way or another an urgent dispatch has managed to be delivered in the small hours every blessed night since we came here. We have tried to avoid it, but still it happens. And you can imagine how I would feel when I have properly waked myself up at 2.00 a.m., rubbed the sleep out of my eyes, and read a dispatch. Then try and gather the cobwebs off the brain, make a decision, find pen and paper, and write a reply! Last night when the inevitable happened (we are beginning to regard it as inevitable), Moss – the typist – half waked, and asked me in a sleepy voice, 'Is it the Auxies?' I said no. 'Well,' he said, 'tis a recognized thing in future that I'm not going to wake up unless they come!' And he promptly went to sleep again. I hope no one calls tonight, but I suppose it is a vain hope. I heard today that a parcel for me is coming out from town tomorrow, so I am hopeful that perhaps I will have a letter from you and that will be the next best thing to seeing you. It's lonely sometimes, and I do look forward to a letter. Soft be your sleep my dear, and sweet and gentle all your thoughts. 'Goodnight.'

## BATCH 7

June 1st, '21

The inevitable did happen again last night. Just as we were undressing for bed a dispatch came. However, that was ever so much better than 2.00 a.m. and we had a peaceable night afterwards. My parcel did not come in the morning post today, and the night one has not come in yet, so I am still awaiting your letter.

I had a letter from Jack Cody this morning, you remember Jack?[32] Well, it started off in this way, 'Dear F., How the hell are you? I heard you were fluttering round the country lately on a horse, doing Buffalo Bill. Do you want an ADC [aide-de-camp], I'd like the job.' Having delivered himself of such noble and profound sentiments, he proceeded in very forcible language to affirm that he was enjoying the country life immensely. He is located somewhere in the mountains west, and is in all probability engaged in growing a moustache (which is the fashion with embryo refugees) and singing songs to his hearts content.[33] Which is not such a bad occupation for the summertime.

My parcel arrived, but alas! Without a letter from you. I had a letter from Nell, written on the 20th in which she said she had got my letter and was waiting for you to call for yours. She told me that you had got back from Youghal all right, and also that she would write again the next day, in which you would probably send a letter also. So that's not too bad. I see from the letter that ye compelled Nell to stay in Youghal until Tuesday morning – and I'm sure it took some compulsion. I am glad of this. I hope she is feeling the better for the holiday, and also that you, yourself had a good time and feel well again.

The weather, which had been wet and wintry here for a few days past, picked up suddenly today, and is now gloriously fine. The 'Hills of Home'[34] as I call those which stood sentinel over my childhood, and were the purple gates through which wandered many a wayward fancy in youth into the rosette which lay undiscovered beyond – these hills stand out, clear-cut and dimly blue, against the bright background of a summer sky. And sometimes my thoughts wander over them now, looking from the other side than childhood's.

2nd June [1921]

Nothing very exciting today except that the inevitable dispatch rider came again this morning 'at the critical hour of dawn'. It was just 4.00 a.m. and the first faint lights, exquisite in form and colour, looked in on the world through the dim windows of the east. I stayed up to see the glorious dawn, and the red sun came up radiant over the hills, which was a compensation indeed for being called so early.

Seán came to see us again today, and as usual, had a good story. It seems another of our lads, as hard a case as himself, and Seán were going home a few nights ago when they met a large flock of geese in a deserted part of the road. Not having had any fresh meat for a couple weeks, Seán suggested that they bring one of the geese home and cook it. The other lad thought it a brilliant suggestion, so they caught one and tried to wring its neck. There their troubles began, they couldn't kill the bird! However, after a terrific struggle they managed to choke it, and started for home triumphantly, carrying the bird between them – a wing each. Everyone was in bed. Next morning the girl in the house asked them where in the name of God they got so-and-so's gander. They explained. It seems the gander was sixteen-years-old, and an institution in the parish! Well, there was nothing to do but make the best of a bad job and cook him. The girl vowed that as fast as she plucked the feathers out of him in one place they grew somewhere else, and there was some serious doubt as to whether he was really dead. Anyway, they boiled him for two days, finally desisting last night, and confessed that the sixteen-year-old gander was too much even for their appetites for fresh meat! As Seán said, 'He was all muscle'!

That reminds me of another good story he told us the last day he was here. A man living back in one of the remotest glens, where he never sees a stranger from year's end to year's end, went in to Cork about a week ago. He has a watch in which he has the most absolute and childlike faith. He compared the time as shown by the watch with Shandon,[35] and they did not agree. He addressed Shandon thusly: 'Be —— , you're wrong this time Shandon – but 'tis seldom with you.'

3rd June [1921]

The weather is absolutely glorious now, and last evening Moss and I had a most delightful tramp over the mountains. There is a very friendly old sheep dog here and he comes with us every evening. It is computed that he is about the same age as Seán's gander! Now each night at 9 o'clock, which is the time when we start for our walk (you have been indoors an hour before that),[36] the dog comes along and wags his tail, and puts his nose in our hands, goes off a short way, looks wistfully at us, and comes back again. I think he's as fond of the ramble in the wild places as we are ourselves.

We went exploring in a new direction last night, and we found a most wonderful rugged and romantic place. On impulse we turned off the little bye-road, along a patch which lost itself among the rocks a short distance away. Soon the path entered a rocky, wooded glen, steep on either side, the trees closing their branches overhead, their burnished leaves making exquisite tracery of light and shade against the sunset-sky. Here and there a break in the rocks gave a glimpse at green valleys, or little glens between the hills, with perhaps only one house in them, sometimes two or three. The houses are usually very white and neat, and look snug and tidy in their setting of dark green trees and purple mountain background. Little fields of every imaginable shape, some tilled, some in meadows or pasture land, stone-fenced and well defined, are jammed in everywhere between heathy barren hillocks or mighty boulders of hard rock upstanding in the landscape. How these fields testify to the unceasing patient toil of these hardy mountainy men! Even at this late hour men were working in the fields.

Following the winding path we came to a brawling mountain stream, that wound its way down with many a leaping rush and fall, and many quiet pools of wine-dark water in the flat stretches, to the wider valley below. As we followed the banks of this stream upwards, it reminded me of the people that live about it, and I thought I saw a similarity in them. Now it was calm and unruffled, deep and slow and gentle, meandering its way quietly and in no hurry; again in another place it sang merrily over the stones, busy and content; at other times again when it roared and leaped from rock to rock, flashing white, stately and strong, it rather awed one, as if to impress the fact that, like the people, though it has its quiet days and its rather sad days of solitude, it has its proud days of leaping strength and power.

Always in my mind was the thought, 'if you were here'. We made a short cut home across the hills with the aid of a compass and arrived just at dark, our heads full of old stories and romance.

In early June, the British Army swept the mountains of West Cork and Kerry, in an operation Republicans dubbed 'The Great Round-up'. Due to its favourable terrain and friendly population, the area served as a sanctuary for different IRA Brigade columns and headquarters staffs, including Florrie's First Southern Division. The British Army decided to use its great numeric superiority to surround the area and bag the Republican forces inside. Thousands of soldiers would search every structure in the area and detain and question the entire male population.

While the round-up strategy seemed unbeatable in theory to British staff officers, it proved clumsy and ineffective in practice. Such complex troop deployments required significant preparations that proved impossible to hide from the IRA's many sympathizers. The rebels were typically tipped off well in advance, allowing them time to escape the encirclement. In the case of 'The Great Roundup', Florrie reported that British General Strickland's order was in the IRA's hands 'almost as soon as it reached his own commanders'.[37] One can only speculate on the source of the intercepted order.

## 4th June '21

Today we have had wars and rumours of wars, in a manner of speaking, or rather raids and rumours of raids. Eight hundred military arrived in Macroom, three Columns, each one hundred fifty strong, camped south in Dunmaway and Clonakilty area. The preparations for a huge sweep are evident, and we have a fair idea of the area it will cover.[38] We are, I think, outside its scope and if we are not we will easily get there. So we don't worry. As Moss said, ''Tis an understood thing that we can't stop 'em.' We were called up at 2.30 a.m. and were sure it was an order to 'hike', but no, it was only the midnight post again.

The weather continues to be glorious, the evenings are waking dreams of heavenly happiness. We go out as usual when our day's work is done, to watch the wondrous sunsets, the beautiful exchanging hues of sky and cloud, and the red sun drawing the purple curtains of the hills across the western doorway of his chamber when he retires to rest. The cuckoos call softly across the valley, and on the still air the voices of children come up from the farmhouses in the valley. How beautiful it would be in your garden this evening!

9ᵗʰ June '21
9.00 p.m.

[Dear sweetheart,]
A hurried line to say I arrived safely at 6.00 a.m. this morning. After a good sleep now and up to the eyes in work. Feeling A-1 too. I hope you got back alright, I had just time for the train.

Your parcel did not come yet, but I'm told this is a usual thing with parcels in this district, as they take almost a week. However it's alright – the cold is practically gone today.

Attached were all written before I went in. Our old friend [The British] did not come near our place at all.

Whenever you are sending next, send me two yards of strong window blind cord – any colour.

F O'D

The 'Great Round-up' ended in frustration for the British. Despite reports of large rebel concentrations in the area, the Crown forces never came to grips with the IRA. Republican flying columns, headquarters staffs, and local Volunteers vacated the area, and the IRA suffered almost no casualties in the operation. Some Volunteers did find themselves caught in the dragnet, but were able to bluff their way past British troops who had no way of identifying wanted men. However, the area remained a dangerous place, as trigger-happy British soldiers shot dead two unarmed Volunteers near Florrie's native Rathmore, and critically wounded an elderly farmer.[39]

Florrie narrowly missed capture during the operation. A party of British troops moved towards O'Donoghue's headquarters, which he would not vacate until the last moment. O'Donoghue buried his typewriter, but refused to abandon his papers, which he bound up and carried with him. By the time his small party left the farm, it found itself nearly surrounded. The group hid from planes and dodged British cavalry and foot patrols until ultimately finding a safe route out of the vicinity. O'Donoghue then directed one of his exasperated scouts to return to the encircled area and guide other IRA fugitives out through the gap.[40]

## June 14th, 1921

Since our return, after the visit of our friends the enemy, we have been so busy that I have not had time to set down a single word. Much work always accumulates after a few days' inattention to it; and the consequent task of getting through it is heavy. However it is now cleared off again, and today is a sort of national holiday in comparison to the last few days.

The recent attempted round-up – officially termed in the reports, military manoeuvres – was a huge fiasco. Fourteen different parties, converging from every point of the compass, took part; all working towards Claydagh, where 1,000 armed rebels were popularly supposed to be encamped.[41] The enemy had between 2,000 and 3,000 men, of all arms, with aeroplanes, etc. But it was a most remarkable thing that those rebels somehow disappeared, and not even the vanishing coat-tails of one could be seen anywhere. But I know that quite a goodly number of amused pairs of eyes (mine were one) watched the weary return of the sweating, footsore English after their gallant but fruitless quest. We really consider that our friends were most discourteous in not even calling at our residence to enquire if we were home! They might indeed have called and not incon-venienced themselves thereby. We were not of course at home to give them greeting, nevertheless we feel disappointed! However, I suppose this is only one little example of man's ingratitude which we must grin and bear. And didn't we grin!

I should report that I had a pleasant journey back after I left you – and an unexpected piece of good fortune. Joe [O'Connor] picked me up, and we decided to continue our journey to the end straight away. It was a glorious night though a bit cold, and we arrived here about 6.00 a.m. After which we went to bed and slept a record sleep.

How did you get home that evening? And how have you been keeping since? I hope you have got the short note I sent in with some things written before I went to town. Joe has gone in again, you may possibly see him, and we are expecting him back tonight or tomorrow. My cold was quite all right yesterday, but for some unaccountable reason we got it back again today. I can't explain it, as the weather is beautiful and fine, and I haven't been out of doors hardly since I returned. Working all the time. But I'm sure it won't last long now either – it's only in the head!

June 15th [1921]

Abuse of the Post Office is popular nowadays, but I had so little dealings with that hoory institution that its shortcomings were unfelt until today. It has indeed surpassed itself by delivering your parcel after a fortnight. I sent you a note on its arrival today, which I hope you will get all right.

It is evident that we are about to have some slight change in the situation in Ireland within the next month. Official reprisals are certainly at an end, which is a big victory for us. The message which has been circulated to enemy police concerning the matter is sufficiently doleful. And no doubt only a very pressing necessity compels the enemy to abandon this weapon, which was really a good one from his point of view, and might have been successful against any other people but the Irish. The enemy has come to the conclusion that he will not beat us by burning the houses and property of our people. His next move will be to try and round-up and intern all the active spirits of the Army, paying special attention to its officers. For this purpose 8,000 troops are being sent to Ballincollig this month, the idea being to use this superiority of force to carry out large scale 'drives' in the nature of that which was so fruitless in this area last week. This plan was also adopted by England in the South Africa War. It was not successful there. It will not succeed here.

I would like to give reasons for my belief. First, the extensive road cutting carried out by us has rendered the enemy's Mechanical Transport practically useless. His smaller posts are now driven in, his bases and stations widely scattered and connected only precariously by rail. Consequently, troops for operations in any particular district will have to be marched long distances. This involves a serious waste of time, a nullification of the important factor of surprise, and a deterioration in the fighting quality of his men – already sufficiently poor. Indeed, so accustomed has his troops become to the assistance of lorry transport that they are already refusing to march long distances.

Secondly, the IRA does not and will not concentrate large bodies of men at any point, except for such short periods as will make it impossible for the enemy to reach them before their operations are over and they themselves scattered. This means that the enemy will have to 'drive' every area separately, and with the difficulties referred to above, our men will have ample opportunity, with good information, of vacating the area he intends to 'drive.'

June 16th [1921]

To continue my faint 'appreciation of the situation' as begun yesterday – and it may be amusing later on to see how far my forecast will be correct.

The enemy is faced with a third serious difficulty in addition to the two mentioned. The men on whom he depended for identification purposes – the old RIC – are almost wiped out, and large areas now exist in which he has nobody to identify prisoners taken. He is then faced with the alternative of interning the whole lot, or releasing them. England's present financial position is so strained that the task of feeding and interning even another 3,000 prisoners would be almost beyond the power of her ability. And 3,000 men would not be by any means a disastrous loss to us. Unless they were mostly officers their loss would scarcely be felt. We have more men than we can possibly utilize.

The enemy can only carry out his projected operations in fine weather and long days. Therefore, supposing he is ready to start on July 1st – which I think he will be – he has two months only in which to effect the capture and internment of an army on its own ground, which is 'everywhere all the time, and nowhere at any given time'. He must keep to his quarters next winter more than ever before, and he realizes that if he does not win before winter he is beaten. Therefore we shall have a warm summer, most probably followed by a cool winter. Supposing even for a moment that he were successful in reducing the activity of the IRA, which increases every day, by interning a large number of the directing minds of the Army, this would not give him victory. Because no matter how many men are interned they must be released some time; and when they are released they will be as intractable as ever. To put it in plain and inelegant language – the enemy is in the very devil of a knot.

All this takes no account of what the civilians may do in the way of making peace in the meantime. It is the most vital necessity for England and she is sparing no effort. We are stronger than she is, we are together now, and we can go on as long as need be. Already she is trying to placate us somewhat in the matter of our prisoners. I think the shooting of men for having arms and levying war is at an end or nearly so.[42] Presently she will recognize our prisoners as prisoners of war, and treat them as such.

June 17th [1921]

I hope when you have read the foregoing two pages you will be of the same opinion as I am that there are only two alternatives for 'Merrie England'. One, the simplest, to clear out; and the other, to roof in the whole damn country and make an internment camp of it! And that wouldn't be the end of all things either.

Well to return to more personal matters again, some friends from Cork were here today, and told me that you were, so to say, on active service one day a while ago. But there was nothing doing, apparently. Of course the person who told me is one of the best, and you need not fear it was just gossip. Nell would know, he called to her. Only that I feel you are so well able to take care of yourself, I would be tempted to indulge in a lecture. You'll be careful, won't you?[43] When Joe arrived back he told me he wanted to give you a call, but, though he actually started to go down, things were so hot he had to abandon the idea. He & L are away again,[44] and I'm more or less alone for a week or so.

June 18th, '21

[Dear Sweetheart,]
Just now I have an opportunity of sending these few notes in to you. Glad to say the cold is quite alright. The bottle was great stuff.

There is absolutely nothing new round here, everything very quiet. No prospect of going in to town for about another fortnight anyway. I may possibly be going to Waterford and could see you at Youghal, but this is indefinite. Will write later regarding it. Any news of Willie and when he is coming? I'd like to arrange things so that I could see him and Kitty before she goes. Give my kind regards to her and Gerald.

With all my love,
F

While headquartered some miles from his hometown of Rathmore, O'Donoghue decided to visit his parents, who had been burned out of their home six weeks previously. This would have been their first meeting since Florrie's marriage to Jo in April. It is unclear if O'Donoghue's parents knew of Jo and Florrie's marriage before the visit.

## BATCH 8

20th June, 1921

Your letter written on the 14th arrived here this morning but from a letter of Nell's which was with it, I see that the delay was in town and not in transit. In fact the transit is very efficient now. I told Nell in a previous letter, which by the way she does not say she got, where to leave stuff in town so that delays will not arise.

Thanks very much for your letter, dear; it is a tonic in itself. To tell you the truth, I was not feeling over well last week. Several things contributed to a depression which is quite unusual with me. I was not entirely rid of the cold, had a more or less continual headache, too much work and too long hours, being almost alone, worrying a bit about you and the idle tongues of other people, and wondering how things were at home and how they would take my changed circumstance. Don't be worried about this at all; you know I always tell you the simple truth as to how I feel.

I am glad I decided to have a holiday yesterday, and to go over. It was a glorious day for walking, fine with a fresh wind and not too hot. We started at 12 o'clock (a guide came with me) and did those first ten miles in a car. Then we had an eight mile tramp, five across the mountain and three on the road at the other side. I found them all well and in great spirits considering what they have been through. It is a sad sight you may be sure, but I was more touched by the spirit in which the calamity is accepted than in the thing itself. People talk about their patriotism, sitting smug and comfortable in their quiet homes, if they give a few pounds that does not hurt them to the cause, or if they help in one way or another without inconveniencing themselves, and I have seen much of this pious humbug. Yesterday it came home to me that this patriotism was a poor mean thing, compared to the calm undaunted faith of these people looking at the ruins of their own homes. I am not referring to my own people merely, I saw and spoke to them all, and I am convinced that there was something supernatural in the unshakable courage and olden Gaelic simplicity of these people. Truly, the hills of Ireland should be levelled to the ground and all her children driven out upon the seas of the world before England can conquer us while we have such faith and such courage.

And the personal side of the visit. They were glad about you. Oh, they made me happy, especially mother and in such a way as only a mother can. They would like to see you, and I wish very much that you could see them. But that cannot be for the present at least. Could you send them a photo of your's, even a small one soon? I showed them the one I had and Jerry's, and they all liked them very much. I have never yet left home without feeling the better for having gone there and without a feeling of sadness too; and yesterday both feelings were more acute than ever before. My sister[45] came with me as far as the boundary of the next parish, across the fields, and saying goodbye to her I felt as if it would have done me much good if I could have cried.

The journey home, or to digs I should say, was uneventful and I arrived just at midnight, very tired. As a result of the hard physical exercise which elated me just as it used to long ago, the keen fresh air, and the mental tonic of seeing those dear to me, I slept a sounder and a happier sleep last night than I had done for two weeks. And today when I was wakened up there was your letter. So I am feeling fit and fresh in mind and body again today.

To return to your letter. I am glad the A and B are gone for a week's holiday. It will do them good, and the weather is glorious. I wish Nell would go for a week later, but it is a bit of a nuisance to Cissie, isn't it?[46] And so you are alone again, with only Poll and the cat. Quite an old maidenish combination, what? I wish I could go in now for a few days quiet, just to rest and talk to you and be happy. But it is not possible for a week or two yet anyhow. By the way, I have just seen in the paper that there was a boating accident in Cork on Sunday, and that there was a youngster in it. I am wondering if it was your party, ye seem to have a pretty taste in accidents of that kind. Glad to see however that nothing worse than a ducking befell anybody.[47]

[This letter is typewritten]

21st June, 1921

[Dear Sweetheart,]
I received your other letter, undated but written apparently on Monday, this morning. I hope Sister K[48] will be able to arrange to get that matter through for you all right. August would be very nice, and I might possibly be able to get a few days off then. Write again when you have any definite news.

Glad to hear you may have a lot of news for me. I am anxious to hear it but I suppose I must suffer on patiently. With regards to the medicine, I have the bottle nearly finished but there is no need to send any more. The cold is quite all right now again. Yes, I got the cord alright thanks.

You do not say you got my letters, but apparently you did. I suppose it is not very easy to remember things and write a connected letter in the circumstances. I can quite understand that A and B and Gerald would make quite a racket between them. However, you will have some peace now that some of the family are gone to Youghal.

Things are just the same here, quiet and uneventful. The work is not so heavy as it was last week, which is a mercy. But feeling alright myself, I don't care how much of it comes along. I don't want anything except a box of tooth powder, and there is no hurry with that, whenever you are writing next will do. I prefer powder to paste if you can get it. If not the paste will do. I am sending a letter to Nell herewith, and she will tell you any news there is about home.

Pardon the impoliteness of typing a personal letter. The sad reason is that we have no paper suitable for writing on, and will not have our supply for a few days. To what sad state this hitherto splendid establishment is reduced!

By the way, ask Nell if she got a letter of mine posted to Jimmy C – Castle St just after I came out. There was a note in it for you.

[I am forever,]<br>F.

## BATCH 9

22/6/21

> To 'G'[49]
> In this hushed hour when calm majestic night
> Comes from the East soft-footed, and from the high
> Of gilded heaven downwards to the horizon's rim
> Drives the last lights, now pale and growing dim,
> That mark where the red sun hath lately set;
> When gathered herds across the rivulet
> Wind homewards through the dewy grass;
> Here in the mountains, watching as they press,
> My heart goes wandering, drifting home again,
> Through wild rough hills and over darkening plain,
> To that quiet place where sweet content and rest
> Awaits it; and where every joy is blest
> By love that makes life beautiful and sad.
> In memory now I see the place where we have had
> So many happy hours, and in your eyes,
> Welcoming me back, the olden glad surprise.
> If this is pain I feel, only heart doth know,
> As I remember how in the after glow
> Of many a city sunset you and I
> Looked from your window on the western sky –
> The touch of your soft hands, the sweet caress
> Your lips gave mine in mutual happiness.

June 23rd, '21

As you are aware, poets, lovers and madmen all suffer from the same species of mental malady. But I hope that instead of imagining that I have suddenly been transformed into any of these by the heat, you will rather choose to think instead that I have some part of all these naturally ingrained in my composition, and so let that be an excuse for the effusion of yesterday. All the same you might let me know if you like it, because if it pleases you it will be excused, whether it is middling or indifferent – I know it cannot claim goodness.

I have been lying out on the heath all day, staring at the horizon and turning the other parts of my anatomy to the sun when one part grew overheated by turns – the reasons of which you shall know. Last evening our good friends the enemy came to Macroom, and it was within the bounds of possibility, as the politicians say, that they would pay us the usual fortnightly visit which is now overdue. Hence the office was officially closed and a national holiday solemnly proclaimed with acclamation this morning. But now we have learned that our friends have taken another direction, and we must go to work again tomorrow and make up for today before the weekend.[50]

24/6/21

[My loyal friend, my sweetheart,]
As I have an opportunity now I send you just a few lines. It is possible that I will be leaving here and going to Kerry for a few days on Wednesday or perhaps Tuesday next. This is not definite, but it is likely, so if you are writing, send it at the latest on Monday evening.

I would perhaps go into town for a day or two, but for certain reasons you will understand, I have postponed the visit unless something turns up. However it is just possible still that I may go in on Wednesday, but if not then, don't expect me for another week. Needless to say I would like to go in, but circumstances do not permit.

Well and how is everybody since? You didn't tell me if you had taken up your new occupation yet. And if so, how do you like it? I suppose the holiday makers are still in Youghal. The faint prospect that I may be able to pay a visit is still on the horizon. Till I see you again. God bless you and keep you in his loving security.

[Forever,]
F

27th June '21

[My loyal friend, my sweetheart,]
I got your letter written on 23rd and also the tooth powder safely yesterday. They were slightly delayed owing to enemy activity in the line of route. I wrote another letter to you since that one. As, on

account of the activity, there was a possibility that it may fall into wrong hands, I was careful not to put anything plainly in it. I would not have written at all only for some things which I expected to happen. And I put the reference to things in the house in Nell's letter so that if they were got and traced no connection could be established between Nell and you. My reference to things in the house was to papers, letters, etc. I hope you didn't mind the way I put it. I will explain when I see you. I don't think the matter I anticipated will occur just yet, so circumstances have arisen to defer it. I'm sure you'll guess what it is, and I know you will keep your own counsel on the matter.[51]

Thanks for your cheerful letter. I'm not in any sense depressed now, it was only a passing mood for a few days at that time. I think it was the cold. In any case I never felt better than I do at present, and as far as your instructions are concerned, they shall be carried out with the utmost attention to detail. Sleep enough! Well, I'd have you know we are all champions, 12 midnight to 10.00 or 10.30 a.m. is the regular thing. And I forgot to mention we have now a Doctor permanently attached to Staff to keep us all in the pink. He is a fellow-countryman of my own, and a decided acquisition apart from his medical qualifications. For one thing he brought a small library of books with him, and I'm prepared to love anybody in advance who does that out here.[52]

I'm glad you are with N & A.[53] It would be very lonely for you by yourself below. How I wish I was in. Well, I'm going neither to Kerry nor to town tomorrow. It became imperative for some of the others to go away today, and I am of necessity to stay here until someone returns – that is some one responsible, there are five officers here, but no 'Great white chief'[54] except poor me. But I'm going to get a few days off and go in at the end of this week or Monday following at latest. So, till then, we'll cheer up and wish the days short. I'll hardly write again before I see you. And I'll be glad if there's nobody but yourself and we can have a quiet few days.

Happily yours,
[Forever 'G']
F.

29/6/21

*Reverie*
Sometimes when I walk home alone
In thoughtful mood, and when the mind is filled
With fragrant memories and gentle thoughts
I see the purpose of our life fulfilled;

And when the Dawn is come, the joyous, golden days
Stretch out in languorous peace,
Across our lives' wide sea
I vision all the days when we are free
To build again in beauty the mansion of our dreams
With shining hope and love.
And I remember what thou has made for me
Of the hard road of Life.
Joyously there comes to my mind the thought
Of a quiet place where we sat and watched the tide
Creep up the rocks and sparkle in the sun,
The hushed, harmonious calm of that sweet day
Comes softly back again.
The dappled sunlight on the shaded path,
Our happiness so deep it never needed words
Save yours to make it perfect; –
'Today was beautiful, but it was very sad.'

F.

8th July, '21

Beloved,

A very hurried line to say we arrived safely here at 1.00 a.m. this morning. Got along first class – no difficulties anywhere. Didn't have to cycle all the way either, got a lift – pony & trap – eighteen or so miles. The usual good luck.

The apples were awfully sweet about midnight, and the caramels caused certain people to invoke blessings on the thoughtful one that keeps the home fires burning! And to think that I nearly refused to bring them.

I'll write a letter when I have about five minutes to spare, which doesn't look as if it will be for a year – there's so much work. However, the holiday was worth it, even if I was abused for taking risks.

God love and guard you,
F.

On 11 July 1921, representatives of the Dáil and the British Government signed a Truce Agreement. The ceasefire was intended to facilitate negotiations for a permanent peace settlement between the two nations. The Truce had been in the works for some time and seemed to have been anticipated by O'Donoghue and a few other high-ranking IRA leaders. However, peace broke over an unsuspecting Irish public like a thunderclap.

From an IRA perspective, the Truce represented a victory. The British Government, it appeared, had sued for peace and recognized the Irish Volunteers as a legitimate military force. Gone was the British argument that the IRA was a 'murder gang' using terrorism to hold the country hostage. The Volunteers were now seen as the vanguard of a united national independence movement supported by a majority of the Irish people.

As the Truce came into effect, soldiers and civilians celebrated. Volunteers who had been on the run for a year or more, now safely returned home to a heroes' reception. Crown forces also welcomed the peace, and there were scenes of jubilation and even occasional fraternization between Black and Tan and their IRA counterparts. For Republicans, it was as if the world had been turned upside down.

12/7/21

[My loyal friend, my sweetheart,]
Well, we have got so far. Hope you are enjoying the truce. 'The spirits of the troops is excellent!' I suppose ye stayed up all night last night, everyone is delighted. I hope it will turn out so well that we will not have to take up our arms again.

I am going to Dublin end of this week or next. I expect I will go into town before going up. Most of our lads here are gone in already, and Joe is going today. I may not be going for a few days, but it is hardly worth your while to write me in the meantime.

I will write that letter for Maggie and send it in a day or two – perhaps tomorrow.[55] In spite of the truce we are a bit busy these days, but expect to be finished up with heavy work tonight.

> With all my love,
> [Good luck and God bless.]
> F.

13/7/21

[My friend, my sweetheart,]
This truce is a great idea. I think we must have one every other year! We are using our motorcars again, and I had a spin down to Kerry this morning. Brought home a carload of school children – somewhere about twenty, I think – anyway there was a heap of them. The whole country is gone mad, cheering, shouting, and so forth. I find it very hard to keep up the normal glum appearance myself. Things certainly are better even than we had hoped, we are on the straight for the finish and winning!

Herewith letter for Maggie. I don't know whether you will be pleased with it, for its awfully hard to write a letter of that sort – especially for me. If you don't like it destroy it, and I'll write another when I go in to town.

Going in, by the way, is uncertain as to time yet. Perhaps next week. I am very gravely remembering the advice you gave and got other people to give me to stay out. Consequentially I'm here all alone. Don't I deserve a special medal?

No news. Write a few lines if you have a chance, dear.

> In great haste.
> [God's Blessing on you.]
> loving you,
> F.

16ᵗʰ July, '21

[My friend, my sweetheart,]
I had a note from Joe yesterday in which he told me that he had called to see you, and you were A-1. He also told me that W. came down, said that he moved him – he did not say where.⁵⁶ I would like to know – it will be quite safe writing you now – and also whether you consider the place suitable. If it is the place we discussed, I hope you will go on there with him, and don't let expectation of a visit from me detain you in town. In fact wherever he is you should be with him.

I may be going in next week – I don't know anything definite yet. In any case wherever you are I can go and see you freely now. We are allowed motorcars, motorbikes etc. and I'm getting my motorbike on Monday.

Am writing this in a hurry as Messenger is waiting. Write soon and let me know how W. is. Give him all my good wishes and Gerald and Kitty too.

> Love to yourself,
> God bless and keep you all safely for me,
> [Sweetheart,]
> F.

By this time, Jo had resigned her position at the Victoria Barracks. The unyielding pressure of her covert work and the likelihood of eventual British arrest likely spurred her decision. Unable to raise two children on Florrie's tiny IRA salary, she would have sought other employment at this time.

27/7/21

[Sweetheart,]

I have received your unexpected letter this morning. I was wondering if you would write, because I forgot in the hustle to make any arrangement. Thanks, dear. I'm sending this to Nell as I am not sure if the address the on paper would find you.

You say too many nice things about me. I don't really deserve any thanks, I only wish I could do more. I've been worrying about my forgetfulness in regard to that motorcar ever since. I promised that you should have it, and I hate breaking a promise. However we will try and make up for that another time.

We got on splendidly – Fred and I.[57] Arrived at 7.30 that evening. There was nearly a riot in the place when he came back. They are all stone crazy about him. Each individual sister came, and, kissed and fussed and made much of him, until I nearly felt jealous. The children were all the same. They all love him. Really you'd be proud of him if you were there! He was a bit lonely leaving me, but he soon forgot it in collecting all the local news since he left, and relating his own adventures. And they didn't suffer from a lack of imagination on his part!

I stayed up there that night, and came back next day. I'm going home on Sunday. Hope weather is fine. I got Miss O'R.' s letter. Same thing as you suggested to me about old position. We'll talk it over when you come back.[58] I'll be in Cork Wednesday night or Thursday morning – probably Wed. night. Hope you'll enjoy your holiday all right. We'll see you when you come back.

With all my love and good wishes,<br>[Forever,]<br>F.

On 21 July 1921, the First Southern Division moved its headquarters to Patrick O'Sullivan's home in Lombardstown, near Mallow. Two weeks later, Dáil President, Eamon de Valera, and IRA Chief of Staff, Richard Mulcahy, traveled through Munster to covertly review IRA units. The inspections proved a great morale booster for all involved. O'Donoghue likely organized the itinerary and arranged meetings between the dignitaries and local Volunteer leaders.[59]

Killarney
16th, August '21

[My friend, my sweetheart,]
I thought I would send you a line or two to let you know how things
are progressing since. After I left you that morning the tour turned out
all right. We had fairly good weather and a very interesting time. It
almost ended in a riot in Mallow Station. There was an immense
crowd, and tremendous enthusiasm. Dev was delighted.[60] 'The spirit of
the troops is excellent.' Well, Sean Hyde[61] and I left immediately on
motorbikes for Killarney. We got there at 7 o'clock, after negotiating
some fearsome things in the way of trenches. We left Killarney on
Sunday morning and we had a fine day and good roads. We got down
to Cahircaveen in the evening, and there was a concert that night to
which we went. The hall would hold about 470. There were about
1,000 in it. Talk about a Turkish bath! The concert was fair to middling
– but it was for the cause. We stayed in Killorglin yesterday, had our
meetings, and finished up last night. We are just back in Killarney now
and having a meeting today, after which we go on to Tralee this
evening. Hope to get to West Limerick on Thursday, and get back on
Friday, so that I will hardly reach Cork until Saturday. We have been
very fortunate so far - good weather, and no trouble with the bikes. It
has really been a sort of holiday.

How have you been keeping since? Well, I hope. How is Jim?[62] Any
news from Kitty? If you have any special news, write to the usual
address on Thursday, and I will get it on Friday morning when I get in.
Give my love to Gerald and Fred, and may God send his Angels to
watch over them and you always. With all my love,

Yours forever,
[Sweetheart,]
F.


Mallow
21/8/21
[Sweetheart,]
A very hurried note written in Hotel in Mallow where we are today, to
say that I got back alright and came on to near here last night.

We are so rushed and mixed up with meetings that I have not time
to write a decent letter. Will do so in a day or two.

You can post any letter for me between now and next Wednesday to
Miss Maggie Callaghan
Lombardstown
Mallow

You can address the inside envelope in the usual way and they will be delivered to me alright. You could post letters in Middleton to me. It will be quite safe, and you know how anxious I would be to hear from you.

Please excuse this hurried note. Give my best wishes to Willie and Gerald, and my best love to yourself. May God keep and guard you, and give you courage and hope.

[Forever]

F.

23/8/21

A line as promised. I'm going to Mallow in a minute and will post this there. I am not going into town on Sat. or Sunday. Going to Kerry on Saturday. Probably won't be back until Monday. So you had better go to Youghal on Sat. and have a Sunday's rest instead of the dissipation that would surely obtain if I went to town! The Skibbereen stunt won't come off after all. M.C.[63] will hardly come, and the piece with Hamlet is not worth motoring to Skibbereen to see. Expect me in Cork Monday night or Tuesday night – if I don't write in the meantime. 'For one night only.'

The Dublin stunt. It is decided that my going is postponed for the moment – or until the situation stabilizes somewhat. So you'll have to get the wallpaper posted up somehow after all! Too bad! It's fairly certain I'll go sometime though, and I have some interesting things to tell you about it too. But don't let the house fall to pieces or anything like that. Don't be amazed at this. I feel it my solemn duty to give the benefit of my mature advice to my 'flighty flapper'.

God bless and keep you,

F.

This ends the primary account of Florence and Josephine O'Donoghue during their nation's War of Independence.

## NOTES AND REFERENCES

1    O'Donoghue's BMH statement. The Genoa gunrunning scheme was an attempt to dramatically alter the military equation in Ireland. The IRA intended to purchase 20,000 rifles in Italy and land them near Union Hall in West Cork. (At this stage the IRA possessed roughly 3,000 rifles in the entire country.) Liam Deasy and Florrie O'Donoghue planned the landing operation, which would have seen the mobilization of most of the Cork No. 1 and Cork No. 3 brigades, and the theft of almost every lorry in County Cork. Mick Leahy,

the Cork No. 1 Vice-Commander and a qualified maritime engineer, travelled to Italy to arrange the shipping of the arms. Deasy and O'Donoghue went to Dublin on 18 December 1920 to discuss the arrangements with GHQ. (On his arrival, O'Donoghue barely escaped arrest on a Dublin train platform, but his alibi withstood police scrutiny.) The smuggling operation was eventually called off, apparently after the British uncovered the plan in Italy. Mick Leahy was angered at GHQ's poor planning and lack of support of his efforts on the continent. His disapproval may have contributed to the Cork IRA's estrangement with Dublin. See Tom Barry, *Guerilla Days in Ireland* (Boulder, CO: Roberts Rhinehart, 1995), pp. 155–7; Tim Pat Coogan, *The Man Who Made Ireland*, pp. 179–82; Liam Deasy, *Towards Ireland Free* (Cork: Royal Carbery Books, 1992), pp. 179–80; O'Donoghue, *No Other Law*, p. 153; O'Donoghue's and Mick Leahy's BMH statements; and Mick Leahy in the O'Malley Notebooks, UCD. Donal Hales, who organized the arms purchase in Genoa, retained some of his coded letters from the operation, which can be found in his papers in the Cork Archives Institute.

2    Some historians are critical of the division scheme. I would argue that while it created additional bureaucracy, the division structure provided IRA GHQ its best option for maintaining some central control over disparate country units. Besides its shortage of arms, the biggest problem facing the IRA was poor leadership in inactive areas. GHQ responded by sending Dublin officers (Andy Cooney, Ernie O'Malley, and Seán MacBride) to assume control of troubled units. Their efforts usually aroused bitterness and resentment since the outsiders typically arrived with no knowledge of local conditions or person-alities. Division staffs, on the other hand, were composed of men from that region who (due to their proximity) could inspect units with much greater frequency than GHQ officers. Already familiar with the units and officers in question, the division staff would possess the native knowledge required to investigate a troubled command and recommend suitable changes. The IRA needed some hierarchy to rid itself of problem leaders, and it made more sense for that structure to exist in the country, rather than emanating from Dublin.

3    For first-hand accounts of the formation of the First Southern Division, see Barry, pp. 157–62; Deasy, *Towards Ireland Free*, pp. 194–5; O'Donoghue, *No Other Law*, pp. 148–57; Ernie O'Malley, *On Another Man's Wound* (Dublin: Anvil, 1979), pp. 306–7; Sean Moylan, *In His Own Words*, pp. 117–20; and O'Donoghue's BMH statement. Participants remembered the Kippagh Meeting for Ernie O'Malley's obnoxious performance as chairman and for Seán O'Hegarty's biting tongue and humorous outfit. ('He looked like an old time music hall artist', recalled Seán Moylan.)

4    Siobhán Lankford, a key Cork No. 2 Brigade IRA intelligence officer operating in the Mallow Post Office, kept many of Florrie's intelligence circulars. They can be found in Lankford's papers in the Cork Archives Institute. Lankford's book about her experiences *The Hope and the Sadness*, holds up well.

5    Ms. 31, 176, NLI.

6    Jo's sister Cecily Hore living in Youghal. This letter could be his announcement of their recent marriage.

7    Next to the British, probably the biggest threat to Volunteers 'on the run' was scabies. Republican accounts typically lamented the appearance of the 'Republican itch'. Outbreaks usually stemmed from primitive living conditions in the countryside, a lack of spare clothes, and tight sleeping arrangements. In his BMH statement, Mick Murphy reports that in May 1921 the Cork No. 1

Flying Column (then residing in Ballyvourney, a few miles from O'Donoghue's headquarters), had to be temporarily disbanded after scabies laid low all its members.

8   'Willie' was the couple's codename for Jo's son Reggie.

9   See the *Cork Examiner* 5 May 1921, and *Cork Constitution* 5 May 1921; Abbott, *Police Casualties in Ireland*, pp. 230–1; Dwyer, *Tans, Terror and Troubles*, pp. 308–11; Moylan, *In His Own Words*, p. 127; and J.J. O'Riordan, *Kiskeam Versus the Empire* (from a typewritten copy in the United Irish Cultural Center, San Francisco), pp. 69–71. According to O'Riordan, two British Army deserters identified Tom O'Sullivan as an informer and a frequent visitor to their barracks.

10   Florrie's elder sister Nell who lived with him above No. 55, North Main Street. Knocknagree is a village near Rathmore.

11   Christian de Wet was the most successful Boer guerrilla 'commando' leader in the Anglo–Boer War. His memoir of the campaign is an early classic in the study of guerrilla warfare.

12   Michael ÓSuílleabháin repeats this anecdote in his memoir *Where the Mountainy Men Have Sown* (Dublin: Anvil, 1965), p. 111. He served with the Cork No. 1 Brigade column in the same area during this period.

13   A quote from Patrick Pearse's address at a Robert Emmet commemoration in 1914.

14   This is probably the Cork No. 1 Brigade Column, made up of many of the most active members of the Brigade. Due to British pressure in Cork city, Seán O'Hegarty moved his Brigade headquarters to the Column's base of operations. A number of O'Donoghue's city colleagues travelled with the Brigade Column, including Seán O'Hegarty, Joe O'Connor, Jim Grey, Seán Culhane, and the column commander Dan 'Sandow' Donovan.

15   That week Eamon de Valera and Northern Ireland Unionist leader, Sir James Craig, met to discuss the possibility of incorporating Northern Ireland into a new Irish state. With the status of Northern Ireland a main stumbling point to a negotiated settlement, this meeting was widely seen to be an 'indication of a movement towards the production of peace in Ireland'. See the *Cork Constitution*, 7 May 1921.

16   They met with representatives from the Cork No. 1 and No. 2 Brigades and Kerry No. 1 and No. 2 Brigades. The purpose of the conference was to finalize distribution plans for the Genoa arms smuggling operation, and to set up a Divisional training camp for Munster IRA officers. The training camp was to be located in the Clydagh Valley (near O'Donoghue's native Rathmore), and commanded by Tom Barry. See Barry, *Guerilla Days in Ireland*, pp. 220–1; Deasy, *Towards Ireland Free*, p. 271; and O'Donoghue, *No Other Law*, p. 154.

17   Father of Patrick O'Connor, Florrie's cousin who was killed in the Easter Rising.

18   The first quote can be found in the *Cork Examiner*, 6 May 1921. The second comes from the *Cork Constitution* 7 May 1921.

19   The Sam Browne belt was worn by British Army officers (and American officers during this period) over their tunics. It was a leather waist belt with a chest strap. IRA flying column members and officers in the field often wore a mixture of civilian and military dress, such as trench coats, Sam Browne belts, and high boots, gators, or leggings. Flying column members also frequently sported bandoliers across their chests and wore their caps backwards to signify 'active service'. In the previous letter O'Donoghue mentions wearing a military-style khaki shirt.

20   Note O'Donoghue's parochialism. Though he grew up less than twenty miles

from the Killarney Lakes and Gap of Dunloe (two of Ireland's most celebrated tourist attractions), this was his first visit.

21    Aggie and Babe are probably his sisters Albina and Margaret (who was the baby of the family).

22    From the Ulster Poet, James Orr (1770–1816). The lines read:
        The Savage loves his native shore,
        Though rude the soil and chill the air;
        Well then may Erin's sons adore
        Their isle, which nature formed so fair!
        What flood reflects and shore so sweet,
        As Shannon great, or past'ral Bann?
        Or who a friend and foe can meet,
        So gen'rous an Irishman.

23    Mrs Isabella Beeton was an expert on cooking and household etiquette in Victorian England. The full title of the book is 'Beeton's Everyday Cookery and Housekeeping Book: Comprising Instructions for Mistress and Servants, and a Collection of Over 1500 Practical Recipes...Showing the Proper Mode of Sending Dishes to the Table'.

24    The captured officer was Seán Moylan, the Cork No. 2 Brigadier and celebrated flying column commander. That evening, British forces encircled Moylan and a group of his officers sleeping in Kiskeam, near Ballydesmond, but Moylan drew off the soldiers, allowing his comrades to escape. Moylan hid atop a fence but was captured the next morning. He was lucky to escape execution. O'Donoghue and Liam Lynch intended to spend the night in the Kiskeam neighbourhood, but were delayed and slept instead in Tournafulla, about a dozen miles from the dragnet. (See Moylan, *In His Own Words*, p. 131; and O'Donoghue, *No Other Law*, p. 169.)

25    Jo's sister and roommate Kathleen 'Kitty' McCoy.

26    Cork No. 1 Brigade officers made three dramatic escapes from British prisons in 1921. In February, Cobh Volunteers used a motor boat to take Seán MacSwiney (brother of Terry) and Limerick IRA leader Tomás Malone off Spike Island Prison in Cork Harbour. On the day of the Truce, 11 July 1921, Matt Ryan and others cut their way through the barbed wire fence at Bere Island Detention Camp. During the Truce period in November, Tom Crofts and a group of Cork officers tunnelled out of Spike Island.

27    The previous day a local IRA unit blew up the bridge at Carrigtwohill, blocking the Cork–Youghal rail line. In addition, 'along the main road in the same vicinity huge trees which were growing at the side of the road were cut and thrown right across the highway, preventing all kinds of traffic from passing through' (*Cork Constitution*, 27 May 1921).

28    Florrie is requesting a dictionary Jo must have taken from the 6th Division Headquarters. Apparently he was still following his School of Commerce teacher's advice to always keep a dictionary handy.

29    The typist was Captain Maurice 'Moss' Walsh of Mitchelstown, who had served as Liam Lynch's assistant-adjutant and staff officer on the Cork No. 2 Brigade staff.

30    Around this time, Joe O'Connor assumed the position of Division Quartermaster and joined O'Donoghue's headquarters. Seán MacSwiney succeeded O'Connor as Cork No. 1 Brigade Quartermaster.

31    The Division Headquarters and O'Hegarty's Cork No. 1 Brigade Flying Column stayed in close proximity to each other for mutual support in case of British attack.

32    Jack Cody, a member of the Reggie Brown kidnapping party. Jo probably met
      Cody when he delivered Reggie Brown to Cork city after their boat trip from
      Liverpool.
33    Later Florrie remembered Cody's 'fine tenor's voice'.
34    The Paps Mountains that overlook Rathmore.
35    The Shandon Church houses Cork's famed clock and bell tower.
36    The British Military Authorities placed Cork city under curfew on 19 July 1920.
      The curfew time changed periodically, responding to both the time of sunset
      and to IRA activity in town. On 22 May 1921, as a collective punishment for a
      fatal ambush of a police patrol in the Blackpool neighbourhood, the British
      Military Authorities lowered the city's curfew from 10.00 p.m. to 8.00 p.m. On 9
      June, they returned the curfew to 10.00 p.m. See the *Cork Constitution*, 23 May
      1921 and 8 June 1921.
37    O'Donoghue, *No Other Law*, p. 177.
38    On 8 June 1921, the *Cork Constitution* reported an 'extensive round-up', with
      British troops converging from Macroom, Ballygarvan, and Millstreet.
39    For details see the *Cork Constitution*, 8 June 1921. Michael ÓSuílleabháin offers
      an entertaining version of 'The Great Round-up' from his vantage point within
      the encircled area. See ÓSuílleabháin, *Where the Mountainy Men Have Sown*,
      pp. 128–38.
40    Patrick Twohig, *Green Tears for Hecuba* (Ballincollig: Tower Books, 1994), pp.
      287–94. Twohig confirmed this version in correspondence with me on 16 March
      2005. Father Twohig grew up in the Macroom area and interviewed numerous
      Seventh and Eighth Battalion veterans over the years. Many of those Volunteers
      had vivid memories of 'the great round-up', which became enshrined in the
      district's folklore.
41    These numbers come from local newspaper accounts, which O'Donoghue had
      apparently read.
42    Beginning in November 1920, British military courts executed a number of
      captured IRA Volunteers for carrying arms. Some of those executions took place
      in Victoria Barracks, so Jo may have heard the firing squads. Seven of
      O'Donoghue's Cork No. 1 Brigade comrades were among the executed.
43    This is a cryptic reference, and one can only speculate as to its meaning. Both
      Jo and Florrie state in this account that Jo worked for the IRA up to the Truce.
      However, this passage could indicate that because of British suspicion, Jo
      became inactive in this last month of the war. Her daughter Margaret believed
      that this was indeed the case. This view is also supported by the fact that Jo
      resigned from Victoria Barracks right after the Truce in July 1921. Since the IRA
      in the Truce period believed that fighting would soon resume, it seems unlikely
      that the Volunteers would lose such an important intelligence asset unless she
      were under heavy British scrutiny. However, the mention of 'nothing doing' in
      the above quote does not make much sense in the context of Victoria Barracks.
      Another possibility is that Jo may have helped with IRA operations, perhaps by
      keeping watch or hiding a weapon. But that would contradict her and Florrie's
      assertion that no-one else in the Cork Volunteers knew of her role. So the
      meaning of this passage remains unclear.
44    Joe O'Connor and Liam Lynch.
45    Elizabeth 'Lizzie' O'Donoghue.
46    'A and B' is likely Reggie and Gerald. It is possible Reggie was living with his
      mother in Cork city at this time.
47    The 20 June 1920 *Cork Examiner* reported the rescue of a boating party of four,

'including a youngster', that had to be rescued after their vessel capsized near Blackrock.

48    Kitty McCoy.

49    As Jo mentioned in Chapter 6, 'G' was her IRA codename.

50    Another large British 'round-up' swept North Cork, east of Florrie's location, centring on the town of Millstreet. See O'Donoghue, *No Other Law*, p. 172.

51    This is probably a reference to the Truce, which was being negotiated at this time. In his senior IRA position, O'Donoghue was likely aware of the negotiations, and he probably recorded his earlier appraisal of the current military situation with this in mind.

52    Con Lucey, who served as the Division's Medical Officer. He may have joined O'Donoghue's headquarters at this time to treat the scabies outbreak in the Cork No. 1 Brigade flying column.

53    O'Donoghue's sisters Nell and Albina.

54    This phrase is probably a relic from Florrie's love of Buffalo Bill stories. 'Great White Chief' was the title used to describe the US President in dealings with American Indians in the Old West.

55    I would speculate this is an announcement of their marriage, addressed to either Jo's or Florrie's sister Margaret.

56    Another coded reference to Reggie. It would seem that Reggie and Gerald lived in Cork at this time, either on Rockboro Terrace with Kitty or with Florrie's sisters Nell and Albina.

57    This is likely Fred Hore, Jo's nephew. Apparently Florrie collected him from his home in Youghal and left him with Florrie's sisters, probably to give Jo, Cecily, and Albert Hore a quiet rest.

58    Refers to her search for a new job. The vacancy may have been in the British Red Cross office, where Jo held a secretarial position upon her return to Cork in 1917.

59    O'Donoghue, *No Other Law*, p. 181.

60    The *Cork Examiner* reported, 'At Mallow, it is learned, President De Valera was recognized, and though his arrival was a great surprise, he received a splendid reception from those in the station at the time.' See the *Cork Examiner* 12/8/21; and *No Other Law*, p. 182.

61    Sean Hyde, an active Cork #1 Brigade officer from the Cobh area, who was promoted to the First Southern Division staff.

62    This could be Jim Grey, the Brigade Transportation Officer. Grey had been in hiding with the Cork #1 Brigade column near Florrie's headquarters.

63    Probably Michael Collins, who occasionally visited his native West Cork during the Truce period.

# PART III
# AFTERWARDS

# 10

## TRUCE AND CIVIL WAR

### John Borgonovo

At the time of the Truce, Jo resigned her position in Victoria Barracks. She probably took another secretarial position until she became pregnant with her and Florrie's first child, Margaret.

Florrie remained at the forefront of the national struggle until the outbreak of the Irish Civil War in the summer of 1922. Unfortunately, he has not written of his first-hand experiences during this crucial phase (at least not to my knowledge), though he covered much of the period in *No Other Law*, his biography of Liam Lynch. A loose record can be established from O'Donoghue's diaries, notes, articles, and books.[1]

In October 1921, Michael Collins and Arthur Griffith led a team of Dáil plenipotentiaries into peace negotiations with the British government. The Irish delegation signed the Anglo-Irish Treaty on 6 December 1921, though the agreement required ratification by the Dáil. Opposition to the settlement appeared immediately when President de Valera and members of a split Irish cabinet repudiated the document.

Under the Treaty terms, Ireland's twenty-six southern counties would secure Dominion Status, a de facto independence enjoyed by countries such as Canada and Australia. However, the new Irish Free State would remain within the British Empire, nominally headed by a Governor-General approved by the British Government. The Treaty recognized Ireland's partition into two states, with six protestant-dominated counties forming Northern Ireland. The Treaty also required members of a new Irish Parliament (to be called the Dáil) to take an oath of loyalty to the King of England. This oath, rather than the partition of Northern Ireland, was the main objection for many Treaty opponents. While most of the IRA's General Headquarters Staff in Dublin supported the settlement, a strong majority of its most active units repudiated the document. O'Donoghue and his First Southern Division Staff colleagues took centre-stage in early December when they issued a letter to GHQ rejecting the Treaty.[2]

The Dáil (with its deputies released from jail and emerged from hiding), deliberated the Treaty in Dublin for three weeks in December and January. Packed galleries watched the emotional debate between national heroes such as Cathal Brugha, Michael Collins, Eamon de Valera, and Arthur Griffith. Treaty supporters were energized by the Irish public's apparent support for the settlement. While few enthusiastically embraced the Treaty, a significant majority preferred compromise to renewed war with Britain.

In a nod to the power of the Cork fighting men, Florrie O'Donoghue, Liam Lynch, and Liam Deasy (the three primary leaders of the First Southern Division) were invited to observe the proceedings.[3] Disappointed and disillusioned, they watched in silence as the Dáil narrowly approved the Treaty, sixty-four votes to fifty-seven.

According to the Treaty terms, the Dáil (known as the Second Dáil because its members had been re-elected in the 1921 General Election), turned over its administration duties to the Free State Provisional Government, selecting Michael Collins as its Chairman. All Anti-Treaty (Dáil) Government ministers resigned (including President Eamon de Valera and Minister of Defence, Cathal Brugha), and were replaced by Pro-Treaty deputies. During these first months, the new Provisional Government acted in tandem with the existing Dáil Ministries (including Defence) which continued to function, though they were now run by Pro-Treaty deputies who often also headed the corresponding department in the Provisional Government.

The complex tenets of the Republican faith obstructed the peace settlement. At the outbreak of hostilities in 1919, the IRA (previously known as the Irish Volunteers) had been a self-governing body dedicated to upholding the Irish Republic proclaimed during the 1916 Rising. In the Autumn of 1919, after the Dáil declared itself the government of that Irish Republic, the Irish Volunteers swore allegiance to the Dáil, and thus became known as the Irish Republican Army. The Volunteer's governing Army Council (the GHQ Staff under the command of Chief of Staff Richard Mulcahy), had subordinated itself to the Dáil's Minister of Defence Cathal Brugha.

By declaring an Irish Free State within the British Empire, the Dáil in effect had voted the Republic out of existence. Having sworn themselves to uphold the Irish Republic, Volunteers no longer felt compelled to obey the non-Republican Dáil government. However, the IRA's ruling Army Council (GHQ) mostly supported the Treaty. Former IRA Chief of Staff Richard Mulcahy now served as the Dáil's Minister of Defence (succeeding Anti-Treaty Cathal Brugha on 10 January 1922), new Chief of Staff Eoin O'Duffy strongly supported the Treaty, and the charismatic IRA/IRB leader Michael Collins was

Chairman of the Free State's Provisional Government. In essence, the IRA's leadership championed a political direction opposed by much of its rank-and-file.

Throughout the country, different IRA units supported the new Provisional Government, many more violently opposed implementation of the Treaty, and some took a neutral stance. The Provisional Government quietly incorporated pro-Treaty IRA officers into a new Free State Army, outside the Irish Volunteer organization. As the British military started to withdraw from Ireland, Pro- and Anti-Treaty IRA units rushed to secure evacuated barracks and bases, resulting in some bloodshed. A compromise was eventually reached where the nearest IRA unit took control of its evacuated barracks, regardless of its stance on the Treaty. This resulted in much of the country coming under the control of Anti-Treaty forces.

Minister of Defence, Richard Mulcahy, called for the loyalty of Anti-Treaty IRA units during the implementation of the settlement. However, the leaders of Anti-Treaty brigades and divisions insisted on following the Volunteer organization by-laws that called for an IRA convention to ratify such a sharp departure in policy. This would allow unit representatives to vote on the body's leadership and its tacit support of a new non-Republican government. Tensions rose with the approach of the IRA Convention. Some feared Anti-Treaty forces would use the meeting to stage a coup against the new Provisional Government, while others assumed the IRA would reject the Treaty and formally break with the Dáil, creating another crisis. Though initially supporting the Convention, Minister of Defence Mulcahy and IRA GHQ asked the Dáil (and adjacent Provisional) Government to prohibit the meeting. The ensuing ban effectively expelled all attending delegates and units from the IRA. Anti-Treaty Volunteers were subsequently cut off from government funds and labelled 'Irregulars' and 'Mutineers'. However, the Convention went ahead as scheduled.

The attempted suppression of the IRA Convention pushed many undecided neutral and moderate IRA leaders to come out directly against the new Provisional Government. Republican militants used the Convention ban as evidence of a secret plot by Richard Mulcahy and Michael Collins to establish a military dictatorship. Suspicion and paranoia on both sides fed the crisis.

Trying to avoid an outright split in the IRA, Defence Minister Mulcahy and Chief of Staff, Eoin O'Duffy, travelled to Cork to confer with the staff of the First Southern Division, including Florence O'Donoghue. The First Southern represented 25 per cent of the IRA's fighting strength, and its Cork Brigades comprised the backbone of the rebellion. Winning over the Division Staff would have done much to diffuse the spiralling military split. While the two sides failed to reach a compromise, both held out hope that they could find a way to bridge the divide.[4]

The banned IRA Convention took place in Dublin on 26 March 1922. Fearing possible arrest, representatives arrived well-armed, including the Cork city contingent which turned up in a stolen armoured car.[5] The body voted to uphold the Republic (rejecting the Treaty and the Provisional Government), and to establish an independent Executive Committee as the IRA's ruling body. The Executive would set its own policy and no longer follow orders from the Dáil. At a second convention two weeks later, delegates elected the new IRA Executive, which in turn selected its own Army Council to replace the Pro-Treaty General Headquarters Staff.

During the IRA conventions, two Anti-Treaty factions became apparent. A moderate wing took a wait-and-see approach to the situation, hoping to find a compromise with its Pro-Treaty counterparts that would reunite the IRA and the rest of the independence move-ment. A smaller militant group vigorously opposed the Provisional Government, and pursued a course that was likely to result in civil war. Florence O'Donoghue became a prominent leader of the moderate faction, and was joined by his First Southern Division colleagues such as Liam Lynch, Liam Deasy, Seán Moylan, Tom Hales, Seán O'Hegarty, and Humphrey Murphy. Both wings were represented on the ruling IRA Executive. In the vote for the IRA Executive, Florrie won the fifth highest vote total, and was subsequently elected Adjutant-General of the reorganized IRA GHQ. His First Southern Division commander Liam Lynch was selected Chief of Staff.

In early April, the Anti-Treaty IRA seized a number of buildings in Dublin, including the Four Courts (the legal centre of the British administration in Ireland,) which became the IRA's new headquarters. Banks were also raided to pay for the upkeep of the IRA's full-time units, which had been cut-off from government funds by the Minister of Defence. As rival armies patrolled Ireland's streets, the spectre of civil war continued to grow.

Militants on the IRA Executive proposed disrupting the upcoming general election, rather than risk a victory by Pro-Treaty candidates. Florrie O'Donoghue, Seán O'Hegarty, and Tom Hales (all from Cork) opposed the plan and threatened to resign from the Executive. Liam Lynch and moderates from the First Southern Division backed O'Donoghue by delaying a vote on the measure. Though O'Donoghue remained on the Executive, he was now considered suspect by the militant faction.[6]

Throughout April, Free State Army and Anti-Treaty IRA forces continued to clash around the country. As the Free State Army gathered strength, militants on the IRA Executive pushed for an aggressive confrontation that would probably ignite a shooting war. Clear public support for the Treaty and the Provisional Government made the IRA position even more difficult. Even if it won a clash with the Free State forces (and during this time the IRA held a strong military advantage), how would the IRA succeed when the British reoccupied the country, as they surely would? There was little public appetite in Ireland for a renewed war with Britain. International support would fall away from the rebels, who had rejected an opportunity for peace. In the countryside, ill-disciplined IRA units were creating local resentment as they commandeered food, vehicles, and supplies from the civilian population. Some locals even talked of welcoming the return of British troops.

To O'Donoghue, the best way out of the impasse was to reunify the IRA so it could act as a brake on the Provisional Government and push the country towards full independence. For he and many of the IRA's most seasoned soldiers, this option also eliminated the growing risk of esteemed colleagues killing one another. The civil war scenario appalled Republicans on both sides of the Treaty divide, especially within the secretive and elite Irish Republican Brotherhood.

On 19 April, the IRB held a tense meeting in Dublin of all county centres, which at one stage saw some opposing members pull guns on each other. Florrie O'Donoghue proposed the creation of a six-man IRB commission (three members from each opposing side) to seek a way to reunite the movement. The measure passed and O'Donoghue co-chaired the commission, though it remained deadlocked and ultimately disbanded after a few sittings. These IRB meetings did lead to another peace conference that eventually produced the controversial Army Officers' Statement.

On 1 May 1922, a group of prominent Anti-Treaty IRA and Free State Army officers (all IRB members), issued a letter calling for Army (IRA) unity. The Anti-Treaty IRA signatories represented the moderate wing of the IRA Executive, and included the Corkmen Florrie O'Donoghue, Seán O'Hegarty, and Tom Hales, as well as Humphrey Murphy (OC of the Kerry No. 2 Brigade) and Dan Breen of Tipperary, who had fired the war's first shots at Soloheadbeg in 1919. Signing on the Pro-Treaty side was the Chairman of the Provisional Government, Michael Collins; Defence Minister, Richard Mulcahy; Chief of Staff, Eoin O'Duffy and Free State generals Gearóid O'Sullivan and Seán Boylan.[7]

The letter stated that civil war was a 'national calamity which would split the country for generations'. It recognized the public's general support of the Treaty, and warned that the current Anti-Treaty strategy would result in Britain's reoccupation of Ireland. The officers called for a reunification of the IRA on the basis of support for the Treaty. They also suggested holding 'an agreed election with a view to forming a Government which will have the confidence of the whole country'. The letter essentially repudiated the IRA Executive position. Appalled militants on the Executive denounced the statement, especially when momentum gathered behind the initiative.

On 3 May, Florrie O'Donoghue and Seán O'Hegarty headed an 'Army Unity Delegation' that was received in the Dáil to present its proposals. Seán O'Hegarty addressed the body, denouncing civil war and appealing for a compromise palatable to both sides. The officers' initiative created some positive peace movement as leaders in the opposing camps tried to back away from the precipice.[8] Hope remained that the forthcoming Irish constitution would meet Republican aspirations (as Michael Collins promised it would). If it did, civil war could still be averted.

The Army Unification Letter further marginalized O'Donoghue within the IRA Executive, though he retained the confidence of Chief of Staff, Liam Lynch.[9] Secret peace talks soon produced an Army reunification scheme. This would allow both Pro- and Anti-Treaty officers to share control of the IRA by placing equal members of each side into a newly integrated IRA GHQ. This reunification effort was supported by Collins and Mulcahy, and Liam Lynch and his First Southern Division colleagues. Lynch nominated Florence O'Donoghue initially as Director of Intelligence (to succeed Michael Collins) and finally as Adjutant-General and a member of the proposed unified Army Council.[10]

In a victory for the militants, the IRA Executive rejected the army reunification plan in a private session. However, Lynch and his First Southern followers planned to bring the measure to a vote in an upcoming IRA Convention scheduled for 18 June – two days after the General Election.

During an IRA Executive meeting on 10 June 1922, the issue of suppressing the General Election was raised again. Despite O'Donoghue's opposition, the Executive passed an election disruption measure. O'Donoghue, Seán O'Hegarty, and Tom Hales once more tendered their resignation from the Executive, but this time their offer was accepted. In his diary, O'Donoghue said that the real issue in his resignation was 'the policy of civil war'. Florrie wrote in disgust, '[The] Executive is discussing this matter in an atmosphere of unreality without any appreciation of the Army's situation.'[11]

On the electoral front, Army unity efforts yielded a compromise in the Dáil between the split deputies. Michael Collins and Eamonn de Valera signed the 'Pact' agreement, which created a slate of Pro- and Anti-Treaty candidates that would form a coalition government after the election. However, the Pact was derailed after the election by a new constitution that fell far short of Republican aspirations, the outbreak of open fighting between Free State and Anti-Treaty troops, and a general apathy towards a coalition from Pro-Treaty leaders who recognized their greater public support. In the 16 June General Election (which was not disrupted by the IRA), Pro-Treaty candidates won a strong majority in the new Dáil.

Two days later, on 18 June 1922, the IRA Convention met for a third and final time. Florrie put forward the Army Unification Proposal (previously rejected by the Executive) to a vote by the full IRA assembly. Amid the long debate, West Cork's Tom Barry submitted a rival resolution to declare war on Britain and attack evacuating Crown forces within seventy-two hours, in the hope of unifying the IRA. Reflecting the disarray of the Anti-Treaty forces, Barry's scheme (which seemed destined for political as well as military disaster), was barely defeated. (In fact it won the first vote, but ultimately lost in a recount after meeting chairman Joe O'Connor noticed the militants had packed the floor.) The militants then walked out of the Convention and reconvened in the Four Courts later that night. They locked Liam Lynch and his First Southern Division supporters out of their Four Courts' headquarters and elected Belfast's Joe McKelvey (who had helped assassinate O'Donoghue's foe District Inspector Swanzy) as the new IRA Chief of Staff. This second IRA split further weakened the Anti-Treaty forces and emboldened the Provisional Government.

For the next nine days, Anti-Treaty militants and the moderates tried to patch up their differences. In the meantime, an event in London dramatically altered the political situation. On 22 June, IRA gunmen in London assassinated Field Marshal Sir Henry Wilson, the former Chief of the Imperial General Staff (British Army). Considerable mystery remains about whether Michael Collins ordered the assassination, or if the gunmen acted on their own in an attempt to unify the London IRA, which was also split by the Treaty.[12] Regardless of the true orgin of the assassination, the British Government blamed the Republican militants occupying the Four Courts, though they were almost certainly not guilty. Prime Minister David Lloyd-George informed the Provisional Government that if the Free State Army did not clear out the Four Courts' Garrison, British troops would.

On the evening of 28 June 1922, Free State Army forces using loaned British artillery attacked the Four Courts. Liam Lynch and the First Southern moderates backed their Anti-Treaty compatriots and Lynch resumed the role of IRA Chief of Staff. Fighting broke out across Dublin, and Lynch headed to Munster to organize Anti-Treaty resistance.

By the time of the Four Courts assault, Florence O'Donoghue had already returned to Cork. On 29 June, he met with fellow moderate IRA leaders Seán O'Hegarty, Gibbs Ross, and Ted Sullivan (commander and vice commander of the Cork No. 5 Brigade).[13] The group travelled to Mallow to try to convince Liam Lynch to stop the fighting, but the Chief of Staff had not yet arrived at his headquarters. Instead they spoke with Liam Deasy, but found him assuming a hard line, due to a recent visit from the Anti-Treaty Sinn Féin leader, Harry Boland.[14]

A few days later, on 3 July 1922, Florrie O'Donoghue formally resigned from the IRA. His loss was considered a significant gain for the Free State.[15]

In his resignation letter to Liam Lynch, Florrie wrote:

> ... My judgment convinces me that out of civil war will come not the Republic, or unity, or freedom, or peace but a prolonged struggle in which the best elements in the country will be annihilated or overborne with the result that the old Shoneen-Unionist groups, who care nothing for Ireland, will be returned to power again, and that in all probability the enemy will reoccupy the country.[16]

O'Donoghue's lack of faith in the Republican position was validated by events during the opening days of the Civil War. The Anti-Treaty IRA leaders had never developed a long-term strategy to defeat the Treaty. When fighting broke out, no war plans existed. The Four Courts' leaders, for symbolic instead of practical purposes, allowed themselves to be boxed up inside an indefensible position and captured en masse. Anti-Treaty forces in Munster and elsewhere made no coordinated attempt to aid the embattled Dublin Brigade, which held Dublin city centre for a week. Even if the Anti-Treaty IRA had defeated the Free State Army, what then? How would they resist a reoccupation by the British? The IRA's response appeared instinctive and reactionary, rather than thoughtful.

O'Donoghue and Seán O'Hegarty recognized what had been unleashed. Almost alone among senior IRA leaders, they both resigned rather than go along with what they considered a dead-end policy. Quitting the IRA took significant moral courage. O'Donoghue knew he would be called a coward by some and a traitor by others. His defection caused Florrie to lose the respect of many of the people he had most closely associated with for six years. It must have been an arduous decision.

Many of the top Anti-Treaty leaders shared O'Donoghue's concerns about the futility of civil war. One can only speculate about what might have happened had other respected fighters like Dan Breen, Dan Donovan, Frank Aiken, Liam Deasy, or Humphrey Murphy likewise resigned. Instead, they reluctantly supported the militants and fought for the next year, but with little of the conviction or passion they displayed in the war against the British. Within a year, the Republicans' defeat was total and their demoralization complete.

As fighting spread into Munster, Cork civic leaders appealed to O'Donoghue and Seán O'Hegarty to help bring an end to the war. O'Donoghue baulked at first, convinced that 'in view of our previous efforts, and the consequent bad odour in which we were with certain prominent people, any movement towards peace would have a better chance of success if we were not connected with it'.[17] But eventually both he and O'Hegarty were persuaded to work to find a peaceful settlement to the conflict.

O'Hegarty and O'Donoghue eventually formed an organization called the 'Neutral IRA', comprised of pre-Truce Volunteers who were staying out of the civil war. This group tried to settle the strife but achieved few significant accomplishments.[18] Interested in peace negotiations, Michael Collins met briefly with O'Donoghue during the former's final visit to Cork, but Collins only spoke in generalities about a settlement. The following day Michael Collins found his fate along the lonely road at Béal na Bláth. With him died any hope for a quick end to the Civil War.[19] Late in 1922, O'Donoghue consulted with Liam Lynch and Liam Deasy about the possibility of reviving the then-defunct Irish Republican Brotherhood to help end the fighting. These efforts were likewise fruitless and quickly abandoned.[20]

By early 1923, hard-pressed Republican forces were in disarray. The well-financed Free State Army knew the location of many of the IRA's sanctuaries and hunted the Republicans mercilessly. The Volunteers were demoralized by the Free State's execution of captured comrades and handicapped by their own lack of support from the Irish public. Senior Anti-Treaty IRA leaders wanted to end the fighting, but had difficulty overcoming their now-intransigent Chief of Staff, Liam Lynch.

By the middle of February 1923, significant progress had been made on a ceasefire proposal championed by O'Donoghue and O'Hegarty.[21] Liam Lynch, however, ordered Eamon de Valera to publicly reject the plan. Outraged, O'Donoghue wrote in his diary, 'De Valera has [a] statement in Press today in reply to us. Dirty trick, simply for propaganda. No truce for him. Wish he were doing some of the fighting.'[22] Neutral IRA peace feelers were further crippled when Lynch forbade his officers from meeting with O'Hegarty and O'Donoghue, who had been shuttling between Munster's discouraged IRA leaders. During this period former TD Liam de Róiste reported rumours that diehard Cork Republicans had 'threatened to shoot the peacemakers of the "Old IRA".'

Free State troops killed Liam Lynch in the Knockmealdown Mountains on 10 April 1923, while he was travelling to an IRA Executive meeting that would debate a ceasefire. Upon Lynch's death, the Anti-Treaty IRA Executive almost immediately declared a cessation of hostilities and ordered its units to 'dump arms'. Much of the ceasefire impetus came from the officers of the First Southern Division, now commanded by O'Donoghue's friend Tom Crofts, who had championed the peace position on the IRA Executive. During this time O'Donoghue consulted with Seán MacSwiney (a Cork city officer on the IRA Executive), Dan Donovan, and Tom Barry[23] (two other prominent ceasefire advocates from Cork).

The war ended with a whimper instead of a bang. The Free State Government had executed seventy-seven Republicans (three times the number of British executions in the Anglo-Irish War), and its army committed appalling atrocities against IRA prisoners, especially in county Kerry (undertaken largely by former members of Michael Collins' 'Squad'). The IRA's economic campaign ruined much of the country's infrastructure and its gunmen had killed the movement's ablest leader in Michael Collins. The nation suffered from the loss of some of its strongest personalities including Arthur Griffith, Kevin O'Higgins,[24] Erskine Childers, Liam Lynch, Harry Boland, Cathal Brugha, and Liam Mellowes. Ireland was split and deep acrimony prevailed. The pride and unity of 1916–1921 seemed a faded memory.

## NOTES AND REFERENCES

1    Much of this chapter is based on various books concerning the Civil War period. Michael Hopkinson's *Green Against Green* remains the authoritative work on the subject (see pp. 52–122). See also Todd Andrews, *Dublin Made Me* (Dublin: Mercier Press, 1969), pp. 220–44; John F. Boyle and Padraig de Burca, *Free State or Republic* (Dublin: University College Press, 2002); Tim Pat Coogan, *The Man Who Made Ireland*, pp. 308–32; Joseph Curran, *The Birth of the Irish Free State*, pp. 162–87; Liam Deasy, *Brother Against Brother* (Cork: Mercier Press, 1998), pp. 32–60; Tom Garvin, *The Birth of Irish Democracy* (Dublin: Gill and Macmillan, 1996), pp. 48–9, and *Nationalist Revolutionaries in Ireland, 1858–1928* (Oxford:

Clarendon Press, 1987), pp. 139–66; C. Desmond Greaves, *Liam Mellowes and the Irish Revolution* (London: Lawrence and Wishart, 1971); Kenneth Griffith and Timothy O'Grady, *Curious Journey, An Oral History of Ireland's Unfinished Revolution* (Cork: Mercier Press, 1998); Dorothy Macardle, *The Irish Republic*, pp. 671–9, 693–6; John O'Beirne-Ranelagh, 'The IRB from the Treaty to 1924', *Irish Historical Studies*, Vol. XX, 1976; Leon O'Broin, *Revolutionary Underground* (Totowa, NJ: Rowman and Littlefield, 1976), pp. 198–205; O'Donoghue, *No Other Law*, pp. 190–246; Meda Ryan, *Tom Barry, IRA Freedom Fighter* (Cork: Mercier Press, 2003), pp. 190–7; and Maryann Valiulis, *General Richard Mulcahy* (Dublin: Irish Academic Press, 1992), pp. 136–52.

2   Mulcahy Papers, P7/A/32, UCD.

3   Deasy, *Brother Against Brother*, p. 32.

4   O'Donoghue, *No Other Law*, pp. 217–18. Details of another meeting during this period between Mulcahy, Lynch, and O'Donoghue can be found in P7B/191, Mulcahy Papers, UCD. See also Valiulis, *General Richard Mulcahy*, p. 136.

5   Mick Leahy, O'Malley Notebooks, UCD; *The Times*, 27 March 1922.

6   This split had been apparent at the formation of the Executive. Liam Deasy wrote, 'Such well-known Republicans as Rory O'Connor, Seamus Robinson, and Liam Mellowes could see no good in Michael Collins, Dick Mulcahy, and Eoin O'Duffy. This distrust even extended to Liam Lynch, Florrie O'Donoghue, Frank Barrett, and myself. We were regarded as being well intentioned but failing in our stand to maintain the Republic.' See Deasy, *Brother Against Brother*, p. 40. See also Greaves, *Liam Mellowes and the Irish Revolution*, p. 308.

7   *Irish Times*, 2 May 1922.

8   Dáil Debates, Vol. S2, 3 May 1922. O'Donoghue's version of the evolution of the peace proposal can be found in *No Other Law*, pp. 236–40.

9   Garvin, *The Birth of Irish Democracy*, pp. 48–9; Greaves, *Liam Mellowes*, p. 326.

10  Hopkinson summarizes and documents the Army Unification Talks in *Green Against Green*, pp. 101–04.

11  O'Donoghue Diary for 1922, 18 June 1922 entry, Ms. 31,187, NLI.

12  O'Donoghue apparently met one of the assassins, Reggie Dunne, while planning the Reggie Brown kidnapping. Both Michael Hopkinson (*Green Against Green*, pp. 112–14) and Peter Hart (*The IRA at War 1916–1923*, pp. 194–220) offer excellent analysis and superb research of the Wilson assassination.

13  The Cork No. 2 and No. 3 Brigades had been reorganized in the summer of 1921, with two new brigades (Cork No. 4 and Cork No. 5) carved out of existing brigade territories. The following year Gibbs Ross was killed leading an IRA attack on the Free State garrison in Mallow.

14  O'Donoghue diary for 1922, 29 June 1922 entry, Ms. 31,187, NLI.

15  See Liam Mellowes' comment, taken from Garvin, *The Birth of Irish Democracy*, p. 49. Also see Liam de Róiste's diary, 3 May 1922, CAI.

16  Letter from F. O'D to Liam Lynch, 3 July 1922, Ms. 31,187, NLI.

17  From O'Donoghue's diary, 2 July 1922 entry, Ms. 31,187, NLI.

18  IRA veteran Todd Andrews recalled, 'the Neutral IRA were despised equally by both sides despite their generous motivation'. See Todd Andrews, *Dublin Made Me* (Dublin: Mercier Press, 1969), p. 275.

19  Collins was killed by members of the First Southern Division, who had been meeting along his convoy route. O'Donoghue's colleagues Tom Crofts, Tom Hales, and Liam Deasy were among those present. O'Donoghue told Ernie O'Malley about his meeting with Collins, in which Collins 'was really talking big'.

See O'Donoghue in the O'Malley Notebooks, UCD; Meda Ryan's *The Day Michael Collins Was Shot* (Dublin: Poolbeg, 1979), p. 92; and Coogan, *The Man Who Made Ireland*, pp. 403–04. Fr Pat Twohig was told by one of Florrie O'Donoghue's sisters that the two men were scheduled to meet on the night of 22 August. See Twohig, *Dark Secret of Béal na Bláth* (Ballincollig: Tower Books, 1991), pp. 132–4.

20    O'Donoghue's efforts to reorganize the IRB apparently prompted Richard Mulcahy and Geroid O'Sullivan to reconstitute the IRB within the Free State Army officer corps. The Free State Army IRB generated resentment among Michael Collins' followers in the Army, which was one of the causes of their Army Mutiny in 1924. For details about O'Donoghue's efforts to jumpstart the IRB, see O'Broin, *Revolutionary Underground*, pp. 218–19 and O'Beirne-Ranelagh, 'The IRB', p. 36.

21    See O'Donoghue's diary entries in February 1923 (Ms. 31,187, NLI) for notes about peace meetings with IRA representatives.

22    O'Donoghue's diary, 28 February 1923 entry, Ms. 31,187, NLI.

23    Though Tom Barry had earlier been a prominent member of the Four Courts militant wing, he now worked to bring about a ceasefire. See Ryan, *Tom Barry, IRA Freedom Fighter*, pp. 190–7.

24    O'Higgins was killed in 1927.

# 11

## 'A LONG LIFE OF DEVOTED LOVE AND MUTUAL HAPPINESS'

### John Borgonovo

After the end of the Civil War, Florrie and Jo O'Donoghue tried to rebuild their lives and take care of their young family. The couple quickly added to their brood. Four more children arrived – Margaret, Patrick, Breda, and Finn Barr. At first the parents tried to make a living by opening a confectionery shop in Cork. However, Florrie secured a more reliable income when he took a position as a rate collector for the Cork County Council. This job provided his family's primary income for the next thirty-five years.

The post-war years were hard times in Ireland. The economy was in poor shape, and thousands of emigrants departed Irish shores. (For example, Jack Cody, Florrie's driver, left for Australia. Christy MacSweeney of the MacNeilus rescue migrated to San Francisco, and Second Battalion Commander Connie Neenan moved to New York.) A career penning collection notes to tardy ratepayers must have been a let down for O'Donoghue, but it did provide him with a steady salary.

During the 1930s, Florrie stayed largely aloof from an unsteady political situation in Ireland. Though a Fianna Fáil Republican, O'Donoghue's children report that he declined a civil service position offered by Eamon de Valera during his first government in 1932. Florrie did remain friendly with cabinet ministers he had known from the War of Independence, such as Seán Moylan, Oscar Traynor, Frank Aiken, and Seán T. O'Kelly. When Fianna Fáil offered government pensions to veterans of the 1916–1923 conflict, Florrie used those contacts on behalf of Cork comrades appealing their pension classifications. He was a national leader of the Old IRA Comrades' Association, an organization of War of Independence veterans that lobbied for Republican aims and assisted former Volunteers regardless of their Civil War loyalties. In Cork, the group was led by O'Donoghue, Tom Crofts, and Liam Deasy, and was considered a threat by the reorganized IRA. Despite some overlapping goals, the two Cork organizations feuded, largely because of the IRA's continued hostility towards the Irish Free State.[1]

In this period O'Donoghue gained his first exposure as a historian. In 1936 he wrote a newspaper article explaining the MacNeilus jail escape, and was then invited to tell the story on national radio. His radio appearance garnered favourable notices and helped establish Florrie's reputation as an authority on the War of Independence period. This led to his second career as a writer and as one of the country's best-known commentators on the Irish independence movement.

When the Second World War erupted in Europe, Florence O'Donoghue joined many of his former IRA colleagues by enlisting in the Free State Army. He was appointed intelligence officer in Munster's Southern Command area, with the rank of Major. With German or British invasion a distinct possibility, O'Donoghue formed a top-secret intelligence auxiliary called the 'Supplementary Intelligence Service'. Intended for counter-espionage against an occupying army, O'Donoghue instructed his team to remain behind enemy lines in the case of invasion. He recruited selectively, choosing many former colleagues from the independence struggle, and organized them along the old IRA battalion areas of the First Southern Division. O'Donoghue's wartime network proved its worth when it uncovered fugitive German spy Herman Goertz's attempted escape by boat from Fenit, Co. Kerry. After the United States entered the war, O'Donoghue also shut down amateurish American intelligence gathering networks in Cork. According to historian Eunan O'Halpin, the success of the Supplementary Intelligence Service, 'hinged on O'Donoghue, whose stature and bona fides were, perhaps uniquely, recognized by old "staters" and "irregulars" alike.'[2]

While serving in the Irish Army, O'Donoghue became prominent in military history circles. He called on his experiences of the independence struggle to teach Irish Army officers the basics of guerrilla war (assuming that upon invasion by either Germany or Britain, the Irish Army would ultimately employ guerrilla tactics). He lectured on the subject and contributed articles to the Army's magazine An Cosantóir, which he edited. Recognizing the lack of serious study of this period, he came up with the idea of a Bureau of Military History to interview former IRA activists and collect their versions of events from the conflict. Taoiseach Eamon de Valera approved the scheme, which was undertaken by the Free State Army from 1947–1957. Due to sensitivity about the independence period, these statements were sealed from public viewing until 2002.[3]

O'Donoghue left the army in 1946 and resumed his position in the Cork County rates office. However, he returned to Cork more dedicated to researching the history of the independence era. It was during this time that Florrie started writing his ambitious biography of Liam Lynch, *No Other Law*. He carefully reconstructed key episodes in the Anglo-Irish War in Cork and the Irish Civil War in an account that remains authoritative today. That impressive book remains a must-read for any student of the 1916–1923 period.

Along with his former IRA colleague Ernie O'Malley, Florrie O'Donoghue was responsible for collecting much of the material that is now essential to the study of the revolutionary era. He frequently met with aging but notoriously reticent IRA comrades, and recorded their thoughts and memories of guerrilla days. The careful review of participants' accounts allowed O'Donoghue to write reliable narratives from a Republican perspective. Along the way he also produced IRA orders, reports, and documents thought to be destroyed during the war, many of them originally hidden by himself. O'Donoghue's work has enabled historians to analyse the success of a small band of rebels against the mightiest military of its time. From those conversations with his colleagues has sprung a scholarship that continues today.

The six O'Donoghue children grew up in a modest but comfortable home on Douglas Road in Cork city. Though money was tight on his rate-collector's salary, O'Donoghue managed to provide an excellent education for them all. In an extraordinary achievement, four of the children eventually became physicians (both Marchment boys, Reggie and Gerald, and Margaret and Finn Barr O'Donoghue; Margaret was one of the few female doctors of her era). Patrick O'Donoghue went on to a career as a dentist, while daughter Breda shared her father's love of art and became a noted painter and sculptor. Breda described the six children as each having sharply distinct personalities, though they remained devoted to each other and their parents. Symbolic of the failure of the Irish state in the 1950s, all six children emigrated.

During my interviews with three of the surviving children, they remembered their childhood fondly. They spent a month every summer at a cottage in Gougane Barra, where Florrie had played hide-and-seek with the British Army so many years earlier. Both parents appear to have been practical and pushed the children to achieve their potential. The children said their mother was passionate, direct, and vivacious, while their father was reserved, yet attentive and devoted to their upbringing. Both were described as supportive and possessing warm and active senses of humour.

O'Donoghue adopted the Marchment boys and apparently integrated them fully into the family. The abduction of Reggie Marchment was never discussed with the children. Dr Margaret O'Donoghue reported, 'It wasn't until I reached the age of twelve that I realized my older brothers had a different last name than mine.'[4] While the children were aware of the story and eventually pieced it together, the full details were first made apparent to them in this narrative. Both Reggie and Gerald Marchment remained close to their parents and siblings. (When I visited the late Dr Margaret O'Donoghue in England in 1996, she had to cut short our interview to nurse the ailing Reggie, who died a short time later.) I have been told that in later years neither of them ever contacted the Marchment-Brown family in Wales.

Josephine O'Donoghue was busy raising six children and remained out of the spotlight. While many Republican insiders knew of her key role during the War of Independence, she insisted on maintaining her anonymity. When Florence O'Donoghue described her activities in *No Other Law*, and even identified her by the codename 'G', she still refused his requests to name her publicly.[5] This was probably due to a variety of factors. Her story contained many private details concerning her children and former husband she probably did not want in the public domain. Five of her children had by then emigrated to England (including Reggie and Gerald), so her silence also shielded them from possible anti-Irish hostility in their new lives. Jo may have also had some conflicted feelings about her activities. She had, after all, betrayed the trust of her superiors and passed information that resulted in many deaths on the British side. Receiving popular acclaim for such profound actions may have been too much for her.

Their twilight years were good to Florrie and Jo. The couple remained active and in good health, frequently travelling to the Irish countryside and occasionally abroad to visit their children and grandchildren in England and Italy. Florrie enjoyed critical and popular success as a historian and was in high demand by scholars and editors. He eventually wrote two full-length biographies (the second on his mentor Tomás MacCurtain), and edited four other books related to the Independence movement. He published numerous articles and book reviews, and appeared on radio periodically. Former IRA colleagues constantly requested his assistance in organizing memorials and to speak at funerals and commemorations for prominent Volunteers.

O'Donoghue remained on good terms with his former IRA comrades. After the early death of his wife, Seán O'Hegarty became an almost nightly visitor to the O'Donoghue home. The two aged rebels would lock themselves for hours in Florrie's study and discuss the old days, only emerging to refill their teapot. O'Donoghue also remained intimate with Joe O'Connor and Tom Crofts. The three men were leaders of the Cork No. 1 Brigade Old IRA Association, which had monthly get-togethers in Cork city.

The O'Donoghues were active in the civic and cultural life of Cork city. Florrie served as Secretary to the Cork Tostal Council, and helped organize its first Cork Film and Choral festivals (both of which continue today). He assisted with the refurbishment of the Cork Gaol, which became a fascinating tourist attraction. O'Donoghue often discussed military history with Irish Army officers stationed at Jo's old employer Victoria Barracks (now renamed Michael Collins Barracks). Florrie and Jo also socialized with Cork's Lord Mayors, business leaders, and TDs, many of whom were former colleagues from the independence struggle.

In 1966, Ireland observed the Fiftieth Anniversary of the Easter Rising. Then seventy-one years old, O'Donoghue played a prominent role in organizing the Cork remembrance ceremonies. His historical accounts of the German arms ship *Aud* and the military plans of the Rising were also incorporated into the elaborate national commemoration activities. He spent the first months of that year participating in and enjoying the Irish nation's last great celebration of its revolutionary generation.

Josephine McCoy O'Donoghue died six months later on 10 November 1966. She had been in good health until she developed a short illness. Cork civic bodies passed motions of condolence on her death, and her obituary made an oblique reference to her activities during the War of Independence.[6] Florence O'Donoghue died a year later on 18 December 1967. His funeral attracted hundreds of mourners and saw the mobilization of his Cork No. 1 Brigade comrades, along with scores of elderly guerrillas and supporters. Tom Barry gave the graveside oration, remembering O'Donoghue as a 'calm, cool, and tenacious man'. Local dignitaries, military officers, and TDs attended from around Cork and Kerry, and President de Valera phoned his condolences to the family.[7]

Looking back in old age, Jo and Florrie's life together must have seemed a blessing to them both. Almost fifty years earlier, Jo was a young war widow who had lost her oldest son seemingly for good. Wandering distraught along the banks of the River Lee pondering suicide, she could not have envisioned the domestic harmony she would enjoy in future years. In 1910, the teenage Florence O'Donoghue arrived in Cork for the first time. As the bewildered farmboy followed a stranger through Cork's bustling streets, how could he have dared to hope for his future lot? He grew up to become a loving husband to a strong and good woman, a father of six fine children, a respected soldier, a celebrated author, and a founder of an independent Irish Republic. It was a remarkable achievement for someone, 'who came to the years of resurgence out of near poverty, without education or training or friends, and who found in the movement worthy ideals and a full life'.

## NOTES AND REFERENCES

1    Brian Hanley *The IRA, 1926–1936* (Dublin: Four Courts Press, 2002), pp. 111–12. Some records from the organization can be found in a section of O'Donoghue's papers lodged in the Cork Archives Institute.

2    For details of the SIS, see O'Halpin's excellent article 'Aspects of Intelligence', in the *Irish Sword* (No. 95 & 96, 1993–1994). In the Goertz episode, O'Donoghue uncovered turncoat Garda Special Branch detective James Crofton, who was working with the IRA to help Goertz escape the country. See Mark Hull, *German Espionage in Ireland, 1939–1945* (Dublin: Irish Academic Press, 1998), pp. 149–50; and J. Bowyer Bell, *The Secret Army* (New Brunswick, NJ: Transaction Publishers, 1997), p. 193. O'Halpin details O'Donoghue's success against the Americans in *Defending Ireland, The Irish State and Its Enemies Since 1922* (Oxford: Oxford University Press, 1999), p. 239.

3    See the Military Archives' 'An Introduction to the Bureau of Military History 1913–1921', p. 1. Correspondence relating to the formation of the Bureau can be found in the O'Donoghue Papers, NLI. When Fine Gael took power in the 1948 Coalition Government, O'Donoghue was dropped from the Bureau's panel of recording officers. This caused some controversy among Republican veterans. For Tom Barry's reaction, see Ryan, *Tom Barry, IRA Freedom Fighter*, pp. 238–9.

4    Interview with the editor at her home in Lincoln, 29 December 1996.

5    O'Donoghue, *No Other Law*, p. 120.

6    *Cork Examiner*, 11 November 1966, 13 November 1966.

7    *Cork Examiner*, 19 December 1967; *Cork Evening Echo*, 19 December 1967.

# APPENDIX

## Cork No. 1 Brigade Order from Florence O'Donoghue, Brigade Information Officer, to all Battalion Commanders[1]

December 22nd, 1920
Cork No. 1 Brigade Headquarters

To All Battalion OCs,
It is beyond question that the Intelligence Service is of supreme importance, and it is the duty of every Volunteer Commander to see that the lead which we secured in this matter against the enemy is properly maintained. The objects of the Intelligence Service are:

1. To discover the intention of the enemy. In the present conflict this intention is political as well as military.
2. To keep in touch with, observe, and report at once, the movement of enemy agents seeking information:
   a. In your own area
   b. In moving from or to your area.
3. To keep under constant observation all enemy bases. It must not be possible for any enemy party to move out from their base without the knowledge of our local intelligence branch.

No. 1 is the concern of every Volunteer and even of every citizen. Conversations of enemy representatives in clubs, in their homes, their movements etc. will indicate enemy intention and will be reported to the immediate superior officer...

No. 2 is of more direct importance and consequence of the individual Volunteer. In this respect Volunteers must always be on the alert. Every stranger in a locality must be kept under observation and his movements carefully noted. Every suspicious individual must immediately be reported to the officer in charge of the area, and if necessary held in custody until instructions have been obtained. Look out for English accents. The index numbers on motor cars should be noted and compared with lists taken by adjoining districts. In this regard the numbers of motor cars of Division Commissioners, County Inspectors, District Inspectors, and Officers commanding troops, should be known to all Volunteers, who will consequently be able to recognize these vehicles directly when they are seen. A Crossley tender conveying a murder gang passes your road, later on you hear of some Irish citizen being brutally murdered. If you have taken the number of that tender you may be able to deal with it the next time you see it.

Get photos of local enemy forces...

Post Offices:

Special attention must be paid to these. The staff of each office or suboffice in your area must be carefully reviewed, and those willing to assist in Intelligence Department carefully selected and kept in constant touch with. Even the smallest office must not be overlooked, as there are scraps of information about the enemy to be picked up even in these, and it is in the assemblage of these scraps that results will be obtained. This Branch of Service must be worked with ceaseless energy, care, and discretion.

A reliable person or persons in each PO should constantly be on the look out for letters addressed to England or Dublin – that is any address or firm with which people do not generally deal...

Telephone and telegram messages...All messages sent by enemy police, soldiers, or agents, should be copied and recorded.

The register number of every motor car and lorry in your area should be noted and a record kept...

...The names and ranks of all officers (enemy) in your area should be known to you, as well as their residences, personal appearance, and general habits. Changes in personnel of enemy organizations should be notified to Brigade Director of Information, and names of successors forwarded...

If the Intelligence service is to be of benefit to you and to the entire organization, no detail can be neglected, nothing which observation can command must be unknown to you. Until you have collected all possible information about the enemy you will not be able to deal with him effectively, or give proper protection to our own people.

As from Friday, December 10th, monthly Battalion reports to be forwarded. This circular should then be destroyed.

Brigade Information Officer

# Florrie O'Donoghue's Resignation Letter to Liam Lynch, Following the Outbreak of the Irish Civil War[2]

2 Rockboro Terrace
Old Blackrock Road
Cork

3rd July, 1922

Liam, a chara [my friend],

I feel it is due to you that I should send you a personal note in explanation of my position, since I did not see you in Mallow on the last occasion I was there. I do not know quite where I stand now with regard to the post I held in the 1st South Division because of the fact that I had worked as AG [Adjutant General] for some time previous to my resignation from the Executive; but lest there should be any misunderstanding about the matter I wish to clear it up by formally tendering my resignation from the post of adjutant. In the present circumstances this of necessity involves also my resignation from the Army.

My reasons are already known to you. I have the same fundamental objections to Civil War now that I had when I resigned from the Executive rather than assent to an action, the logical result of which would have been civil war. I have thought over the matter carefully and at length, and to my mind there is nothing in the circumstances of the origin of the present conflict which would justify my taking part in it. It is true that my sympathies are entirely with you, but my judgment convinces me that out of civil war will come not the Republic, or unity, or freedom, or peace but a prolonged struggle in which the best elements in the country will be annihilated or overborne with the result that the old Shoneen-Unionist groups, who care nothing for Ireland, will be returned to power again, and that in all probability the enemy will reoccupy the country.

In no circumstances could I be a party to a conflict which would bring about such deplorable results, and it is only in the event of the return of the English that I could take up arms again. Should that happen, as I think it will, I'll be somewhere in the ranks. Meantime I have to find the means of living.

This decision of mine is the hardest that I have been forced to take since I joined the Army, not because it will leave me misunderstood and derided (though it will do that) but because I have to part with you all, and lay aside the work I had hoped to do for Ireland.

May I assure you, and all the other Divisional officers, that I have no feelings other than of esteem and regard for each and all of you; and if at anytime I can be of any use I hope you will call on me. As I cannot wish for your success I will hope that your work will in its result help to bring us nearer to the ideal we have at heart.

[Your friend,]
F. O'Donnachadha

P.S. Use your own discretion in showing this to other officers.
F.

## Seán O'Hegarty's Note to Florence O'Donoghue, Announcing his Resignation from the Cork No. 1 Brigade and the Irish Republican Army

30/6/22

F O'D,
Like yourself I am now out of a job.

In a meeting of 24, 19 were for war, 4 against, and one (OC 9th Bn.) had no opinion.

Dommy [O'Sullivan] and I resigned and I don't know who's carrying on.

S O'H

### NOTES AND REFERENCES

1    The full order can be found in Ms. 31,202, NLI.
2    Ms. 31,187, NLI.

# GLOSSARY

**6ᵗʰ Division (British Army)**
British Army formation composed of all British military forces in Munster. Headquartered in Cork city's Victoria Barracks, the division eventually commanded 15,000 British troops stationed in counties Clare, Cork, Kerry, Kilkenny, Limerick, Tipperary, Waterford, and Wexford.

**Anglo-Irish Treaty**
Peace agreement between the British Government and Dáil Éireann signed on 6 December 1921. It established the Irish Free State as a Dominion of the British Empire. This gave twenty-six of Ireland's thirty-two counties a form of self-government similar to that of Australia or Canada. The Dáil's narrow passage of the Anglo-Irish Treaty in January 1921 subsequently sparked a civil war between rival factions of the IRA. Opposition to the Treaty centred on the issue of Ireland remaining within the British Empire, which would disestablish the Dáil's self-declared Irish Republic. The Treaty also ratified the partition of the country between north and south, though this division was largely ignored in the ensuing debate.

**ASU**
Active Service Unit. IRA formation of armed, full-time Volunteers employing guerrilla tactics. An ASU had the same function as a flying column, and was used to describe columns operating in Dublin and Cork city. In IRA battalion areas, an ASU was typically a full-time unit with a strength smaller than a flying column.

**Auxiliary Cadets**
Special division of the RIC composed of 1,500 former British military officers, intended to act as shock troops in the country. Formed into companies of about 100 constables, the Auxiliary Cadets (also known as 'Auxies') were stationed in Ireland's hotspots, where they quickly became known for their superior fighting skills and

frightening reprisals. In late 1920, Auxiliary Cadets set fire to a large section of Cork city's commercial centre, and fired into a crowd of Gaelic football fans at Croke Park in Dublin. The Auxies wore distinctive Glengarry caps, and were supplied with the latest military weapons and transportation.

**Battalion**          Intermediate IRA formation. A number of companies formed a battalion, and a number of battalions composed an IRA brigade. Battalion areas typically encompassed a large town or a rural district with a number of parishes. Cork city Volunteers were organized into two battalions, the First and Second.

**Black and Tans**     Non-Irish RIC reinforcements recruited mainly from Great Britain's demobilized war veteran population. The British constables were given the Black and Tan moniker due to the motley mixture of uniforms they wore upon their arrival in Ireland in the winter of 1920.

**Commandant**         Military rank for IRA officers at the Battalion, Brigade, and Division level.

**Company**            The basic IRA territorial formation. A company encompassed a small geographic area, such as a city neighbourhood, a village, or a rural parish. Company members elected a captain to command the unit, as well as a first lieutenant and a second lieutenant to assist the captain.

**Cork City**          Second largest city in the Republic of Ireland and the commercial centre of the province of Munster. Set on the River Lee on the edge of one of the world's great natural harbours, Cork boasted a population of about 76,000 during the 1916–1921 period.

**Cork No. 1 Brigade** Florrie O'Donoghue's brigade, also known as the **(IRA)** 'Mid-Cork' Brigade. Composed of nine battalions stretching from the Macroom area in the west to Youghal in the east, the Brigade included the two Cork city battalions. The Brigade area extended east to west in a band across the middle of County Cork, below the Cork No. 2 Brigade and above the Cork No. 3 Brigade area.

**Cork No. 2 Brigade (IRA)**  Also known as the 'North Cork' Brigade, lying north of the Cork No. 1 Brigade area. Its leaders included Liam Lynch, and Seán Moylan.

**Cork No. 3 Brigade (IRA)**  Also known as the 'West Cork' Brigade, lying south and west of the Cork No. 1 Brigade area. Its leaders included Tom Hales, Charlie Hurley, Liam Deasy, and Tom Barry who gained fame commanding the Brigade flying column.

**Cumann na mBan**  Republican women's organization. The militant body supplied key assistance to the IRA during the Anglo-Irish conflict, most notably in logistics, intelligence, and communications. Its members also provided essential grassroots assistance to Sinn Féin and the Dáil Government. To better assist the Volunteers, the Cumann was organized into geographic units corresponding with the IRA's brigade, battalion, and company areas.

**Dáil Éireann**  Parliamentary assembly initially composed of Sinn Féin MPs elected in the 1918 general election who declared Ireland's independence from Great Britain. Banned by the British authorities, the Dáil ran its own shadow government that undermined the British Administration in Ireland from 1919–1921. The Dáil Minister of Defence (Cathal Brugha) nominally commanded the Irish Volunteers, which became known as the Irish Republican Army. After the Anglo-Irish Treaty, the Dáil became the Irish State's national parliament.

**First Southern Division (IRA)**  IRA formation commanded by Liam Lynch and composed of adjoining brigades in Munster. In the spring of 1921, the IRA started structuring groups of its brigades into division areas under the command of a division staff reporting directly to IRA GHQ. The First Southern Division was composed of all the IRA brigades in counties Cork, Kerry, and Waterford, along with the West Limerick Brigade.

**Flying Columns**  Mobile bands of IRA guerrillas that struck vulnerable British forces. Members were full-time Volunteers who had typically been trained by a Volunteer with British Army experience. Flying columns usually numbered between ten and sixty riflemen, and were supported by the nearest local Volunteer company or battalion, which provided logistical and scouting assistance.

**GAA**    Gaelic Athletic Association. Popular sports organization that celebrated Irish culture. It played a key role in the 'Gaelic revival' of the early twentieth century and was considered strongly nationalist. Most IRA leaders were members.

**GHQ (IRA)**    IRA General Headquarters Staff in Dublin. Its members commanded the IRA and formed its ruling Executive Council. GHQ was led by Chief of Staff Richard Mulcahy and heavily influenced by Director of Intelligence Michael Collins.

**GPO**    General Post Office.

**Home Rule**    Form of limited autonomy, similar to the government structure used in Scotland and Wales today. Home Rule in Ireland was one of the most pressing political issues in Britain from 1880–1920, and nearly sparked a civil war in Ireland in 1914. Under Home Rule, Ireland would have assumed some self-government funct-ions, but would not control its own military, foreign affairs, or taxation structures.

**IRA**    Irish Republican Army, also known as the Irish Volunteers. The independent militia initially formed in 1913 to secure Irish Home Rule. The Volunteers eventually evolved into an under-ground army sworn to use physical force to secure an independent Irish Republic. Historians cannot agree on a reliable membership figure, though 60,000 seems likely. However, due to an acute weapons shortage, the number of armed IRA guerrillas was a fraction of that. At the time of the July 1921 Truce, the IRA possessed just 3,000 rifles.

**IRB**    Irish Republican Brotherhood. Secret society committed to winning Irish independence through physical force. Founded in the 1860s, its members were called Fenians. In the early twentieth century, the 'organization' was revived in Ireland, and its leaders planned the 1916 Easter Rising. Afterwards, the IRA largely overshadowed the IRB, though most senior Volunteer leaders retained membership in both bodies. Michael Collins served as President of the IRB's ruling Supreme Council, and used his IRB position to build support for the Anglo-Irish Treaty. The IRB collapsed at the outbreak of the Irish Civil War. In December 1922, Florrie O'Donoghue failed in his attempt to revive the body to help settle the Civil War. Senior Free State Army officers briefly reorganized the Brotherhood, but it was permanently dismantled following the 'Army Mutiny' Crisis of 1924.

**IO**  Intelligence officer

**Irish Parliamentary Party**  Also known as the IPP and the Nationalist Party. Founded by Charles Stuart Parnell and later led by John Redmond, this moderate party attempted to win Irish self-government through constitutional means. It championed Irish Home Rule rather than outright independence, and dominated Irish politics from 1880 until its defeat by Sinn Féin in the 1918 General Election.

**Irish Volunteers**  Independent militia also known as the Irish Republican Army in the 1920–1921 period. 'Volunteer' is a term used to describe an IRA member.

**MP**  Member of the British Parliament at Westminster.

**NCO**  Non-commissioned officer in the British Army. Corporals and sergeants rank as NCOs.

**OC**  Abbreviation for 'Officer Commanding'. In the IRA, units above the company level were commanded by an OC. Unit executive officers (the second-in-command) were called Vice-Commanders or Vice OC.

**RIC**  Royal Irish Constabulary. Ireland's national police force, organized into a well-armed paramilitary body stationed in protected barracks. The Irish force was similar to France's Gendarmerie or Italy's Carabinieri. The RIC numbered 10,000–15,000 constables during the 1919–1921 conflict. It was disbanded in 1922.

**Sinn Féin**  Irish separatist political party that demanded full independence from Britain. After sweeping the 1918 general election, Sinn Féin MPs (now known as TDs) formed their own national parliament called Dáil Eireann. British officials generically called Republicans 'Shinners'.

**The Truce**    Ceasefire between the British Government and the Irish Republican Army, declared on 11 July 1921. The Truce allowed Volunteers to move about openly, though without 'provocative' gestures such as parading with arms. The ceasefire continued through Britain's evacuation of the twenty-six county area in 1922.

**TD (Teachta Dála)**    Member of the Irish parliament, Dáil Éireann, in Dublin.

**Vice-Commander**    Second-in-Command of an IRA division, brigade or battalion. Also called Vice-Commandant or Vice OC.

# BIOGRAPHIES

**Tadg Barry**

Prominent Cork city Volunteer and Sinn Féin official. An early leader of Cork's Volunteer movement, Barry transitioned into the political sphere and was elected a city Alderman for Sinn Féin. He spent 1921 as a British prisoner at Ballykinlar Camp in County Down. During the Truce period in November 1921, a British sentry shot Barry dead while he stood with a group of prisoners speaking to departing colleagues.

**Tom Barry**

Commander of the Cork No. 3 Flying Column. Belligerent, yet brilliant, the British Army veteran led the West Cork column at its famed Kilmichael ambush in December 1920. Barry's flying column dodged British troops for the rest of the war, punishing them at Crossbarry, one of the conflict's largest engagements. During the Truce period he was promoted to First Southern Division Training Officer. Barry joined the militant faction of the Anti-Treaty IRA, though in early 1923 he changed his position and advocated peace. He later returned to the IRA and stayed active until his resignation as Chief of Staff in 1937. O'Donoghue helped Barry research his classic memoir *Guerrilla Days in Ireland,* and the Cork city residents remained friendly. Barry delivered O'Donoghue's graveside oration.

**Reggie Brown (Coleridge Marchment Jr)**

Son of Josephine McCoy and Coleridge Marchment Brown. In later years he retained his baptismal name Coleridge Reginald Marchment, though he was known as Reggie to his family and friends. He studied medicine at University College, Cork and subsequently practised in Lincoln, England, where he raised his family. He died in 1998.

**Cathal Brugha**

Dáil Minister for Defence 1919–1922. Brugha gained fame for his heroism during the 1916

Rising, when he single-handedly held a position against British troops, despite being critically wounded. An ineffective administrator, he was overshadowed in the IRA by Michael Collins and Richard Mulcahy. His personal dislike of Collins probably contributed to Brugha's prominent opposition to the Anglo-Irish Treaty. During the opening days of the Civil War, Brugha was killed in Dublin after making a brave but suicidal one-man charge against a group of Free State soldiers.

**Sir Roger Casement** Leader of the 1916 Rising. As a consul in the British Foreign Office, Casement was knighted for uncovering atrocities in the Belgian Congo. After his retirement, the Irish nationalist travelled to Germany to gain military assistance for the 1916 Rising. He subsequently failed in his attempt to raise an Irish brigade from Irish born British prisoners of war. On the eve of the Rising, a German submarine landed Casement at Banna Strand on the Kerry coast, but he was captured within a few hours. Convicted of treason, he was hanged in the summer of 1916.

**Peadar Clancy** Vice-Commander of the Dublin Brigade and prominent GHQ officer. A printer by trade, Clancy is largely forgotten today, but in 1920 he was a strong and charismatic leader. Todd Andrews said Clancy left him with 'an indelible impression of the superman' (Andrews, *Dublin Made Me*, pp. 148–9). Clancy was captured with Dick McKee, and tortured and killed in Beggars' Bush Barracks following the Bloody Sunday shootings.

**Jack Cody** Active Cork No. 1 Brigade Volunteer. Cody served as a driver with the Brigade's Transportation Section. In the fall of 1920, he joined Pa Murray's squad in London that planned to assassinate members of the British Cabinet in response to Terence MacSwiney's hunger strike. O'Donoghue chose Cody as his driver for the Reggie Brown kidnapping, and Cody and his sister later brought the boy back to Cork in December 1920. During the spring of 1921, Cody joined the Brigade flying column near Macroom.

**Michael Collins**

The War of Independence's most celebrated leader. The West Cork native spent his early adulthood in London working as a bank and postal clerk. There, Sam Maguire introduced Collins to the GAA, Irish cultural groups, and eventually the Irish Republican Brotherhood. Collins returned to Dublin to fight in the Easter Rising, and emerged from prison as the Volunteer movement's key leader. He subsequently headed the IRB, organized the IRA's Intelligence Department, and served as the Dáil Minister for Finance. A leader of the Irish delegation to the Anglo-Irish Treaty negotiations, he championed the agreement and was largely responsible for its passage. The first Chairman of the Free State Provisional Government, he took charge of the Irish Army at the outbreak of the Civil War. On 22 August 1922, he was killed in an ambush of his convoy while he toured Cork.

**Tom Crofts**

Leading Cork No. 1 Brigade officer and OC of the Cork city Active Service Unit. Arrested in April 1921, he tunnelled out of Spike Island Prison with other Cork officers in the Truce period. During the Civil War, Crofts commanded the Anti-Treaty First Southern Division and served on the IRA Executive. In early 1923, O'Donoghue and Crofts worked together to end the Civil War. The two remained good friends in Cork over the years. Crofts was active in Cork's Fianna Fáil politics and became future Taoiseach Jack Lynch's election agent.

**Seán Culhane**

Prominent Cork city Brigade officer. The shop clerk acted as intelligence officer in the city, serving as O'Donoghue's head of operations. He organized and led the assassinations of RIC District Commissioner Smyth in the Cork Conservative Club in July 1920, and District Inspector Swanzy in Lisburn the following month. He fought with the Brigade flying column at Coolavokig, but was captured in May 1921. Culhane joined the staff of the First Southern Division during the Truce, and succeeded O'Donoghue as Division Intelligence Officer.

**Liam Deasy**

Commander of the Cork No. 3 Brigade. A carpenter, Deasy succeeded Charlie Hurley as OC of the West Cork Brigade in the spring of 1921 and also served as Cork's IRB Secretary. He and Florence O'Donoghue collaborated closely in planning the proposed Genoa arms shipment. After the Truce in July 1921, Deasy joined the First Southern Division as Vice-Commander and later commanded the unit. During the Civil War he was promoted to Anti-Treaty IRA Deputy Chief-of-Staff. After his capture in early 1923, Deasy issued a unilateral call for surrender, which caused the IRA considerable dissension and morale problems. After the war Deasy renewed his friendship with O'Donoghue. Deasy's War of Independence memoir *Towards Ireland Free* is a worthwhile read.

**Liam de Róiste**

Sinn Féin TD for Cork city. As President of the Cork Gaelic League, de Róiste helped lead the city's Irish cultural revival. A deeply religious man, he questioned the morality of the 1919–1921 guerrilla war which he witnessed first-hand. He kept a compelling diary of his experiences during the conflict, which can be found in the Cork Archives Institute. In April 1921, drunk Black and Tans tried to assassinate de Róiste in his home, but instead killed a Catholic priest houseguest. A moderate Republican, de Róiste voted for the Anglo-Irish Treaty despite death threats from Seán O'Hegarty. De Róiste later became a vehement anti-communist and leader of the Catholic Front movement in the 1930s.

**Eamon de Valera**

President of Sinn Féin and Dáil Éireann from 1918–1922, longtime Taoiseach and President of Ireland. The mathematics teacher ably led Sinn Féin and the political wing of the Independence movement. After his escape from Lincoln Jail in early 1919, de Valera spent the next two years in America raising Republican funds. He rejected the Anglo-Irish Treaty and was one of the driving forces behind Irish Civil War. He and O'Donoghue probably became acquainted during De Valera's tour through Cork and Kerry during the 1921 Truce. De Valera founded the Fianna Fáil Party in 1926, and led its first government in 1932. The dominant Irish political figure of the twentieth century, he headed Fianna Fáil governments from 1932–1948, 1951–1954, and 1957–1959. In 1959, de Valera was elected President of Ireland, serving two terms until his retirement in 1972.

**Dan 'Sandow' Donovan**

Organizer of many Cork city actions and commander of the Cork No. 1 Brigade Flying Column. A carpenter and highly-regarded Gaelic footballer, he was nicknamed 'Sandow' for his resemblance to a famed circus strongman of the period. A tough fighter, Donovan commanded the city's First Battalion and later organized the Brigade Flying Column, leading it to victory in the Coolavokig ambush in the winter of 1921. Donovan later helped plan the massive weapons seizure from the British ship *Upnor* in the Truce period. During the Civil War he commanded the Cork No. 1 Brigade and led some of the Anti-Treaty IRA's largest flying columns.

**Reggie Dunne**

Leader of the IRA's London Battalion. Dunne and London Volunteer Joseph O'Sullivan (both ex-British soldiers) gained infamy in an episode that sparked the Irish Civil War. In June 1922, the two men assassinated former British Army Chief of Staff Field Marshal Sir Henry Wilson, outside his London home. O'Sullivan (who lost his leg in Flanders) and Dunne were captured by a crowd of bystanders, and subsequently tried and hanged.

**Michael Fitzgerald**

Commander of the First (Fermoy) Battalion, Cork No. 2 Brigade, who died on hunger strike in October 1920. Fitzgerald was involved in some of the North Cork Brigade's early successes. Arrested in late 1919, he was jailed without trial through the summer of 1920. He undertook a hunger strike to protest his detention, and died sixty-seven days later in Cork Gaol.

**Jim Grey**

Cork No. 1 Brigade Transportation Officer. A car mechanic, Jim Grey was a favourite driver of the Brigade staff and participated in many actions.

He later joined the Brigade flying column in the hills near Macroom and fought in the Coolavokig Ambush. His brother Miah was also a highly regarded Brigade driver.

**Arthur Griffith**
Skilled propagandist, founder of the Sinn Féin Party, and the intellectual leader of the independence movement. From 1919-1920, Griffith acted as Dáil President during Eamon de Valera's absence in America. With Michael Collins, Griffith led the Anglo-Irish Treaty negotiations and later championed the Treaty. He subsequently succeeded de Valera as President of Dáil Éireann, and served as the de facto president of the Irish Free State. Overworked and stressed by the outbreak of the Civil War, Griffith died of a cerebral haemorrhage in August 1922.

**Hales Brothers**
Tom Hales founded the Volunteer organization in the Bandon area. He was OC Cork No. 3 Brigade at the time of his capture in July 1920, which resulted in his torture by British Army officers in Victoria Barracks. (A photo of his experience can be seen on the cover of Peter Hart's *The IRA at War, 1916–1923*.) His brother Seán commanded the Bandon Battalion in the Cork No. 3 Brigade. Seán was a Free State Army General and Pro-Treaty TD when he was assassinated in response to the execution of IRA prisoners in 1923. (His death prompted the Free State's execution of Liam Mellowes, Joe McKelvey, Rory O'Connor and Dick Barrett.) Another Hales brother, Donal, helped organize the aborted Italian arms shipment in Genoa, which Florrie O'Donoghue also worked on.

**Pat Higgins**
Adjutant, Cork No. 1 Brigade. A close associate of Tomás MacCurtain since the founding of the Cork Volunteers, Higgins left the Brigade staff in 1917 and was succeeded by Florrie O'Donoghue. He remained active in Sinn Féin and the Dáil Ministry of Local Government in Cork.

**Alfred Hore**
Josephine Brown's brother-in-law. Husband of Cecily McCoy and father of Fred and Clara Hore.

**Charlie Hurley**
Commander of the Cork No. 3 Brigade. An office clerk, Hurley succeeded Tom Hales as OC of the

Cork No. 3 Brigade. Florrie O'Donoghue, Liam Deasy, and Tom Barry all claimed Hurley prophesied his own death. On 19 March 1921, Hurley was hiding in a farmhouse recovering from wounds he received leading an IRA ambush at Upton Railway Station. In the early morning, British troops stormed the house. With a pistol in each hand, Hurley climbed from his bed, rushed downstairs to the kitchen, and fired on a group of British soldiers, wounding three of them. He was shot down as he tried to escape through the yard. See Tom Kelleher in *Rebel Cork's Fighting Story*, pp. 158–9; Barry, *Guerrilla Days in Ireland*, p. 136; and Deasy, *Towards Ireland Free*, p. 250.

**David Lloyd-George** British Prime Minister, 1916–1923. Leader of the Liberal Party, Lloyd-George headed a coalition government with the Conservative Party. Key members of his government included Winston Churchill, Austin Chamberlain, and Lord Birkenhead.

**Con Lucey** First Southern Division Medical Officer. Lucey graduated from University College, Cork and was a member of the IRA's 'College Company'. He later saw action with the Cork No. 3 Brigade's flying column. Lucey joined O'Donoghue's First Southern Divison Headquarters in the spring of 1921, most likely to treat a scabies outbreak in neighbouring flying columns. During the Civil War, he headed the Anti-Treaty IRA's medical services.

**Liam Lynch** Commander of the Cork No. 2 Brigade, OC of the First Southern Division, and Chief of Staff of the Anti-Treaty IRA. The former shop clerk led some of his brigade's most successful sorties, including the kidnapping of British Brigadier-General Lucas and an assault on British soldiers attending church in Fermoy. A capable administrator, Lynch impressed colleagues with his unwavering dedication to the Republican cause, which seemed almost religious in its intensity. Lynch was O'Donoghue's commanding officer in the First Southern Division, and became the primary Republican leader during the Civil War.

He led Anti-Treaty IRA forces until his death at the hands of Free State troops in Tipperary on 10 April 1923.

**Tomás MacCurtain**    Commander of the Cork No. 1 Brigade and Lord Mayor of Cork. A long-time clerk, Irish teacher, and traditional musician, MacCurtain played a key role in the city's Gaelic revival. He commanded the Cork Brigade since its founding in 1914. During the 1916 Rising, MacCurtain failed to put his brigade into action, due to confusion over orders from Dublin. After his release from Frongoch Detention Camp in 1917, he left the IRB, believing the organization interfered with the Volunteer's chain of command. In late 1919, MacCurtain pressed GHQ to allow the Cork No. 1 Brigade to initiate guerrilla operations, and his units produced some of the earliest Volunteer triumphs of the conflict. A charming man possessing considerable organizing ability, MacCurtain combined the political, military, and cultural aspects of the Independence movement. Shortly after being elected Lord Mayor of Cork, MacCurtain was assassinated by members of the Cork police.

**Tomas MacDonagh**    Poet, author, and literature professor at University College Dublin. One of the seven signatories of the 1916 Rising Proclamation, he was executed following the rebellion.

**Denis MacNeilus**    Prominent Cork No. 1 Brigade Volunteer officer who broke out of Cork Gaol in November 1918. He served on the Brigade staff throughout the War of Independence, and during the Civil War commanded the Anti-Treaty forces' First Northern Division. MacNeilus later moved to Sligo and O'Donoghue helped erect a memorial to him there following his death in 1954. See Ms. 31,144, NLI for details.

**Terence MacSwiney**    Commander of the Cork No. 1 Brigade, TD for Mid-Cork, and Lord Mayor of Cork. A teacher by profession, MacSwiney helped Tomás MacCurtain organize the Volunteers in Cork. He succeeded MacCurtain as both OC of the Cork No. 1 Brigade and Lord Mayor of Cork. A playwright and intellectual, MacSwiney became the movement's most celebrated martyr following his death on hunger strike in October 1920. His siblings continued to play an important role in Cork's Republican movement. His sister Mary successfully toured America on behalf of Sinn Féin, was elected TD in Cork city, and became a prominent and vocal opponent of the Anglo-Irish Treaty. With another sister Anna, she also was a key organizer of the Cumann na mBan. Brother Seán was a leading Brigade officer who dramatically escaped from Spike Island Prison by boat in the spring of 1921. Briefly a TD for Mid-Cork, Seán joined the Anti-Treaty IRA Executive and supported its 1923 ceasefire.

**Sam Maguire**  Leader and organizer of the IRA and IRB in Great Britain. A Corkman and one of the few Protestants in the Volunteer Movement, Maguire acted as Michael Collins' mentor during his time in London. Maguire became a dean of London Republicans, while remaining active in the Irish cultural movement. His contributions to the GAA are still recognized by the All-Ireland Cup bearing his name.

**Coleridge Marchment Sr.**  Husband of Josephine McCoy, father of Gerald and Reggie Marchment, killed in action on the Western Front in October 1917. Before his marriage and after his business went bankrupt, he changed his surname from Brown to Marchment.

**Cecily McCoy**  Sister of Josephine McCoy, wife of Alfred Hore. Cecily 'Cissie' McCoy Hore frequently cared for Gerald Marchment, and took in Reggie Brown Marchment after he was brought to Ireland in 1920. She lived in Youghal with her husband Alfred and their two children Fred and Clara.

**Kathleen McCoy**  Sister of Josephine McCoy. A nurse, Kathleen 'Kitty' McCoy lived with Jo in their home at Rockboro Terrace, Cork.

**Dick McKee**  Key IRA GHQ leader and OC of the Dublin Brigade. The printer was an effective and charismatic leader, who rivalled Michael Collins as the strongest figure in the IRA. He and Peadar

Clancy were arrested in Dublin on the eve of Bloody Sunday (the shooting of British Army intelligence officer which they helped plan), and were tortured and killed the following night in Beggars' Bush Barracks.

**Joe McKelvey**     Commander Belfast Brigade and Anti-Treaty IRA leader. McKelvey helped organize the assassination of District Inspector Swanzy in Lisburn. He was a key opponent of the Anglo-Irish Treaty within both the IRB and the Anti-Treaty IRA's militant faction. Captured in the Four Courts, he was executed by the Free State Government as a reprisal for the assassination of Pro-Treaty TD Seán Hales.

**Seán Moylan**     Prominent leader and successful flying column commander of the Cork No. 2 Brigade. A carpenter by trade, Moylan led his column to victories at Tureengarriffe and Clonbanin, and succeeded Liam Lynch as OC Cork No. 2 Brigade. As TD, he voted against the Anglo-Irish Treaty, and was associated with the First Southern Division's moderate faction during the run-up to the Civil War. After the war, Moylan enjoyed a long career as a Fianna Fáil TD and Minister for Lands. Moylan and O'Donoghue remained friendly over the years, and O'Donoghue helped organize an annual Moylan commemoration in Mallow.

**Richard Mulcahy**     IRA Chief of Staff from 1917–1922, TD for Dublin, and Free State Minister of Defence from 1922–1924. A former medical student, Mulcahy led the successful Ashbourne Ambush during the 1916 Rising, which proved to be a precursor to the IRA's guerrilla campaign. As IRA Chief of Staff, Mulcahy often clashed with his superior Cathal Brugha but worked well with Michael Collins. Mulcahy supported the Anglo-Irish Treaty and became Free State Minister of Defence in 1922. After the death of Michael Collins, he was the primary leader of the Irish Army. An excellent organizer without much personal charisma, he later headed the Fine Gael Party, and served as Minister for Education in the Fine Gael governments of the 1940s and 1950s.

**Humphrey Murphy**   Commander of the Kerry No. 2 Brigades and Anti-Treaty IRA Leader. Schoolteacher 'Free' Murphy was the personable commander of the Kerry No. 2 Brigade, which adjoined the Cork No. 1 Brigade's western boundary. In the run-up to the Civil War, Murphy supported O'Donoghue's IRA and IRB peace efforts. In May 1922, Murphy signed the Army Officers' Statement which called for IRA unity. He remained committed to the Anti-Treaty side throughout the Civil War, and helped organize a bitter guerrilla campaign against Free State Forces in Kerry.

**Leo Murphy**   Commander of the Third Battalion, Cork No. 1 Brigade and close associate of Florrie O'Donoghue. Murphy apprenticed with Florrie O'Donoghue in Michael Nolan's drapery shop, and the two men joined the Cork city Volunteers together. Murphy organized the Brigade's Third Battalion and led a number of attacks on Crown forces in 1920 and 1921. He was killed on 26 June 1921, when British forces surrounded his battalion council meeting in Waterfall. Murphy sprinted from the encircled pub, firing as he ran, and almost broke through the cordon, but was shot down in a close-by field. Forty years later Florrie O'Donoghue helped organize a memorial to him near that spot and delivered its commemoration address. (See Ms. 31,444, NLI for details.)

**Mick Murphy**   Leading Cork city officer, who organized many attacks and ambushes. A carpenter, Murphy commanded the city's Second Battalion until his capture in the spring of 1921. He subsequently took the Anti-Treaty side during the Civil War. Murphy was also a famed hurler who led the county to three All-Ireland championships.

**Patrick 'Pa' Murray**   Commander of the Cork city Active Service Unit and leader of many ambushes and attacks. The nephew of First Battalion commander Fred Murray, 'Pa' commanded IRA forces in Cork city during 1921 and kept them active despite intense British pressure. Murray earlier headed an assassination team sent to London to kill members of the British Cabinet during Terence

MacSwiney's hunger strike. He also led the shooting team that tracked down the informer 'Croxy' O'Connor in New York City in early 1922. During the Civil War, he sided with the Anti-Treaty forces and became the IRA's OC Britain.

**Art O'Brien**

President of the Irish Self-Determination League in London. An early organizer of the Irish Volunteers, O'Brien had transitioned into a more political role by 1920. He met with reporters, contacted sympathetic politicians, and as president of the Irish Self-Determination League tried to mobilize Britain's significant Irish population in support of the Republican campaign.

**Fr Dominic O'Connor**

Cork No. 1 Brigade Chaplain. Fr Dominic was a source of great spiritual and occasional physical assistance to city Volunteers. A Capuchin priest and former British Army chaplain who saw combat in Salonika, he was also a zealous Republican and the brother of Brigade Quarter-master Joe O'Connor. Fr Dominic stood sentry during the MacNeilus prison escape, acted as Terence MacSwiney's chaplain during his hunger strike, served a one-year stretch in a British prison, and ministered to the Anti-Treaty Four Courts garrison under artillery fire at the outbreak of the Civil War. In 1922, the Capuchin Order banished Fr Dominic to the United States. O'Connor served out his days ministering in Eastern Oregon's remote high desert, dying there in 1935. In the ensuing years, Florrie O'Donoghue, Joe O'Connor, and Seán O'Hegarty led a difficult campaign to return Fr Dominic's remains to Cork. (Fianna Fáil leaders Eamon de Valera, Seán T. O'Kelly, and Oscar Traynor initially opposed the effort.) In 1958, after a number of years of lobbying, Fr Dominic was brought home to an enormous funeral hosted by the Cork No. 1 Old IRA Association. 500 IRA veterans marched alongside the remains of their former chaplain. Breda O'Donoghue Lucci reported that her mother walked behind Fr

Dominic's casket weeping. See Ms. 31,306 and 31,449, NLI for details.

**Joe O'Connor** Cork No. 1 Brigade Quartermaster and capable leader on the Brigade staff. Joe O'Connor was Florrie O'Donoghue's close friend and colleague, first on the Cork No. 1 Brigade Council and later on the staff of the First Southern Division, where O'Connor served as Division Quartermaster. In 1922, he chaired the tumultuous third IRA Convention, which resulted in a temporary split in the Anti-Treaty forces. During the Civil War, O'Connor became the Anti-Treaty IRA's Quartermaster General. In later years he lived in Cork and remained good friends with Florrie throughout his life.

**Patrick O'Donoghue** No relation to Florrie O'Donoghue. Leader of the IRA in Manchester, UK. Patrick O'Donoghue was one of Michael Collins' important IRB contacts in Britain and helped organize IRA escapes from Lincoln Jail and Strangeways Prison in 1919.

**O'Donoghue Sisters** Florrie O'Donoghue maintained close relations with his four sisters. Three of them (Nell, Albina, and Margaret) lived with him above Michael Nolan's shop at 55 North Main Street in Cork city. They sheltered him while O'Donoghue was 'on the run', and often cared for Gerald and Reggie Marchment. Sister Elizabeth remained with his parents in Rathmore.

**Patrick Sarsfield (P.S.) O'Hegarty** A founder of the Sinn Féin Party and effective Republican propagandist. The brother of Seán O'Hegarty, P.S. managed the Cork Post Office until his dismissal for Republican activities. He remained close to Arthur Griffith, supported the Anglo-Irish Treaty, and became the Irish Free State's first Postmaster General. An author of numerous books and academic articles, his work *The Victory of Sinn Féin* was an early first-hand account of the independence struggle.

**Seán O'Hegarty** Commander of the Cork No. 1 Brigade. The pugnacious, opinionated, and strict leader succeeded Terence MacSwiney as Brigade OC in August 1920. Old by IRA standards (he was in his early thirties), O'Hegarty's atheism and alcohol abstinence likely contributed to his reputation as an eccentric and sometimes difficult character. Due to a sharp and sarcastic tongue his men called him (with irony) 'The Joker', though they were devoted to him. The former postal clerk brought discipline and an aggressive fighting spirit to the brigade, but frequently feuded with GHQ leaders in Dublin. In the run-up to the Civil War, O'Hegarty gained headlines by organizing the capture of the British arms ship *Upnor*, threatening the lives of pro-Treaty TDs, and abducting a hostile British journalist. However, O'Hegarty stayed neutral during the Civil War and with O'Donoghue laboured to negotiate an end to the conflict. O'Hegarty's wife was also an active Republican, and she served a short jail sentence while helping to organize the Cork Cumann na mBan. Seán O'Hegarty and Brigade Quartermaster Joe O'Connor were probably O'Donoghue's closest personal friends to survive the 1916–1923 period

**Gearóid O'Sullivan**    IRA Adjutant-General from 1919–1922. The West Cork schoolteacher was a senior leader in both GHQ and the IRB, and a close associate of Michael Collins and Richard Mulcahy. Though efficient, O'Sullivan often displayed a condescension that annoyed visiting country officers. During the Civil War he served as a top general in the Free State Army.

**Charles Stuart Parnell**    Charismatic leader of the Irish Home Rule movement during the 1880s. At the height of his success, his Irish Parliamentary Party was shattered when Parnell married a divorcee named Katherine O'Shea, with whom he had carried on a long affair. A Protestant, Parnell was denounced by the Catholic Church and his party split amid great recriminations. Parnell died abruptly in 1890 and it took over a decade for his party to reunite.

**Patrick Pearse**    Educator, writer, and leader of the 1916 Rebellion. He acted as President of the Irish Republic and Commander-in-Chief of the insurgent forces, and was executed following the end of the Rising. An intellectual, he founded St Enda's school in Dublin, which produced many of the top Volunteer leaders of the 1919–1921 period.

**Seán Phelan**	IRA Volunteer in Great Britain. Seán Phelan was a teacher and the son of Irish immigrants living in Liverpool. After helping Florrie O'Donoghue kidnap Reggie Brown, Phelan joined the Cork No. 3 Brigade flying column. His first action was the disastrous Upton Train Station Ambush in March 1921. Acting on information provided by Josephine O'Donoghue, the column intended to ambush a small detail of British soldiers travelling by train from Kinsale to Cork. However, a second and much larger detachment of British troops unexpectedly boarded the train at Kinsale Junction. In a bloody affair, Phelan and two Volunteers were killed, along with six passengers. According to Florrie O'Donoghue, British soldiers shot and bayoneted Phelan as he tried to escape through the station bathroom window. Phelan was buried in the Republican plot at St Finbarr's Cemetery in Cork city. See Deasy, *Towards Ireland Free*, p. 222; and O'Donoghue's article and notes on the ambush, Ms. 31,301, NLI.

**Matt Ryan**	Intelligence officer associated with the Cork No. 1 Brigade leadership. Ryan and O'Donoghue were members of the city's 'G' Company, and became close friends. Captured in 1921, Ryan escaped from Bere Island Detention Camp on the day of the Truce, 11 July 1921. He took the Anti-Treaty side during the Civil War, served on Liam Lynch's General Staff, and was leading Republican forces in his native Tipperary when he was killed on 29 March 1923.

**General Sir Edward Peter Strickland**	Commander of the British Army's 6th Division at Cork's Victoria Barracks. Strickland (1869–1951) was a distinguished infantry officer and veteran of Britain's colonial wars in the Sudan and West Africa. He led the British 1st Division through the latter half of the First World War, including its Somme and Passchendaele campaigns. After leaving Ireland in 1922, he commanded the British 2nd Division, and retired as a Lieutenant General in command of British troops in Egypt. O'Donoghue and Seán O'Hegarty tried to kill General Strickland in September 1920.

**Dominic Sullivan** Prominent Cork No. 1 Brigade staff officer. He succeeded O'Donoghue as Brigade Adjutant in April 1921. Sullivan resigned from the IRA at the outbreak of the Civil War, and stayed neutral during the conflict.

**District Inspector Oswald Swanzy** Active RIC commander in Cork city. The Monaghan native fiercely opposed the Volunteers in Cork. Swanzy helped arrest Denis MacNeilus after he shot Head Constable Clark in November 1918, and later led police reprisal parties following the shooting of District Inspector MacDonagh. Strong circumstantial evidence linked Swanzy to the killing of Tomás MacCurtain, and a Cork Coroner's Jury indicted him for murder. He subsequently left the city for Lisburn, Northern Ireland. The Cork No. 1 Brigade tracked him there and assassinated Swanzy as he left church, sparking a three-day Anti-Catholic riot in the town.

**Nora Wallace** Communications Officer for the Cork No. 1 Brigade. Wallace appears to have been the only woman during the conflict to hold a Brigade-level IRA officer's commission. Nora and her sister Sheila ran a newsagents just off Patrick Street in the Cork city centre that served as Brigade head-quarters until almost the end of the Anglo-Irish war. In May 1921, the British Army closed the Wallace shop and ordered the sisters out of the city.

**Maurice 'Moss' Walsh** Staff officer with the Cork No. 2 Brigade and the First Southern Division. He acted as a typist and assistant in Liam Lynch's Brigade Headquarters. In April 1921, he joined the First Southern Division Headquarters staff in a similar capacity. During the Civil War, Walsh served with the Anti-Treaty forces as a member of Lynch's General Headquarters Staff.

**J.J. Walsh**

Sinn Féin TD for Cork city. A former head of the Cork GAA and a co-founder of the Irish Volunteers in Cork, Walsh was elected TD in 1918 and helped organize the Dáil government in Cork. Walsh voted for the Anglo-Irish Treaty and later served as Free State Minister of Posts and Telegraphs.

# BIBLIOGRAPHY

**PRIMARY SOURCES**

CORK

*Cork Archives Institute*

Liam de Róiste Diaries
Seamus Fitzgerald Papers
Robert Hales Papers
Donal Hales Papers
Roibeárd Langford Papers
Siobhán Lankford Papers

*Cork City Library*

Guys Cork Directory, 1920

*Cork Public Museum*

Terence MacSwiney Papers
Tomás MacCurtain Papers
Seán Hegarty Papers

*University College, Cork*

Alfred O'Rahilly Papers
Public Records Office, British in Ireland Series [microfilm]

DUBLIN

*National Library of Ireland*

F.S. Bourke Collection
Department of Defence Archives [microfilm]
Frank Gallagher Papers
Joseph McGarrity Papers
J.J. O'Connell Papers
Florence O'Donoghue Papers
James O'Donovan Papers

## University College, Dublin

Richard Mulcahy Papers
Ernie O'Malley Papers
Ernie O'Malley Notebooks (included in Papers): Interviews with Stan Barry, Charlie Brown, Mick Burke, Dan Corkery, Martin Corry, Tom Crofts, Seán Culhane, Seán Daly, Dan 'Sandow' Donovan, Eamonn Enright, Seamus Fitzgerald, Dan Healy, Seán Hendrick, Ray Kennedy, Michael Leahy, Pat Margetts, James Minihan, Mick Murphy, Seamus Murphy, Patrick 'Pa' Murray, Connie Neenan, Florence O'Donoghue, Paddy O'Reilly, George Power, Connor Reilly, Mick O'Sullivan.

## Military Archives (Cathal Brugha Barracks)

Bureau of Military History: Statements of Robert Ahern, Seán Culhane, Dan Donovan, Daniel Healy, Mick Murphy, Patrick 'Pa' Murray, Florence O'Donoghue
Department of Defence Correspondence Relating to Disappearances in Cork City
'Executions by IRA'
'British Casualties, Military'
Statement of Captain O'Dwyer

## LONDON

### Imperial War Museum

Gen. E.P. Strickland Papers – *History of the 6th Division in Ireland*, official history covering 1919–1921, written by the division staff; *Summary of Important Orders to the 17th Infantry Brigade from HQ 6th Division*, a booklet prepared by brigade staff; *Sinn Féin and the Irish Volunteers*, booklet prepared by the General Headquarters staff of the Irish Command; Miscellaneous correspondence and material relating to Strickland in Ireland 1920–1921; Stickland Diaries.
Lt Gen. Sir Hugh Jeaudwine Papers
Lt Gen. A.E. Percival Papers

### Kings College, Liddell Hart Centre for Military Archives

Papers of Maj. Gen. Howard Foulkes

## INTERVIEWS/CORRESPONDENCE

Breda O'Donoghue Lucci
Emilio Lucci
Seán O'Callaghan
Dr Margaret O'Donoghue
Dr Patrick O'Donoghue
Dan O'Donovan
Donal O'Donovan
Father Patrick Twohig
Pat Whooley

## MISCELLANEOUS MATERIAL

Untitled Article Relating to Tadhg O'Sullivan and the MacCurtain
  Inquest, courtesy Dr Seamus O'Donoghue, Cork
*Cork Chamber of Commerce and Shipping Annual Reports, 1919–1922,*
  courtesy Cork Chamber of Commerce
*A Brief History of the Diocese of Baker,* by Father Dominic O'Connor and
  Rev. Patrick Gaire, Baker Diocesan Chancery, Oregon, 1930

## NEWSPAPERS AND PERIODICALS

*An Cosantóir*
*An tÓglac*
*An tÓglac (1961–1971)*
*Cork Constitution*
*Cork County Eagle and Munster Advertiser*
*Cork Examiner*
*Cork Weekly News*
*Freeman's Journal*
*Irish Bulletin*
*Irish Times*
*New York Times*
*Old Ireland*
*South Wales Echo*
*The Times*
*Weekly Summary*
*Western Bulletin*
*Wolfe Tone Annual*

# PAMPHLETS

*American Commission on the Conditions in Ireland Interim Report*, American Commission on Conditions in Ireland (London: Hardin & Moore Ltd, 1921)

*Cuimhneachán 1916–1966* (Dublin: Department of External Affairs, 1966)

*An Introduction to the Bureau of Military History 1913–1921* (Dublin: Military Archives, 2002)

*Who Burnt Cork City?* (Dublin: Irish Labour and Trade Union Congress, 1921)

# SELECT BIBLIOGRAPHY

Abbott, Richard, *Police Casualties in Ireland 1919–1922* (Cork: Mercier Press, 2000)

Andrews, C.S., *Dublin Made Me* (Dublin: Mercier Press, 1969)

Augusteijn, Joost, *From Public Defiance to Guerrilla Warfare* (Dublin: Irish Academic Press, 1996)

— (ed.) *The Irish Revolution 1913–1923* (New York: Palgrave, 2002)

Barry, Tom, *Guerrilla Days in Ireland* (Boulder, CO: Roberts Rinehart Publishers, 1995)

Béaslaí, Piaras, *Michael Collins and the Making of a New Ireland, Vol. I* (Dublin: Phoenix Publishing Company, 1926)

Borgonovo, John, 'Informers, Intelligence and the "Anti-Sinn Féin Society": The Anglo-Irish War in Cork City, 1920–1921', MA Thesis, University College, Cork, 1998

Bowden, T., 'The Irish Underground and the War of Independence, 1919–1921', *Journal of Contemporary History*, VIII, No. 2 (1973)

Bell, J. Bowyer, *The Secret Army* (New Brunswick, NJ: Transaction Publishers, 1997)

Boyce, D. George, *Nationalism in Ireland* (London: Routledge, 1985)

— *The Irish Question and British Politics, 1868–1996* (London: Macmillan, 1996)

Boyle, John F. and de Burca, Pádraig, *Free State or Republic* (Dublin: University College Press, 2002)

Brewer, John D., *The Royal Irish Constabulary: An Oral History* (Belfast: Institute of Irish Studies, Queens University, 1990)

Callwell, C.E., *Field-Marshal Sir Henry Wilson: His Life and Diaries* (London: Cassell, 1927)

Campbell, Colm, *Emergency Law in Ireland, 1918–1924* (Oxford: Oxford University Press, 1994)

Chavasse, Moirin, *Terence MacSwiney* (Dublin: Clonmore and Reynolds, 1961)

Clarke, Olga Pyne, *She Came of Decent People* (London: Methuen, 1986)

Conlon, Lil, *Cumann na mBan and the Women of Ireland, 1913–1925* (Kilkenny: Kilkenny People Press, 1969)

Coogan, Tim Pat, *The Man Who Made Ireland, The Life and Death of Michael Collins* (Niwot, CO: Roberts Rhinehart, 1992)

Costello, Francis J., *Enduring the Most, The Life and Death of Terence MacSwiney* (Dingle: Brandon Books, 1995)

— *The Irish Revolution and Its Aftermath* (Dublin: Irish Academic Press, 2003)

Crozier, Brig. General F.P., *Ireland Forever* (Bath: Cedric Chivers Ltd, 1971)

— *Word to Gandhi* (London: Williams and Norgate, 1927)

Curran, Joseph, 'Decline and Fall of the IRB', *Eire/Ireland*, Winter, (1975) pp. 14–23

— *The Birth of the Irish Free State* (Alabama: University of Alabama Press, 1980)

Dangerfield, George, *The Damnable Question, A Study in Anglo-Irish Relations* (Boston: Little, Brown and Company, 1976)

Deasy, Liam, *Towards Ireland Free* (Cork: Royal Carbery Books, 1992)

— *Brother Against Brother* (Cork: Mercier Press, 1998)

Doherty, Gabriel and Keogh, Dermot (eds), *Michael Collins and the Making of the Irish State* (Cork: Mercier Press, 1998)

Dwyer, T. Ryle, *Michael Collins, The Man Who Won the War* (Cork: Mercier Press, 1990)

— *Tans, Terror and Troubles, Kerry's Real Fighting Story 1913–23* (Cork: Mercier Press, 2001)

Fallon, Charlotte Mary, *Soul on Fire, The Biography of Mary MacSwiney* (Cork: Mercier Press, 1986)

Fitzgerald, Seamus, 'East Cork Activities', *Capuchin Annual*, 1970

Fitzpatrick, David, *Politics and Irish Life 1913–21: Provincial Experiences of War and Revolution* (Dublin: Gill and Macmillan, 1977)

— (ed.) *Revolution in Ireland?* (Dublin: Trinity History Workshop, Trinity College Dublin, 1990)

— ' "Unofficial Emisaries": British Army Boxers in the Irish Free State, 1926', *Irish Historical Studies*, XXX, No. 118 (November 1996)

Foster, R.F., *Modern Ireland 1600–1972* (London: Allen Lane, 1988)

Garvin, Tom, *The Evolution of Irish Nationalist Politics* (Dublin: Gill and MacMillan, 1981)

— *Nationalist Revolutionaries in Ireland 1858–1928* (Oxford: Clarendon Press, 1987)

— *1922: The Birth of Irish Democracy* (Dublin: Gill and Macmillan, 1996)

Greaves, C. Desmond, *Liam Mellowes and the Irish Revolution* (London: Lawrence and Wishart, 1971)

Griffith, Kenneth and O'Grady, Timothy, *Curious Journey, An Oral History of Ireland's Unfinished Revolution* (Cork: Mercier Press, 1998)

Gaughan, J. Anthony, *The Memoirs of Constable Jeremiah Mee* (Dublin: Anvil Books, 1975)

— *Alfred O'Rahilly, Vol. II, Public Figure* (Dublin: Kingdom Books, 1989)

Hamilton, Nigel, *Monty, The Making of a General, 1887–1942* (New York: McGraw Hill Books, 1981)

Hart Peter, *The IRA and Its Enemies, Violence and Community in Cork, 1916–1923* (Oxford: Oxford University Press, 1998)

— (ed.) *British Intelligence in Ireland, 1920–21, The Final Reports* (Cork: Cork University Press, 2002)

— *The IRA at War 1916–1923* (Oxford: Oxford University Press, 2003)

Hopkinson, Michael, *Green Against Green: The Irish Civil War* (Dublin: Gill and Macmillan, 1988)

— *The Last Days of Dublin Castle, the Mark Sturgis Diaries* (Dublin: Irish Academic Press, 1999)

— *The Irish War of Independence* (Dublin: Gill and Macmillan, 2002)

Hull, Mark, *German Espionage in Ireland, 1939–1945* (Dublin: Irish Academic Press, 1998)

Keogh, Dermot, *Twentieth-Century Ireland, Nation and State* (Dublin: Gill and Macmillan, 1994)

Keogh, Dermot and Doherty, Gabriel (eds), *Michael Collins and the Making of the Irish State* (Cork: Mercier Press, 1998)

Lankford, Siobhán, *The Hope and the Sadness* (Cork: Tower Books, 1980)

Lee, Joseph, *Ireland 1912–1985: Politics and Society* (Cambridge: Cambridge University Press, 1989)

Lieberson, Goddard, *The Irish Uprising* (New York: CBS Records, 1968)

Lyons, F.S.L., *Ireland Since the Famine* (New York: Charles Scribners, 1971)

MacEoin, Uinseánn, *Survivors* (Dublin: Argenta Publications, 1980)

McDermott, Jim, *Northern Divisions, The Old IRA and the Belfast Pogroms 1920–22* (Belfast: Beyond the Pale Publications, 2001)

Macardle, Dorothy, *The Irish Republic* (Dublin: Irish Press, 1951)

Macdonald, Lyn, *They Called it Passchendaele* (London: Michael Joseph, 1978)

McDonnell, Kathleen Keyes, *There is a Bridge at Bandon* (Dublin: Mercier Press, 1972)

Mackay, James, *Michael Collins: A Life* (Edinburgh: Mainstream Publishing, 1996)

Macready, Gen. Sir C.F.N., *Annals of an Active Life* (London: Hutchinson, 1924)

Maher, Jim, *Harry Boland, A Biography* (Cork: Mercier Press, 1998)

Mansergh, Nicholas, *The Irish Question 1840–1921* (Toronto: University of Toronto Press, 1975)

— *Unresolved Question, The Anglo-Irish Settlement and Its Undoing, 1912–1972* (New Haven: Yale University Press, 1991)

McCoole, Sinéad, *No Ordinary Woman, Irish Female Activists in the Revolutionary Years 1900–1923* (Madison: University of Wisconsin Press, 2002)

Mitchell, Arthur, *Revolutionary Government in Ireland* (Dublin: Gill and MacMillan, 1995)

—'Alternative Government: "Exit Britannia", The Formation of the Irish National State, 1918–1921' in Augusteijn (ed.), *The Irish Revolution, 1913–1923*, pp. 70–84

Moylan, Seán, *Seán Moylan: In His Own Words* (Millstreet: Aubane Historical Society, 2004)

Mulcahy, Gen. Richard, 'Chief of Staff 1919', *Capuchin Annual* (1969)

Neeson, Eoin, *The Civil War in Ireland 1922–1923* (Cork: Mercier Press, 1969)

Nelligan, David, *A Spy in the Castle* (Dublin: McGibbon and Kee, 1968)

Norway, Mary, *The Sinn Féin Rebellion as They Saw It* (Dublin: Irish Academic Press, 1999)

O'Beirne-Ranelagh, John, 'The IRB from the Treaty to 1924', *Irish Historical Studies*, Vol. XX, p. 26 (1976)

O'Brien, Joseph, *William O'Brien and the Course of Irish Politics 1881–1918* (Berkeley, CA: University of California Press, 1976)

O'Broin, Leon, *Revolutionary Underground, The Story of the Irish Republican Brotherhood* (Totowa, NJ: Rowman and Littlefield, 1976)

O'Callaghan, Seán, *Execution* (London: Frederick Mueller, 1974)

O'Connor, Frank, *An Only Child* (London: MacMillan & Co., 1970)

O'Donoghue, Florence, 'We Need Trained Guerrilla Fighters', *An Cosantóir*, Vol. III, No. 5 (May 1943)

— *Tomás MacCurtain, Soldier and Patriot* (Tralee: Anvil Books, 1955)

— (ed.) *Rebel Cork's Fighting Story* (Tralee: Anvil Books, 1961)

— 'Guerrilla Warfare in Ireland', *An Cosantóir* (May 1963)

—'The Reorganization of the Irish Volunteers', *Capuchin Annual* (1967)

— (ed.) *Sworn to Be Free, The Complete Book of IRA Jail Breaks* (Tralee: Anvil Books, 1971)

— *No Other Law* (Dublin: Anvil Books, 1986)

O'Faolain, Seán, *Vive Moi* (London: Rubert Hart Davis, 1965)

O'Kelly, Donal, 'Ordeal By Fire – How the City Faced the Terror of 1920 and 1921', in O'Donoghue (ed.) *Rebel Cork's Fighting Story*, pp. 19–25

O'Halpin, Eunan, 'Aspects of Intelligence', *Irish Sword* (No. 95 & 96, 1993–1994)

— 'Collins and Intelligence 1919–1923' in Doherty and Keogh (eds) *Michael Collins and the Making of the Irish State*, pp. 68–80

*Defending Ireland, The Irish State and Its Enemies Since 1922* (Oxford: Oxford University Press, 1999)

O'Hegarty, P.S., *The Victory of Sinn Féin* (Dublin: Talbot, 1924)

O'Malley, Ernie, *On Another Man's Wound* (Dublin: Anvil, 1979)

Ó Snodaigh, Pádraig and Mitchell, Arthur (eds), *Irish Politcal Documents 1916–1949* (Dublin: Irish Academic Press, 1989)

Ó Suílleabháin, Michael, *Where the Mountainy Men Have Sown* (Dublin: Anvil, 1965)

Russell, Liam, 'Some Activities in Cork City 1920–21', *Capuchin Annual* (1970)

Ryan, Meda, *Michael Collins and the Women In His Life* (Cork: Mercier Press, 1996)

— *Tom Barry, IRA Freedom Fighter* (Cork: Mercier Press, 2003)

Steel, Nigel and Hart, Peter, *Passchendaele, The Sacrificial Ground* (London: Cassell and Co., 2000)

Townsend, Charles, *The British Campaign in Ireland 1919–1921: The Development of Political and Military Policies* (London: Oxford University Press, 1975)

Twohig, Patrick, *Blood on the Flag* (Ballincollig: Tower Books, 1996) [English translation of Seamus Malone's *B'Fhiu An Broin*, first published in 1958]

— *Green Tears for Hecuba* (Ballincollig: Tower Books, 1994)

Valiulis, Maryann Gialanella, *General Richard Mulcahy* (Dublin: Irish Academic Press, 1992)

Walsh, J.J., *Recollections of a Rebel* (Tralee: The Kerryman, 1944)

Wilson, Trevor and Prior, Robin, *Passchendaele, The Untold Story* (New Haven: Yale Note Bene Press, 2002)

Winters, Sir Ormonde, *Winters Tale* (London: Richards Press, 1958)

# INDEX

6ᵗʰ Division (British Army)   70, 89, 114–116, 216
  Headquarters (Victoria Barracks) 71, 78, 115–116, 142–143, 188
  Intelligence Staff 34, 70, 116, 120, 122–123, 141, 143–144
  'Round-up' operations   160, 168–172, 188–189
  Strength and command area, 122–123
Anti-Treaty IRA   195–203
  Conventions   195–199
  Executive 196–199, 202, 203
  militant faction 196–200, 203
  moderate faction   196–200, 203
Army Unity Delegation (IRA) 197–198
Army Unity Plan (IRA)   198–199
*Aud*   19, 20, 45, 209

Ballyquirk Aerodome attack   64–66
Barry, Tadg   42, 221
Barry, Tom   44, 45, 186, 199, 202, 204, 209–210, 221
Blarney Barracks attack   82, 102–103, 109
Boer War 17, 22–23, 152, 171, 186
British Army 16, 17, 84, 87, 98–99, 122, 141, 158–160, 171–172, 178, 189
  anti-insurgency operations,   143, 154, 158–160, 171–172, 178, 189
  attitudes towards Irish   94, 89, 171
  quality of soldiers   17, 70, 100, 171
  Irish Command   115–116, 122
Brown, Charlie (Macroom)   104, 107, 109
Brown Family (in-laws)   112–116, 131, 135, 137

Brown, Maude   113
Brown, Reggie – *see* Coleridge Marchment Jr
Brugha, Cathal   55, 58, 97, 100–101, 108, 194, 221–222

Canny, Christy   61
Carrigadrohid Barracks attack   82, 102–105
Carrigtwohill Barracks attack   81–82
Casement, Sir Roger   42, 45
Catholic Young Man's Society (CYMS) 14, 26, 111
Civil War   193–204
  Ceasefire negotiations 201–202, 204
Clancy, Peadar   56, 73, 222
Clarke, Captain (arms raid on) 27–28
Cody, Jack   78–79, 128–134, 136, 166, 188, 205, 222
Cohalan, Bishop Daniel   54, 72–73, 86, 109, 115, 122, 142, 145
Collins, Michael   55–58, 68, 75, 97, 100–101, 105, 107, 126, 128, 136, 146, 184, 189, 193–195, 197–199, 223
Connors, Patrick 'Croxy'   83, 88–89, 143
Conroy, Con   123, 144
Conscription Crisis   36, 44, 46–47
Coolavokig Ambush   143, 145
Cooper, Major   114–115
Cork No. 1 Brigade   32, 39, 43, 61, 93–94, 145–146, 161, 185–187, 209, 213, 216
  arms   27, 28, 50, 70–81, 86, 100
  Brigade Council   34, 37, 38, 51, 81
  and civilian informers   69, 83–84, 89, 141

communications  34, 35, 38, 47, 48, 62
Conscription Crisis  36, 44, 46, 47
contacts with GHQ  21, 56, 57, 68, 73, 74, 76, 81, 83, 92–93, 100–102, 107–109
Cyclist Company  30–32, 34, 36
establishment of  57, 86
flying column  74, 87, 143, 145, 153, 186, 188, 189
goes into action  80–82
rank and file  26, 27, 37, 42, 70, 71, 79, 83, 102, 103
reluctant officers  41, 51, 53, 60, 81–82
reorganization after 1916  28, 30–34, 40, 42
tensions with IRB  21, 31, 58–61, 74, 91
training  28, 30, 31, 33, 36, 39, 56, 80
Cork No. 2 Brigade (IRA)  57, 64, 74, 88, 147, 203, 204, 216
Cork No. 3 Brigade (IRA)  57, 64, 74, 136, 185, 216
Cork City  11, 12, 13, 71, 97–98, 161, 173, 216
and 1916 Rising  19–21, 23
Barrack Street ambush  98
burning of  142, 145
curfew  98, 142, 167, 188
Dillon's Cross ambush  142
martial law  142
Parnell Bridge ambush  143, 145
population and the conflict  67, 68, 71, 77, 89, 91, 95, 99, 102, 141
Cork Gaol Rescue  50–53, 56, 61, 62, 66, 72, 206
Cork Grammar School Raid  81, 87
Cork Post Office  29, 67, 70, 83, 100
Cork School of Commerce  13, 17, 26, 30
Cork Volunteer Hall  20, 25, 30, 33, 48
Corkery, Daniel  96–97, 103–104
Crofts, Tom  68, 69, 75, 77, 85–86, 89, 106–107, 161, 187, 202, 204, 205, 209, 223
Culhane, Sean  87, 96–97, 107, 108, 186, 223

Cumann na mBan  29, 37, 39, 42, 44, 55, 71, 148, 216

Deasy, Liam  64, 185, 194, 196, 200, 201, 203–205, 224
De Róiste, Liam  54–56, 73, 145, 202, 224
De Valera  38, 54, 58, 109, 153, 182, 186, 189, 193–194, 199, 202, 224
Doherty, Jim  42, 205, 209
Donovan, Dan 'Sandow'  65, 66, 74, 87, 103, 106, 108, 109, 127, 143, 161, 186, 202, 224
Donovan, Jerome  52–53
Donovan, Martin  52–53
Dowling, Des  102–103
Dunne, Reggie  129, 203, 224

Easter Rising  18–21, 24, 25–25, 31–33, 38, 43, 209
Enright, Eamon  71, 76

Ferris, Sgt.  85–86
First Southern Division (IRA)
formation  147–148, 185
headquarters  147–149, 160–161, 163, 165, 182–183, 188
headquarters staff  147, 150, 165, 178, 193, 195, 168, 170, 173, 181, 195, 203
moderate faction within Anti-Treaty IRA  196, 198–200, 202
opposes Anglo-Irish Treaty, 193–194–196
Fitzgerald, Michael  34, 44, 88, 136, 224
Fox, George  97
French, Viscount  81, 88, 96

Garvey, Sgt Dennis  96, 107, 109
Genoa Gunrunning Plot (Italian Arms Shipment)  147, 185
Golden, T.J.  38
'Great Round-up, The'  168–170
Grey, Jeremiah ('Miah')  66, 78–79, 103
Grey, Jim  57, 58, 65, 66, 77–79, 87, 103, 186, 189, 225–226
Griffith, Arthur  38, 101–102, 109, 136, 193–194, 226

Hales, Tom 38, 64, 112, 144, 196–198, 204, 226
Harley, Keane 14, 26
Harrington, Constable Daniel 96, 107, 109
Harrington, Father Gabriel 61
Healy, Mary 12–13, 28
Healy, Paddy 52–53, 64
Higgins, Pat 33, 35, 38–40, 44, 45, 226
Hore, Alfred 111, 113–114, 126, 147, 226
Hore, Clare 113
Hore, Fred 113, 183, 189
Hudson, Rev. George 117
Hurley, Charlie 94, 107, 227
Hyde, Seán 182, 189

Inchigeela RIC Barracks Attack 66, 74, 82
Irish Republican Army (IRA) 18, 19, 37, 39, 54, 102, 126, 185, 187, 218
  Army Unity Delegation (Civil War) 197–198
  Army Unity Plan (Civil War) 198–199
  chain of command 55, 97, 100–101, 147, 194
  Civil War split 193–195
  development of guerrilla tactics 56, 80–82, 97, 101, 143, 171–172
  establishes divisions, 147–148, 185
  financial assistance to local units 69, 74, 76, 94, 107–109, 196
  General Headquarters (GHQ) 47, 55–57, 73, 74, 81, 83, 100–102, 119, 126, 147, 185, 193–195
  growth of 30, 40, 47, 157
  Intelligence efforts 56, 67–72, 75, 105, 119
  organization structure 26, 39, 41, 54, 55, 126, 147
  policies 28, 30, 32, 42, 55, 60, 80, 92–93, 102, 194
Irish Republican Brotherhood (IRB) 16, 19, 21, 24, 29, 42, 43, 58–60, 74, 80, 126, 147, 197, 204, 218–219
Irish World 31–32, 43

Kelleher, Tom 64

Kelly Captain (6th Division Intelligence officer) 88, 108, 118, 122, 123,
Kenmare, Earl of 10, 21
Kennedy, Denis 32, 36, 39
Kerry Volunteers 42, 155–157, 186
Kilmurray RIC Barracks Attack 81–82

Langford Robert (Riobard) 44, 87
Lankford, Siobhan 45, 185
Leahy, Michael 38, 107, 127, 185
Lisburn (Anti-Catholic riots) 97, 107–108
Lloyd-George, Prime Minister David 60, 96, 98, 128, 200, 227
Lucey, Dr Con 78, 189, 227
Lynch, Liam 64, 88, 147–148, 165, 189, 193–194, 196, 198–199, 201–203, 297, 213–214, 227
Lynch, Ned 48

MacCarthy, Frank 52–53
MacCurtain, Eilís (wife of Tomás) 90
MacCurtain, Tomás 19–21, 23, 29, 33–35, 43, 47, 49, 50, 55, 57, 58, 67, 68, 71, 81, 208, 228
  assassination and inquest 86, 90–91, 96, 105–106, 126
  Cork No. 1 Brigade revenge for 87, 96–97, 101, 107–108, 126, 136
  funeral of 90–91
  leadership qualities 34, 37, 40, 58, 64
MacDonagh, District Inspector 85–86, 89, 106
MacDonagh, Thomas 25, 43
MacSwiney succeeds 91–92
MacNeill, Eoin 16, 19, 20, 23
MacNeilus, Denis 30, 32, 36, 43, 50–53, 62–64, 228
MacSweeney, Christy 52–53, 94, 106, 205
MacSwiney, Mary 29, 44, 111, 229
MacSwiney, Seán 29, 123, 161, 187, 188, 202, 229
MacSwiney, Terence ('Terry') 20, 29, 30, 33, 35, 37–39, 43, 51, 55, 58, 60, 90–91, 94–96, 102, 111, 229
  as military leader 38, 64–65, 92, 95

arrest and hunger strike   34, 121,
    127–128, 146
succeeds Tomás MacCurtain   91–92
Marchment, Sr Coleridge   111–115,
    117, 122, 135, 229
Marchment, Gerald (Brown)
    113–114, 118–119, 151, 164, 173,
    175, 181, 182, 184, 189, 207–208
Marchment, Coleridge Jr (Reggie
    Brown)   112–117, 125–126,
    129–134, 137, 147, 151, 173, 175,
    181, 184, 186, 189, 207–208, 221
McCardie, Lord Justice   117
McCorley, Roger   87, 97
McCoy, Bridget (mother)   110–112
McCoy, Cecily (Cissie Hore)
    110–114, 117, 147, 150, 175, 186,
    229
McCoy, Head Constable Henry
    110–114
McCoy, Kathleen ('Kitty')   110, 114,
    120–121, 125, 161, 173, 175, 181,
    183, 187, 229
McCoy, Josephine (Brown)   105,
    125–126, 134–136, 141, 143–144,
    207–209
    contacts Terence MacSwiney   121,
        127
    custody of Reggie   113–117, 135
    education   111
    hostility of Brown family towards
        112–114, 116, 118, 135
    IRA spy   119–121, 123, 135, 141,
        144, 173, 188–189
    marriage to Coleridge Marchment
        112–116
    meets Florrie O'Donoghue
        119–120, 125–126
    secretarial experience   111,
        113–115
    and 6th Division Staff,   115–121,
        182, 193
    sympathizes with IRA   117–118
Maguire, Sam   129, 229
McKee, Dick   56, 73, 230
McKelvey, Joe   97, 199, 230
Moylan, Sean   37, 44, 187, 196, 205,
    230
Mulcahy, Richard   55–57, 73, 91, 97,
    100–101, 108, 148, 182, 194, 198,
    203–204, 230

Murphy Family (Cardiff)   131–132
Murphy, Humphrey   196–197, 201,
    230
Murphy, Jerry   42
Murphy, Joe ('G' Company)   52–53
Murphy, Joseph (hunger strike)   44,
    136
Murphy, Leo   15, 25, 28, 43, 48, 107,
    141, 230
Murphy, Mick   107, 144, 161, 186,
    230
Murphy, Seán   38
Murphy, Dr Tadg   90, 106
Murphy, William   115
Murray, Fred   44, 48, 51, 53, 59, 61,
    72
Murray, Patrick 'Pa'   72, 74, 88, 96,
    106–109, 136, 231
Murtagh, Constable Joseph   85, 90,
    105–106

Neenan, Connie   71, 107, 109, 144,
    205
Neutral IRA   22, 201–203
Nolan, Michael   11–15, 47, 86

O'Brien, Art   128–129, 232
O'Connor, Fr Dominic   44, 49, 74,
    90, 118, 119, 125, 145, 232
O'Connor, Joe   38, 41, 42, 44, 48, 60,
    61, 65–66, 91, 100, 103, 107, 119,
    126–127, 163–165, 170–171, 173,
    180–181, 186, 188–189, 199, 209,
    233
O'Connor, Patrick   24–25, 42–43, 186
O'Connor, Patrick 'Croxy' (see
    Connors, Patrick 'Croxy')
O'Donoghue, Albina   15, 86, 157,
    178, 187, 189
O'Donoghue, Nell   9, 15, 86, 144,
    151, 155, 157, 163, 166, 173–176,
    178, 186, 189
O'Donoghue, Elizabeth 'Lizzie'   86,
    175, 189
O'Donoghue, Florence
    accepts death   48–49, 94
    Brigade adjutant   40–41, 47, 60,
        62, 77
    Civil War peace efforts of
        197–202
    concerns for family   49, 86, 94,

155, 157–158, 175
contacts with GHQ   98, 100–102,
   108–109, 126, 147, 164,
   184–185,
develops intelligence network   56,
   66–72, 75–76, 81, 83–84, 99–100,
   147, 211–212
discusses early organization of the
   Volunteers   25–30, 41–42
first impressions of Jo   125–126
frustration at poor planning
   65–66, 104
impact of Easter Rising   25–26
IRB membership   31–32, 58–61,
   74, 80, 147, 197, 204
joins Brigade Council   34, 37–38
joins the Volunteers   25–26
member of the Anti-Treaty IRA
   Executive   196–199, 213
on the development of guerrilla
   tactics   28–30, 32, 66, 80–81,
   92–93
on morality of killing   48, 94
organizes Brigade
   communications   34–37, 40,
   47–48
personal feelings towards British
   48, 69–70, 75–76, 151, 155
relationship with Seán O'Hegarty
   48–49, 59–60, 66, 91–92, 128,
   153, 162, 201, 208–209
relationship with Tomás
   MacCurtain   34, 58–60, 67, 89
Republican faith of   32, 48
views of democracy   32, 41, 54
views of Sinn Fein   41, 42, 54–56,
   83
World War II Army Service   67,
   206–207, 210
O'Donoghue, Josephine – see
Josephine McCoy
O'Donoghue, Margaret   86, 144, 157,
187, 189
O'Donoghue, Patrick   10–11, 29,
154, 173–175
O'Donoghue, Patrick (Manchester)
130, 133, 137, 233
O'Donoghue, Seán   26, 43
O'Duffy, Eoin   195
O'Hegarty, P.S.   31, 43, 100, 102, 109,
111, 233

O'Hegarty, Sean   21, 29, 37, 41,
   43–44, 48, 50–52, 55, 57–60, 64, 66,
   73–74, 80, 84, 90–91, 98, 100,
   103–105, 111, 126–128, 143,
   153–154, 162, 165–167, 186,
   196–198, 200–202, 208, 214, 234
O'Mahoney, Denis   104–105
O'Suílleabhain (O'Sullivan), Michael
   87, 186
O'Sullivan, Geróid   56, 73, 100–101,
   198, 204, 234
O'Sullivan, Patrick (Kilnamartyra)
   77, 87, 107
O'Sullivan, Seán   30, 38, 51, 53,
   81–82, 89, 106

Paps Mountains   11, 21–22, 166, 188
Parnell, Charles Stewart   15, 41, 45,
   234
Pearse, Patrick   25, 186, 234
Perry, Mrs   113, 117, 135
Phelan, Sean   130–132, 136, 234
Power, George   64

Quinlisk, Timothy   67–69, 75, 84

Rathmore   9, 18, 21–23, 25, 29, 154,
   169,
Rathmore Ambush and reprisals   43,
   151, 154–155, 173–174, 186, 188
Redmond, John   15, 18–19, 29, 45
Royal Irish Constabulary (RIC)   28,
   39, 47–48, 54–55, 60–61, 77–78,
   82–83, 97,100, 102, 111, 172, 219
as intelligence force   47, 61, 68,
   82–83, 97, 172
Auxiliary Cadets   98, 100, 141–146,
   153, 165
Black and Tans   98, 141, 145, 151,
   180
IRA attacks on   59, 81–82, 85–86,
   96–98, 102–106, 108, 142–145, 151,
   188.
IRA intercepts coded messages of
   67, 68, 70, 76, 127
members assist IRA   47–48, 71, 72,
   76, 97, 108
reprisal by,86, 89–92, 94, 98–99,
   141–142, 145–146, 154, 171
Ryan, Matt   27, 42, 48, 68, 85, 161,
   187, 235

Sinn Féin  38, 39, 41–42, 44, 54–56,
    72–73, 83, 98, 219–220
Smyth, District Commissioner Gerald
    98, 108
Stack, Austin  58
Strickland, General Sir Peter Edward
    98, 108, 116, 135, 142, 146, 168, 235
Sullivan, Dominic (Dom)  48, 66, 71,
    214, 236
Swanzy, District Inspector Oswald
    51, 87, 89, 96–97, 107, 109, 136, 235

Terry Family (Cardiff)  126, 129–132
Terry, Kathleen  131–132

Ulster Volunteer Force  15–16
Upton Train Ambush  136, 235

Varien, Harry  59–60, 74

Wallace, Nora  48, 71, 236
Wallace, Sheila  48
Wallace's Newsagents (Brigade HQ)
    48, 62, 68, 71, 90, 100
Walsh, Maurice 'Moss'  163, 165, 167,
    169, 186, 236
Walsh, Mickey  17
Walsh, J.J.  54–56, 73, 237